SPITFIRE SAGA

SPITFIRE SAGA

RODNEY SCRASE DFC

ANGUS MANSFIELD

This book is dedicated to the ground crews who so effectively provided the back up to their pilots, these chaps on the Squadron for years gave the Squadron its teeth. Not glamour but at all times complete support.

Rodney Scrase

Parts of this narrative have been published previously in *Barney Barnfather: Life on a Spitfire Squadron* by the same author. This is inevitable because Rodney Scrase and Barney Barnfather both flew with 72 Squadron. Their log books are of course different but in the period they flew together the ORB and developments in-theatre are the same.

Front cover: Painting of Rodney Scrase's Spitfire by Barry Weekley

First published 2010
This paperback edition published 2019

The History Press
The Mill, Brimscombe Port
Stroud, Gloucestershire, GL5 2QG
www.thehistorypress.co.uk

British Library Cataloguing in Publication Data.
A catalogue record for this book is available from the British Library.

ISBN 978 0 7509 8921 3

Typesetting and origination by The History Press
Printed and bound by CPI Group (UK) Ltd

CONTENTS

ABBREVIATIONS

ACM	Air Chief Marshal
AFC	Air Force Cross
AM	Air Marshal
AOC-in-C	Air Officer Commanding-in Chief
ATA	Air Transport Auxiliary
AVM	Air Vice-Marshal
BAT	Blind Approach Training
CFI	Chief Flying Instructor
DFC	Distinguished Flying Cross
DSM	Distinguished Service Medal
EFTS	Elementary Flying Training School
F/Lt	Flight Lieutenant
F/O	Flying Officer
F/Sgt	Flight Sergeant
Gp Capt	Group Captain
MO	Medical Officer
ORB	Operations Record Book
OTE	Operationally Tour Expired
OTU	Operational Training Unit
P/O	Pilot Officer
RAAF	Royal Australian Air Force
RAFVR	Royal Australian Air Force Reserve
RCAF	Royal Canadian Air Force
RNZAF	Royal New Zealand Air Force
R/T	radio telephony
SAAF	South African Air Force
Sgt	Sergeant
Sqn	Squadron
Sqn Ldr	Squadron Leader
u/s	unserviceable
USAAF	United State Army Air Force
Wing Cdr	Wing Commander
W/O	Warrant Officer

FOREWORD

We met at the Operational Training Unit at Grangemouth and Balado Bridge where we both flew the Spitfire. Rodney had been trained in America and I had been a flying instructor at RAF College Cranwell before I managed to wrangle out of Training Command by way of a Night Fighter Training unit. It was easy to pick out the pilots who could fly a steady formation and Rodney was one of the best.

It was quite interesting to find out that we were both posted to No. 611 Squadron to learn all we could about the Spitfire IX before joining a ship waiting on the Clyde with a dozen other pilots. One of these was F/Lt Edward Mortimer Rose DFC & Bar, who had already won a DFC and Bar in Malta. He drew his revolver and fired at a nearby seagull perched on the mizzen mast but he missed! It was Mortimer who collided with Wing Commander Gilroy right over Souk el Khemis just as Rodney and I arrived there two months later. After an uneventful trip to Gibraltar we joined Wing Commander Gomez who was in charge of assembling both Hurricanes and Spitfires that had arrived by sea in wooden crates. We were detailed once or twice to join a party of aircraft on a ferry trip to Oran or to Maison Blanche, the main base for Algiers. We were both pretty pleased to be sent from Gibraltar to Algiers to await a posting to one of the 'mobile' fighter squadrons. We did not have long to wait. We flew to Souk el Arba and then by open truck to a new strip at Souk el Khemis. It was from this truck that we got our first glimpse of two Spitfires spinning into the ground followed by just one parachute. It was our friend from the ship on the Clyde: Mortimer Rose who had collided with the Wing Leader. Many years later 'Sheep' Gilroy blamed condensation on the inside of the cockpit after returning from a sortie at high altitude.

Shortly after joining the famous No. 72 (Basutoland) Squadron we all went back to Gibraltar to be re-equipped with Mark IX's. Rodney and I thought a clever postings clerk in the Air Ministry had planned our route to No. 72 Squadron but we never breathed a word!

I returned to University in 1945 from my prisoner of war camp in Germany and as I walked down Kings Parade I wondered at old friends who had survived. I went one day to try the lunch in the Air Squadron Mess. There in the visitors' book was a name I dearly wanted to find. Rodney had written in very small print, his decoration. He certainly deserved it and we have remained friends to this day.

Tom Hughes – August 2010

CHAPTER ONE

LOVE AT FIRST FLIGHT

How much I owe to my logbooks. Without the dates and cryptic notes which appear within, the memory of what happened over 60 years ago would be hard to disentangle. So for starters there is the first time I flew in a Spitfire. In my case this was on 16 September 1942. I was on a course at No. 58 OTU Grangemouth.

I had done a 35-minute Spitfire Check in a Master III. My instructor F/O Beardsley felt I was OK to go and I did. The next 55 minutes in a Spitfire Mark 1 was a gingerly completed exercise, doing circuits, pretending I was landing on top of a feathery white cloud and building up my confidence. At that stage there were no aerobatics and certainly no sideslip approach to a landing. But I got over the first stage and my landing was a three pointer. So I was away and my love affair with the Spitfire could truly be said to have begun.

Just a month later and doing a climb to 30,000 feet I came near to being a casualty. Something went quite wrong with my oxygen supply and I came around at 5,000 feet flying straight down towards the hills, fortunately in time for me to recover. I was in a bath of sweat but with the confidence that builds up after a narrow escape.

Next it was to discover the power of a Spitfire Mark IX. On a short-term attachment to 611 Squadron at Biggin Hill I gained some experience on type flying not only a later model, but one that was full of operational urge. The responses were immediate, the power inspiring and the confidence it built up in me was perhaps too soon for a new boy.

That confidence was to suffer a rude awakening when I joined my first squadron, No. 72 Squadron at Souk el Khemis in Tunisia. On my first day, 28 January 1943, we were driven down to dispersal to see the team taking off on a sweep as part of a wing. At less than 1,000 feet two Spitfires collided. The Wing Leader 'Sheep' Gilroy was hit from below by a very experienced pilot, F/Lt Mortimer Rose DFC. Gilroy baled out but Morty crashed and was killed. No fault was attributed to the Spitfires.

In February the Squadron returned to Gibraltar to collect our Mark IXs. On our return flight, 6 hours in all, in loose formation and with an overnight stop at Maison Blanche we arrived at Souk el Khemis in the midst of a heavy rainstorm. Landing on a darkened airfield was no fun: no lights but I had the thrill of a safe landing. Such was not to be the case for all my colleagues. One fatal casualty and a number of damaged new Mark IXs did not speak well for our skill as pilots. But the improved performance of the Mark IX spoke loud and clear about our ability to combat the enemy. They were flying from concrete runways on the outskirts of Tunis and Bizerte, we flew from muddy strips covered with Sommerfield tracking. This resembled chicken wire and did give us some help in taking off and landing but many were the occasions when an airmen sitting on your tail was a requirement when taxiing.

From Malta and later Sicily my love affair with the Spitfire built up. Partly this was a case of combat success but there was very much an improved awareness of what you could with the aircraft and how she would respond to your handling of the controls. Also in part it was due to the gradual reduction in enemy resistance.

One black mark was my hitting a tree at Cassala. I had a 90-gallon overload tank and just did not allow sufficient height over the airfield boundary. The undercarriage collapsed and the propeller blades were broken off. The aircraft was a 'Gift of War' with only a few hours flying time and was declared Category III damaged. Yes, I did feel I had let the plane and its donor down. For me, a bruised forehead and a bloody nose but I was back flying the next day.

17 September was a day to remember. As Black Two I was on patrol over the Salerno beaches. We engaged two Do 217 bombers that had discharged their 3000lb radio controlled bombs against our warships. I was having trouble with my supercharger and lost speed. Roy Hussey, my No. 1 carried on and shot down both of the Do 217s. As I got things back under control and rejoined him, I passed close by to one of the Do 217s on fire and with the crew baling out, one after the other. Poor chaps I thought.

In 1944 the bombing of Monte Cassino on 15 February will always be a sad memory. Flying at 15,000 feet as Red 1 in my own Mark IX–RN–N MH 669 I was leader of the escort to the Maurauders flying in two groups of six. We all saw clearly what was happening and my comments that this was a wonderful show were widely reported in the press back home. Little did we realise that it would be another three months before the Allies could finally break through on the road to Rome.

And that flight in 1944 was to be the end of my tour with No. 72 Squadron. I had completed 200 operational flights – in all 275 hours. Of that total 199 hours were in a Spitfire Mark IX, a love affair I hold very dear.

Rodney Scrase

CHAPTER TWO

THE EARLY YEARS

Rodney Diran Scrase was born on 8 April 1921 in South Croydon, the first of three boys to his parents Ralph and Adrienne. The Great War had come to an end on 11 November 1918 and his father had been in the British Army that had been sent to Salonika, Greece and Serbia to assist the Serbians. Once the war had ended he had been sent across with the 28th Division of the British Army to Constantinople. They had been despatched to serve as the Army of Occupation in Turkey. Ralph Scrase, with the rank of Company Quartermaster Sergeant, was stationed on the Asiatic side of the Bosphorus at Scutari.

The Army found themselves in some difficulty because of the language barrier. It had to find interpreters to help them communicate so adverts appeared in local papers inviting anyone who could speak French, Turkish and English to work for the British Army. As well as standard pay the interpreters would also receive supplies in kind: tea, coffee, sugar and flour. This was a sound proposal accepted readily by the families and daughters of professional people. Adrienne was the beautiful daughter of a Doctor of Medicine in Constantinople. She was from an Armenian family, aged 24 and a competent pianist but did not know what she wanted to do with her life so became an aide to the British Army now resident in her country as an interpreter.

Rodney's father Ralph kept a diary in his Army Logbook:

MONDAY 18 MAY 1919

Our lady clerk Miss Adrienne Gasparian, an Armenian, commenced work today and I think she will be a great success. She has a very cheerful nature, is a nice respectable girl, in fact it is a treat to have her working in the same office. One would hardly know her for anything but an English girl. She knows thoroughly the Armenian, Turkish, German and French languages and is now learning English although she is already well versed in it and will no doubt improve greatly now that she will have English drummed into her ears all day long!

Their romance blossomed quickly.

THURSDAY 5 JUNE 1919

Adrienne was absent from duty today, as she is a witness in some lawsuit and had to attend the tribunal (Law Courts) at Scutari. I felt her absence most keenly as she is the ray of sunshine in the office – in fact I would go as far to say that whereas I was 'dying' to get home a few weeks ago, I shall now be very sorry to leave in one way, much as I desire to get out of the Army. I should be very happy if Adrienne could only come home to England with me but it seems so impossible and there are so many obstacles in the way of anything like that. My mind seems full all day long of nothing else but Adrienne, Adrienne, Adrienne. Perhaps it is because I am so young and consequently sentimental and emotional. Anyway it seems to me I've got a bad attack of lovesickness. And yet one can hardly contemplate really giving all one's love to a person who it seems will be so impossible ever to gain for one's own. For one thing she is an Armenian girl and her customs, habits, upbringing, may all be different to ours, although it does not seem so at present. Then I have reason to believe, judging from her conversation, that her parents are very conventional and strict and they could hardly be expected to give their daughter away to a perfect stranger and foreigner without being assured of her own happiness, not to mention such questions as financial standing and my own character, of which, even Adrienne knows very little. Yet again there is a question of religion, she belongs to the Armenian Church whereas I am a Wesleyan Non Conformist. There is then the question (one which should interest both parties when contemplating marriage to my way of thinking) of health and pedigree. As far as I am concerned I am in first class health and there is nothing to stand in my way as far as that is concerned, but of Adrienne I know practically nothing. I only know that her character and general disposition, so full of cheer and 'bonhomie' sympathy have attracted me to an extent more than I care to admit in as much I know I love her yet am restrained by the knowledge that if I show my love and gain hers for me, the obstacles in the way are so great, that our affections on each other would have been wasted and then our parting when I go home would be such a cruel tug to us both, especially for her being a girl if she did grow to really love me.

SATURDAY AND SUNDAY 7 AND 8 JUNE 1919

Two of the happiest days of my life, by some inexplicable means Adrienne has read all through this journal and has learned of my feelings and my own mind. After leaving Adrienne I went to see the photographer and left a film to be developed and printed. Then I went to the Naval and Military Club and had dinner. Afterwards I had a wash and brush up and had my boots cleaned and after looking in the shops I got on a tram for GHQ where I thought I would perhaps meet Adrienne again. Fortunately I noticed her in another tram going in the opposite direction just as my tram reached GHQ. We had previously arranged to meet at the Bon Marche and I was trying to meet her a little ahead of time. Anyway when she saw me Adrienne got off her tram and we walked together back to Pera and she took me to an Armenian theatre for a drama by Sir Arthur Conan Doyle. Of course I could not understand the 'lingo'. After leaving the theatre we went by the 'tunnel' railway and caught the ferry to Adrienne's home at Moda arriving there about 8 p.m. I was now introduced

> to her mother, a dear lady who I instantly began to like, and shortly afterwards to her father, whom I also like immensely. It is easy to see that they are good parents and that their little family forms a home where there is love and sympathy – just as it should be. Conversation with them was difficult because I don't know Armenian, nor they English. They both know French however and I wished I had taken more trouble when at school to learn that language but I did not then realise how useful it would have been to me. However, Adrienne acted as interpreter and we were soon on good terms. It was so nice to feel myself in a real home again after so long in exile. Everything was quite cosy and snug. Just before dinner Adrienne and I went for a short walk down to the sea front and I wish it were in my power to express here on paper all my thoughts. If these pages were ever read by a third person they will have perhaps realised that there is something stronger than ordinary common acquaintance between Adrienne and I. We have both mutually realised that we have kindled in each other hearts the flame of love – deep soul-filling holy love. My heartfelt emotions are touched like they have never been touched before and I feel I know that in spite of all the obstacles Adrienne will one day be my beloved wife, the dear girl who will share my whole life. During our walk we discussed the matter and I learned what I had hoped to be the case and that is Adrienne returns my love to the full and that I am the first man to whom she feels she can be really happy with. Oh God! I am humbled to the dust. To know that I have won the love of such a pure noble girl fills me with thanks to thee Oh God and I pray that thou will help me to return her love and to be to her the man she thinks I am. The thought of her fills me with inspiration and the desire is so strong within me to possess her for my own dear wife. God grant that we may be guided right and that all obstacles may be overcome. She is for me, the one girl in the world with whom I can be truly happy. Her nature is exactly suited to me and I feel for her that awe and reverence and respect that is essential for true love.

Ralph and Adrienne became engaged on 16 August 1919. The parents of both were anxious about the developing relationship, so much so that Adrienne's parents sent a good friend of theirs to London to find out what type of family the Scrases were. Ralph was one of seven children born to George Burton Scrase and Alice Sewell. They had been married at Horsham but moved to Burgess Hill where George became a Commercial Traveller with a pony and trap working for his brother Alfred in a mineral water business. Working as a traveller suited George and he built up an agency travelling for a number of firms. George and Alice had a large family of six boys and Ralph had been born on 15 September 1897. The family friend sent by Adrienne's parents spoke well of the Scrase family and their standing in the community so they were married on 24 January 1920 in Croydon after their return to England.

Rodney arrived a little over a year later and was born on 8 April 1921 in South Croydon. He would be the first of three brothers, Roy was born on 29 August 1922 and Ralph arrived on 21 December 1923.

Adrienne's parents were, by now, living with the Scrase family in Lansdowne Road Croydon, as they had had to leave Constantinople because of troubles there. Rodney slept in a cot at the end of his grandparents' bed. Ralph worked for his father's company, known as Sun D'or, but with several sons working for the same business it was not a job in which there would be opportunities for progress.

Croydon was an interesting and a very desirable place to live in the 1920s. Its fashion and architecture flourished when the suburbs were at the peak of their popularity between the world wars. Croydon began to expand massively in the late nineteenth century and this expansion reached a peak in the 1920s and 1930s, when families desperate for their own home away from the grime of London flocked to the fresh air and space outside the capital.

By 1927 a new opening arose and he was offered a job with H.S.Whiteside and Co. Ltd as Regional Sales Manager in the North of England. The Company H.S. Whiteside and Co. Ltd was a snack foods and confectionery manufacturer, their most famous products the Sun Pat Range of chocolate coated peanuts and raisins, and their peanut butter products.

Ralph Scrase's job with H.S.Whiteside and Co. took the family from Croydon to Nottingham when Rodney was around seven and they lived in a rented house overlooking the Arboretum, a large park in Mansfield Grove. They lived happily there for almost ten years and Rodney attended the Mundella Grammar School. His father was then promoted and moved back to Dulwich in London, still with H.S.Whiteside and Co. Ltd, and based at the Park House Works in Camberwell.

There Rodney attended Alleyn's school, an independent, fee-paying co-educational school situated in Dulwich, South London. It was originally part of the historic Alleyn's College of God's Gift charitable foundation, which also included James Allen's Girls' School (JAGS), Dulwich College and their feeder schools (JAPS and Alleyn's Junior School). The official religion at the school was and is Church of England. At Alleyn's Rodney joined the Officer Training Corps or Cadet Corps to gain his first experience of life in the Military.

> In the summer of 1939 I went along to the Alleyn's School notice board to see what Higher School Exam results I had achieved: four passes, sufficient to get a place at University. I had already planned on studying for a B.Com degree from the London School of Economics. In those days admission to University was relatively straightforward, you went along to the College in Houghton Street, Aldwych, and sat through a 20–30 minute chat with one of the Professors.

So Rodney went onto to study at the London School of Economics. There he learnt to row, Houghton Street was close to the River Thames and there had been a rowing club for the LSE established in 1895. The boathouse was actually at Chiswick and Rodney became captain of the club. With the outbreak of war students were evacuated to Cambridge. Rodney was in the rather unusual position of rowing at Cambridge University without quite belonging there. Most people at Cambridge rowed at some time during their career, even if only in a rugger boat. The LSE crew took to the water again, this time from Bonham's Yard. They were not exactly in the class of the Phaeacians, but what they lacked in skill they made up for in enthusiasm. Other evacuated colleges did likewise and the Cambridge University Boat Club allowed them, together with the 'Rob-nines' (a composite town club) and the RAF to compete in the Inter College Bumps. The first of these occurred in the Lent term of 1940. The Bart's eight registered two bumps in three nights, over Rodney's London School of Economics boat and Christ's boat.

Bumping races were typically raced over several days. Each day the boats were lined up bow-to-stern, along the bank of the river, with a set distance between each boat and the next (this was usually about one-and-a-half boat lengths of clear water). The starting positions were marked by a rope or chain attached to the bank, the other end of which was held by each boat's coxswain. Boats waited along the bank, and were poled out just in time for the start, to avoid any drifting. At the start signal the coxswain let go of the rope and the crew started to row, attempting to catch the boat in front while simultaneously being chased by the one behind. A crew that caught the boat ahead of it was said to 'bump' it. A bump was made when any form of contact was made with the boat in front, or when the stern of the boat behind completely passed the bow of the boat in front.

> It was a glorious day and at the start our coach and bank party leader – gave us some sage advice and stirring words of encouragement. It was almost Churchill-like. So with a clear aim in sight we waited for the gun to launch us into flight. And row we did. We looked marvellous for the first few strokes as we pulled away. Then something literally unheard of happened: a whistle was blown which was aimed at us, not the team behind.
>
> Now whistles are used by bank parties to let their boat know they are gaining on the boat in front. One means you are one length behind, say 60ft – which means you are gaining on them. The boats start 90ft apart. Two whistles means a half a length – three means three-quarters and four means you are on them – then its continuous for bumps.
>
> Now this one whistle was like a red rag to a bull and we stirred like a mighty beast and dug deep. One whistle, it was like a symphony to us. Another – still just one but we were keeping close.
>
> That moment – that feeling is what the whole competition is all about. Brilliant.

While also at Cambridge, Rodney joined the Cambridge University Air Squadron. Marshal of the Royal Air Force, Sir Hugh Trenchard, had originally conceived the idea of University Air Squadrons. Cambridge University was the first squadron of its kind anywhere in the world, and was formed on 1 October 1925. All its members were undergraduates of the University, the very first member being G.H. Watkins, the famous explorer who pioneered expeditions on the Arctic air routes in Greenland.

Initially, the squadrons were equipped with such front-line aircraft as the Bristol F2B Fighter, still in service from the First World War, but these soon gave way to more modern training aircraft, such as the Avro 504N and the Avro Tutor, which became standard equipment for all University Air Squadrons until 1939. The Munich Crisis and the period of re-armament just prior to the Second World War required a massive increase in the number of pilot and officer recruits, and many more University Air Squadrons were formed before and during the war years to provide for this need. During the war most squadrons were flying de Havilland Tiger Moths, and these were supplemented with North American Harvards, a type that was to remain in University Air Squadron service to the end of the 1950s.

After two years at Cambridge and having earned his degree at the London School of Economics, Rodney volunteered to join the RAF. He was driven out to the airship sheds at Cardington where he took the King's Shilling. He would receive instructions on becoming an active member of the service at a future date and actually enlisted on 6 May 1941.

CHAPTER THREE

RAF TRAINING, 1941

Rodney Scrase's life in the RAF began at Cardington in May 1941. Then he became LAC Scrase with service number 1432590 – a number he would never forget.

It was another 3 months before his call up papers came through with instructions to proceed to No. 1 ARC (Aircrew Reception Centre) at Regent's Park, London. Rodney was one of a group of fifty, all members of University Air Squadrons from Cambridge, Oxford and Edinburgh who had spent the previous academic year attending lectures, in his case at the Cambridge University Air Squadron. There he had a few brief flights in a Tiger Moth, and he underwent medical tests and interviews to judge his suitability for training as a pilot. Because of this he and his colleagues skipped attendance at an Initial Training Wing, which would normally have lasted between 6 and 8 weeks and where they would have been expected to undertake physical training, drills and ground school subjects – learning to fly without actually seeing an aeroplane. Memories of this early time are of living in a requisitioned luxury flat overlooking Regent's Park and marching across Prince Albert Road to London Zoo's restaurant for meals. The evenings were spent visiting London's West End.

Within three weeks the group was transferred to No. 4 PD (pre-deployment) Wing at Wilmslow to be kitted out and provided with civilian suits and berets. They were to go to the USA to do their flying training at one of the six newly opened British Flying Training Schools (BFTS) there because of the lack of training airfields in England. It had been agreed by President Roosevelt in May 1941, well before the United States entered the war later that year after the Japanese attack on Pearl Harbor, that RAF pilots could be trained in the open and safe skies of the United States as opposed to the war torn skies in Britain and that such training would be carried out at these six British Flying Training Schools:

1 BFTS Terrell in Texas. Opened 9 June 1941
2 BFTS Lancaster in California. Opened 9 June 1941
3 BFTS Miami in Oklahoma. Opened 16 June 1941
4 BFTS Mesa in Arizona. Opened 16 June 1941
5 BFTS Clewiston in Florida. Opened 17 July 1941
6 BFTS Ponca City in Oklahoma. Opened 23 August 1941

After a few days leave he embarked on HMT *Stratheden* at Glasgow bound for the port of Halifax in Canada. From Halifax he went by train to Montreal and on to

Toronto. When they arrived in Canada they were all amazed by the amount of fruit available to them, nobody had seen bananas or oranges for ages. From No. 1 Manning Pool he travelled by train down through the US via Detroit and Atlanta to his BFTS in Florida, a journey of two, maybe three days.

Training was similar at each BFTS and occupied 28 weeks. His flying training took place under the blue skies of Riddle Field, Clewiston. Clewiston is midway between Fort Myers to the west and Miami to the east. Billed as 'America's Sweetest Town', Clewiston is a community of vast open spaces on the southwest shore of Lake Okeechobee in Hendry County that was a major producer of sugar cane. As it was about 50 miles from these resorts they used to hitch hike when leaving camp at weekends. There was always a camp bus to bring them back.

The base at Riddle had been constructed in record time. After being officially opened in July 1941, by mid-August construction had been started on almost every building associated with the airfield. The buildings were constructed squarely in the middle of a 4-mile tract that formed the airfield. The layout of the building complex was in the shape of a huge diamond, the ends of the diamond pointing north and south, with space earmarked at the northern end for any buildings required in the future. A large steel hangar to house about 30 aircraft was erected at the southwestern end. All the buildings were of concrete block construction on reinforced concrete foundations. The roofs were made of heavy slate over felt and the exterior of all the buildings was painted white. Between the two large barrack blocks for the cadets were outdoor recreational facilities: tennis courts, basketball and volleyball courts together with a swimming pool. The barrack block facilities were for cadets only, the facilities for about 100 or so instructors, mechanics and other technicians were located in private facilities away from the airfield. For the period the airfield was open, between 17 July 1941 and 25 August 1945, about 1,800 Royal Air Force cadets on 24 courses were to pass through Riddle Field. About 1,400 graduated as pilots, 300 as commissioned pilot officers and 1,100 as sergeant pilots. Those that did not qualify or who were 'washed out' were generally sent to Canada for record evaluation and placement either as bomb aimers, navigators, wireless operators or gunners.

The instructors at the Flying Training Schools were American civilians, very often chaps in their 20s, and who were always addressed very politely as 'Mr'. At the BFTS there were perhaps four or five RAF personnel commanded by a CFI (chief flying instructor). At No. 5 BFTS it was RAF Wing Cdr Kenneth Rampling – a much decorated bomber pilot. A tall jovial man who was labelled a 'regular guy' by the Americans, he was keen to see course graduations take place on time. 'Let's move it on lads' was on of his stock phrases and he encouraged the staff to get the cadets airborne from 6 o'clock in the morning until 7 or sometimes 8 o'clock in the evening.

The cadets were issued with a little blue book that gave them a very comprehensive view of life in America. It was not as hectic as life in the Hollywood movies but the outstanding hospitality the book warned them about measured up fully to expectations. The cadets mostly came from carefree undergraduate days and entered into flying with little knowledge but with immense enthusiasm. Some fell by the wayside and some had hair-raising experiences. They took back many things – amongst them a new vocabulary and a strange accent. There were new tastes like fried chicken and sweet potatoes and lots of memories. Swimming in the warm Atlantic, Saturday nights and Florida sunsets, the moon over Miami and the southern girls – the movies weren't wrong about them. The one thing that dismayed them was the treatment of the young negroes who worked on the airfield. Most of these young workers were very helpful but poor and occasionally they would accept tips or items of clothing. The Americans treated them with disdain.

Rodney's logbook records his first flight at No. 5 BFTS on 9 October 1941 in a PT17 Stearman. This was the primary training aircraft and the American Stearman Biplane was similar to the British Tiger Moth. Mr Clark was his instructor pilot on No. 3 BFTS Course. The sortie lengths were generally very short, 25 minutes on the first flight and only one sortie of over an hour up to his first solo sortie. This occurred after 11 hours and 54 minutes dual on 30 October for 16 minutes with a note 'First solo – take-offs into wind'. The course progressed with glide approaches, turns, stalls, spins and onto instrument flying interspersed with solos over the next 10 hours. Mr Hunziker took his Progress Check after 40 hours in two parts.

His time on the course continued with ground school learning and actual flying. They were allowed off every other weekend when most of them spent time in Miami or West Palm Beach. The hospitality of the American people was tremendous. Frequently they would be invited to stay with American families in their homes. Most of them had swimming pools and tennis courts and they were nearly always assured of a marvellous weekend on these occasions. The trouble with the weekends away was that they did not get much money so they were so grateful to the families for their generosity.

Navigation and low flying with advanced aerobatics followed through November and in December he undertook some night flying before completing the Primary part of the course on 9 December 1941.

> It was at this time, 8 December, that the Japanese raid on Pearl Harbor took place. We had been out for the day, and on returning to camp realised something exceptional was taking place. Armed people, their equivalent of our Dad's Army, surrounded the camp. We had gone off for the week-end without identity documents and each had to be vetted back into camp by the RAF personnel.

Rodney moved onto the BT13A Vultee on 12 December and started to use the Link trainer for instrument flying practice. Cross-country flights entered the course syllabus with sorties of about 1 hour 30 minutes as the normal length and more instrument and night flying from December to January.

CHAPTER FOUR

TRAINING COMPLETED, JANUARY 1942

In late January, now with over 120 hours experience, Rodney progressed to the AT6, a far more advanced machine we know as the Harvard. The same round of exercises was now flown at an increased airspeed and more advanced manoeuvres introduced until his final sortie on 7 March 1942 at which time he had just over 82 hours dual and almost 98 hours first pilot time and 15 hours in the link trainer.

> As we look back over the six months down here in the heart of Florida, surely long enough, we feel, to have qualified us as 'crackers' it is interesting to compare our experience with what we imagined it would all be like when we first learned we were coming here to train. Our idea about America then probably came from two sources. One was by now the quite famous 'little blue book' issued to us, which, along with its strict instructions for our deportment, gave us the impression that the USA was a land where the people were very different from us, and where we should feel that we were foreigners. The other source was the Hollywood flicks on which we had all been brought up from our cradles. From these we gathered that America was inhabited mainly by gum chewing gangsters and their speak easies, hot bands, dashing reporters with slouch hats and jitter bugs.
>
> But now looking back, one feels that the diplomatic author of that little blue booklet was a little too apprehensive, we seem to have got by without causing an international incident and on the other hand we have not found life in America as hectic as they would have us believe, which is a good thing. As after all, we did come over here to learn to fly. In fact we found the people were really very much like us. They even spoke the same language as us practically, although some of us have had some difficulties with certain differences in pronunciation experienced with our instructors at one end of the intercom and us at the other. One thing the little blue book did not exaggerate. It warned us about American hospitality and boy it was right! We have been entertained right royally wherever we have gone, at Fort Myers, at Palm Beach, at Miami and even one man inadvertently at Tallahassee. To those that have shown us such good times we can only say 'come over and be our guests' after the war.

The Americans treated the cadets who trained in the USA like sons and brothers. A pilot who had completed his training at Clewiston wrote these words in 1942.

Wherever the British flag is flown
With the Stars and Stripes above
You'll find a kindred unity
of friendship and of love;
Each British heart beneath those flags
Whoever it may be
Says 'Thank you' to America,
'For what you've been to me.'

Our return to the UK was much the same as the outward journey. We returned to Halifax with a two-day stopover in New York. Of course we went to the top of the Rockefeller Tower, were bowled over by the glamorous Rockettes and wondered where we could ever expect to meet such tall sprightly lasses. On by rail to Moncton, our holding camp in New Brunswick, brought us face to face with reality. A heavy snow-fall to coincide with my 21st birthday meant we were locked in to camp as the sergeant on guard duty would not let us off base with dirty boots!

For our return to the UK it was a ten-day return in a fast convoy to the UK. Never have I seen such lovely green hills as we did cruising up the Clyde to Gourock, and once ashore the delightful accents of our welcoming committee of Scottish lasses serving tea and cakes made us realise we had been away for nearly 6 months.

Down to Bournemouth by rail to learn of my promotion to pilot officer, a new service number – 123465, and to order my uniforms from Gieves who had tailors on duty in a nearby shop. Also to learn of the procedure for pay and allowances, and to be told I now had a bank account with Glyn Mills Holt's Branch in Kirkland House Whitehall. My first leave at home as a sprog pilot and the embarrassment of having to say to all the well-wishers that I was just a new boy.

My return to Bournemouth coincided with Fw190 bomber attacks on the town. So off we were sent to Harrogate. It was there I was told of my posting and not to a single engine AFU (Advanced Flying Unit). That was what I had selected and most of my colleagues were going to Tern Hill.

So off Rodney went to No. 12 (P) Advanced Flying Unit (AFU) at Grantham in Lincolnshire, on No. 10 Course, where he started to fly the twin engine Airspeed Oxford advanced trainer. No. 12 Flying Training School had been formed at Grantham back in 1938 and it was the first FTS to receive the North American Harvard Trainer. In 1939 it had been re-designated No. 12 Service Flying Training School and the Harvard had been replaced by Harts and Oxfords and concentrated on the training for twin engine pilots. The following year the training had been standardised on Oxfords and the unit was re- designated again to No. 12 (P) Advanced Flying Unit. It was conceived as a finishing school for pilots trained in North America or elsewhere in the Commonwealth who would have had no experience otherwise of flying in the often inclement European weather, the blackout over England or just basic map reading over a congested English landscape. After 40 hours flying on the Oxford that Rodney took in his stride, he moved to 1511 Blind Approach Training (BAT) Flight at Upwood in Huntingdonshire, for a further 11 hours, still on the Oxford. Returning to Grantham in July 1942 he completed his course with another 14 hours on the Oxford. Not all were as fortunate as Rodney. Under stress or inexperienced on type, it was all too easy for accidents to happen and though he never suffered the indignity himself, it was not unusual to see an accident on the ground when the hapless pilot, who may have been intent on pulling up the flaps, retracted the wheels instead and drop the Oxford onto its belly to the amusement of all onlookers.

Another incident at Grantham derived from its unsuitability for night flying. Like most RAF bases it was clearly marked on German maps and flare paths used for training inevitably made natural targets, as did slow, unarmed training aircraft doing predictable circuits. The night flying element of the course was therefore conducted from a nearby satellite where the flare path was delineated by paraffin flares and a chance light. Other facilities were however minimal. The tiny watch office on the field situated on the opposite side of the valley to Grantham was usually staffed by AFU pupils who approached the task with little enthusiasm because it was so boring. As the Oxfords endlessly pounded the circuit, there was little to do except wait for a request for landing when the pupil would scan the skies, and assuming there was no other traffic in the circuit, give the aircraft a green light to land. On one particular occasion just such a request to land almost led to an accident when a Lancaster bomber returning from a raid from the Ruhr requested permission to land thinking the satellite airfield was its home base. The bigger bomber only just got down on the satellite's shorter runway with the crew cursing their navigator since he had managed to persuade the pilot that they were over their own base!

> On arrival at Spitalgate, Grantham, I had made the case about what I thought was a mis-match in my posting. Half way through the course came news that I was to go to Tern Hill but only after I finished my training. At least I would be able to follow my preference.
>
> When I finally got to No. 5 (P) AFU my BFTS friends who were just finishing the course told me it had been thought I had done a 'runner' and the RAF Police were out looking for me. I always took this as a bit of 'let's frighten the silly old sod'!

At the end of July he was posted to No. 5 (P) AFU at Tern Hill in Shropshire where he started to fly the Miles Master Marks I and III. Some of the sorties were flown from the satellite field at Calveley in Cheshire and the pace of the course was brisk. On 4 September he flew a Hurricane for the first time for 50 minutes. His first flight in a single engine fighter was something most pilots remembered for the rest of their lives and Rodney was no exception. His initial assessment of the Hurricane with the famous Merlin engine was that it was the most powerful engine he had encountered. The Miles Master was a wooden two-seat trainer powered by a Rolls-Royce Kestrel, Bristol or Pratt and Whitney radial engine, but the Hurricane and Merlin engine gave him 1,000hp for the first time and an airframe with which he was totally unfamiliar, except perhaps in theory.

In an unfamiliar cockpit and strapped in for the first time it was evident that there was something very different about the Hurricane straight away. Brakes released and a cautious taxi and Rodney recalled, 'having to swing the tail from side to side' in order to see ahead because forward visibility was non-existent over the nose while the tail was on the ground. Once the Hurricane had arrived cross wind for the final pre-take-off checks, he experienced a further impression of the power of the engine when it was run up to full throttle in order to test for magneto drop and pitch control; then a smooth opening of the throttle with the left hand and he was away. He felt like he had been dealt a swift blow on the back of the head as the Hurricane surged forward and he was away quicker than he thought and in a short time the wheels left the ground. Then came something that was a standing joke with old-hand Hurricane pilots, a climb like a porpoise because he had to manually raise the undercarriage and with an inexperienced pilot this inevitably meant a seesaw movement in the Hurricane until about 1,000 feet, when the undercarriage had been retracted. The drill was then to execute a dummy approach and landing onto cloud with wheels and flaps down for the approach and 'landing' at about 4,000 feet. It also showed him how quickly the airspeed fell away as the throttle was pulled back and a pronounced change in attitude as the flaps were lowered for a successful landing. Job done.

NO. 58 OPERATIONAL TRAINING UNIT

Rodney was shortly afterwards posted to No. 58 Operational Training Unit (OTU) at Grangemouth in Stirlingshire. Prior to the Second World War, aircrew completed their operational training on their squadrons but once the war had broken out and operations had begun, it became obvious that this could not be carried out by units and or personnel actively engaged on them. At first squadrons were removed from operations and were allocated to the task of preparing new pilots and/or crews, but before long these training squadrons were re-designated 'Operational Training Units'.

The airfield had opened originally on 1 May 1939 as Central Scotland Airport. No. 35 EFTS had used it with their Hawker Harts and DH Tiger Moths and No. 10 Civilian Air Navigation School with Ansons. Until March 1941 the airfield was operational as it was also strategically vital for the protection of the Forth Bridge and Rosyth Docks, where many Royal Navy vessels were based or repaired, so 602 squadron Spitfires, 141 squadron Blenheims and Gladiators and 263 squadron Hurricanes were all stationed there. No. 58 OTU had been formed at Grangemouth on December 2 1940 with Wing Cdr J.R. Hallings-Pott DSO, posted in from 7 OTU at Hawarden, as chief flying instructor, bringing with him a wealth of experience in Spitfire training.

Rodney was posted to No. 26 Course at 58 OTU at Grangemouth where the new chief flying instructor was Sqn Ldr G.W. Petre. The large number of Polish pilots at Grangemouth necessitated a completely 'Polish Squadron', designated A Squadron.

The British squadron, or B Squadron, had seven instructors; F/Lt Humphrey, F/Lt Tofield, F/O West, F/O Beardsley, P/O Porteous, P/O Pocock and Sgt Morrison.

10 SEPTEMBER 1942

Logbook: Master III P/O Pocock and Self. Circuits and Landings.

ORB: After 12 weeks of training at Grangemouth and Balado Bridge 40 pupils from Course 23 passed out on Monday 7 September. Course 26 arrived to start training on Tuesday 8 September. This course comprises 20 Officers and 22 sergeants with 12 British, 19 Polish, 3 American, 7 New Zealand and 1 Rhodesian.

After a short local check out over three trips in a Master III aircraft and a local navigation trip in a Dominie Rodney went solo in a Spitfire I X4899 on 16 September 1942. The Mark I, equipped with a Rolls-Royce Merlin II engine, with a 1,030 hp, a single speed supercharger, glycol cooled and a two-position, variable pitch, three-bladed metal propeller with a top speed of 362mph at 19,000 feet and a service ceiling of 34,000 feet. It was able to climb at 2,500 feet per minute and could reach 20,000 feet in 9 minutes.

He was taken through the various cockpit instruments, knobs, levers and the operation of the reflector gun sight and firing mechanism with its fire safe switch. It was a vast array of gadgets and he had to identify each before he would be allowed to fly the Spitfire. After checking, and checking again, testing the controls, the radio, the oxygen and fuel states, practising rolling the Perspex hood back and forth, switching on the gun sight, testing the range bar, he was ready. With the propeller in fine pitch, he primed the engine, switched on, gave a nod to an airman by the external starter battery, he pressed the starter button and the Merlin engine burst into life. Recounting that moment, years later, some aspects of that first flight were as vivid as if they had been yesterday.

16 SEPTEMBER 1942

Logbook: Spitfire I – X4899- Solo 55 minutes.

> I had done a 35-minute Spitfire Check in a Master III. My instructor F/O Beardsley felt I was OK to go and I did. The next 55 minutes in a Spitfire Mark I was a gingerly conducted exercise, doing circuits, pretending I was landing on top of a feathery white cloud and building up my confidence. At that stage there were no aerobatics and certainly no sideslip approach to a landing. But I got over the first stage and my landing was a three pointer. So I was away and my love affair with the Spitfire could truly be said to have begun.

One of the features of the Spitfire, he discovered, was the wonderful handling characteristic at low speeds and at high 'g' close to the stall. With full power in a steep turn, she would judder, but as long as she was handled correctly, she would not spin. Rodney recalled coming into land on that first flight some years later. He put the airscrew into fine pitch, lowered the undercarriage, turned cross wind, lowered the flaps and straightened out for a final approach before the Spitfire 'floated' down onto the grass airfield again for his 'three pointer'. It was a description that many pilots would come to use about the Spitfire: she tended to 'float' because of her clean lines with a minimum of drag. She was an absolute delight to fly.

> Just a month later and doing a climb to 30,000 feet I came near to being a casualty. Something went quite wrong with my oxygen supply and I came around at 5,000 feet flying straight down towards the hills, fortunately in time for me to recover. I was in a bath of sweat but with the confidence that builds up after a narrow escape.

11 NOVEMBER 1942

Logbook: Spitfire 11B – Grangemouth to Balado Bridge.

Rodney signed off his OTU course having flown 58 hours in a Spitfire. His wing commander signed off his logbook on 1 December and confirmed he passed as 'average'.

ORB: Sqn Ldr G.W. Petre Chief Flying Instructor [CFI] has been posted to an operational squadron. A skilful pilot, a capable instructor and an outstanding gentleman, Sqn Ldr Petre was one of the most popular members of the station. Sqn Ldr P. Davies DFC who arrived from 52 OTU has filled his place as CFI.

The pupils of Course 26 completed their training at 58 OTU. 16 of the pilots of this course are proceeding overseas on completion of their embarkation leave.

From October, all Polish fighter pilot pupils had been sent to No. 58 OTU and it became the only operational training unit where British and Polish flying instructors worked alongside one another.

At the end of 1942, the OTU was able to summarise in its ORB: 'A year of achievement, a year of development and a year of change. In the course of the last 12 months, 400 fighter pilots have passed out from Grangemouth, men of many nations, men of varying skill and character, all imbued with a high fighting spirit, trained to the last degree, replacing the gaps in the old established squadrons, forming new squadrons, serving at home and overseas. Some have given their lives, some are prisoners of war, and others have won renown with their skill and courage.'

Two of the pupils from No. 26 Course at Balado Bridge, Rodney and Tom Hughes, were both sent on attachment to 611 Squadron down at Biggin Hill. Born in 1922 in Rugby, Warwickshire, Tom attended the town's famous school as a day pupil. Aged 18 in 1940, he had joined the RAF Volunteer Reserve as a pilot and started his flying training on DH Tiger Moths at 7 Elementary Flying Training School at Desford in Leicestershire that October. There he flew in a mix of civilian and service-registered machines before moving on to No. 8 Flying Training School at Montrose, Scotland, to fly Miles Masters.

Tom was assessed as 'above average' and was posted to the Central Flying School at Upavon, Wiltshire joining No. 82 Flying Instructors Course flying Airspeed Oxfords and Avro Tutors. After flying for a further 92 hours, and a total of just 202 hours flying, he qualified as a flying instructor on 15 June 1941. Tom then joined No. 11 Service Flying Training School at Shawbury, Shropshire, in June 1941, flying Oxfords. That October he was posted to the College Flying Training School at Cranwell, Lincolnshire, still flying the Oxford, but in December he had moved to the Advanced Flying Unit and started flying Masters as well. In March 1942, he had moved to 60 Operational Training Unit at East Fortune, Scotland, and started to fly a wider range of aircraft types, including the Bristol Blenheim and Bisley, Beaufighter II, DH Dominie, Fairey Battle and Miles Magister.

Finally in September 1942 he moved to 58 OTU at Grangemouth, Scotland, where he met Rodney. Tom now had over 900 hours on nine types of aircraft and was more experienced than some of the instructors. Here, after a few trips in a Master, he first flew a Supermarine Spitfire and gained a further 66 hours on Mark Is and Mark IIs.

Little did Rodney know at this stage, but this was to be the start of a wonderful and long-lasting friendship with Tom, something that would last a lifetime.

CHAPTER FIVE

A WEEK AT THE BUMP, NOVEMBER 1942

In November 1942, with 345 hours flying experience I came to the end of my training and was assessed as 'fighter pilot – good average'. And that was probably why I was sent on attachment to 611 Squadron at Biggin Hill to gain 'some experience on type'. During a week stay I made two trips on a Mk IX – total flying time 1hr 25 minutes. Just about enough to have those responsible for postings to mark my records as 'send him off to North Africa', there to join one of the two squadrons which it was planned were to be equipped with a more effective Spitfire fighter than the Mk V.

Biggin Hill had been at the forefront of the Battle of Britain in 1940 and the RAF actions over Northern France in 1941 and 1942 when the RAF started to take the offensive back to the Germans. The first forays into occupied Europe had been by fighters operating in pairs on so called 'Rhubarb' sorties, looking for targets of opportunity and who took advantage of cloud cover to evade the defending fighters. Spitfires were soon flying in wing-strength formations over Northern France in an attempt to draw up German fighters into a battle of attrition where it was hoped the RAF would prove the merits of having large numbers of fighters. The Germans were by and large reluctant to counter pure fighter sweeps and often stayed on the ground or kept a watching brief from a distance. The general lack of reaction led to the development of 'Circus' Operations where a small number of bombers were escorted by large numbers of RAF fighters on raids into Northern France. The destructive strength of the bombers was small but their presence encouraged the German fighters into the air to fight.

Circus operations had begun to grow in strength and complexity. The core of a force known as the 'beehive' would take the form of three or four squadrons acting as close escort to the bombers, each stepped at 1,000-foot gaps with three more squadrons of the escort as a cover wing that could provide protection to the close escort and the bombers. In addition, further squadrons flew as target support and would clear a route for the bombers and provide close escort to the intended target and were given a free rein on enemy formations that were likely to be climbing to get above the incoming bomber force. Finally, one or more wings would act as withdrawal cover and meet the force on its way home and deal with any further fighters as the escorts could be short of fuel.

Biggin Hill was perhaps the most famous RAF fighter station of them all. It was situated on a plateau on the North Downs to the south of Bromley and had first been developed as a landing ground by the Royal Flying Corps in 1917 for wireless telegraphy experiments. Its proximity to London meant it had played a strategic role in the defence of the capital and its ability to take considerable punishment during the Battle of Britain had been an inspiration. Still bearing the scars of battle it was now home to 611 Squadron that formed part of the Biggin Hill Wing.

The squadron leader at Biggin Hill was Jamie Rankin, a forthright Scotsman born in Edinburgh in 1913, who joined the RAF in 1935. After brief service with the Fleet Air Arm he became an instructor with No. 5 OTU. Early in 1941 he had been promoted to squadron leader and attached to No. 64 Squadron to gain operational experience. He then took command of No. 92 Squadron, then equipped with the new Mark V Spitfire. During the fighter sweeps of the summer, his score had mounted rapidly and in June 1941 he was awarded the DFC for nine victories. In September 1941 he had become Squadron Leader at Biggin Hill and received the DSO the following month. In December 1941 Rankin was posted to HQ Fighter Command, and in April 1942 returned to lead the Biggin Hill Wing for a second time. Blessed with superb eyesight, Jamie, like Sailor Malan, was always fully aware of all that was going on in the squadron he was leading. All the pilots knew that with Jamie in the lead, they would never get jumped: attacked yes, but never bounced by an unseen enemy.

The wing commander for RAF Biggin Hill at the time was Gp Capt A.G. 'Sailor' Malan, probably one of the most famous fighter pilots in the RAF. A South African by birth, he had joined the Merchant Marines in 1924, which earned him his nickname. He joined the RAF in early 1936 and was posted to No. 74 Squadron with whom he fought as a flight commander through the Battle of Britain. The cold winter of 1940/41 and poor weather meant that operational flying was kept to a minimum, a few patrols and scrambles. The lack of activity enabled newer pilots to get some concentrated training and pay some overdue attention to the weaknesses in tactics that had become evident during the clashes with the German fighters in the summer of 1940 and the Battle of Britain. Malan was instrumental in changing Fighter Command into an up-to-date fighting force, by throwing out the old set pattern attacks and tight formations and developing new and effective ones. He became famous for his 10 commandments of engagement in aerial combat, which became well known and used by nearly all RAF squadrons that eventually became part of RAF official doctrine.

1. Wait until you see the whites of his eyes. Fire short bursts of one to two seconds only when your sights are definitely 'ON'.
2. Whilst shooting think of nothing else, brace the whole of your body: have both hands on the stick: concentrate on your ring sight.
3. Always keep a sharp lookout. 'Keep your finger out'.
4. Height gives you the initiative.

5. Always turn and face the attack.
6. Make your decisions promptly. It is better to act quickly even though your tactics are not the best.
7. Never fly straight and level for more than 30 seconds in the combat area.
8. When diving to attack always leave a proportion of your formation above to act as a top guard.
9. INITIATIVE, AGGRESSION, AIR DISCIPLINE, and TEAM WORK are words that MEAN something in Air Fighting.
10. Go in quickly – Punch hard – Get out!

With the acceptance that fighter operations over France were to be carried out in wing strength of up to 36 aircraft or three squadrons it was clear that each wing would need an experienced leader and someone who possessed a high degree of tactical awareness and was capable of leading that many aircraft in such a way that the formation maintained its integrity during operations. The post was called 'Wing Commander Flying' although those promoted to such a role were inevitably called 'Wing Leaders' and Sailor Malan had been promoted from his role as CO of 74 Squadron to command the Biggin Hill Wing when it was set up in 1941.

Wings were the vanguard of the RAF air offensive over German-occupied Europe, becoming more important elements of the Tactical Air Forces formed later in 1943 and increasing use of them was made in North Africa and Italy, where Rodney would play an important role.

611 (West Lancashire) Squadron Royal Auxiliary Air Force had been formed at Hendon in 1936 five days after Liverpool City Council had granted a tenancy to the Air Ministry of five acres of land to the east of Chapel House Farm Speke near Liverpool, on which the new airfield was to be constructed. The Squadron was formed as a unit of the Auxiliary Air Force, a reserve organisation similar to the Territorial Army where the majority of officers and men were recruited from geographical areas local to the unit and who trained at weekends and on an annual two-week training camp. The squadron commanding officer was an Australian, Sqn Ldr Hugo 'Sinker' Armstrong, who had assumed command in November 1942 from Edward 'Jack' Charles, a Canadian who had been the CO from April 1942.

611 Squadron was among the first to take the new Spitfire Mark IX into combat receiving their new aircraft in July 1942, just after 74 Squadron had received its new batch in June 1942. The early production Mark IX standard was fitted with a Merlin 61 engine, E Type wing and large cannon blisters that allowed for the fitting of four 20mm cannon. The Mark IX had been developed because the Spitfire Mark V had been no match the for the new German Fw190 fighter and was essentially a Spitfire VC modified to incorporate the Merlin 61 engine with the latest negative G carburettor. The main difference between the two aircraft were the slightly longer nose due to the larger engine, a four-bladed Rotol constant speed propeller, two thermostatically controlled radiators and two-speed superchargers which were automatically controlled as well as pressurised fuel tanks.

During its trials it had made a profound impression on those developing it at the Air Fighting Development Unit: 'The performance of the Spitfire IX is outstandingly better than the Spitfire V especially at heights above 20,000 feet. On the level the Spitfire IX is considerably faster and its climb is exceptionally good. Its manoeuvrability is as good as the Spitfire V up to 30,000 feet and above that it is much better. At 38,000 feet it is capable of a true speed of 368mph and is still able to manoeuvre well for fighting'

A few months after the Spitfire IX was pitted against a captured FW190 and the report on that comparative trial revealed that the two aircraft were indeed closely matched. It was at this point that the Germans began high altitude operations of a more serious nature and modified some Junkers 86P and Junkers 86R into high altitude bombers that could operate over England during daylight hours with impunity. The Spitfire IX with its high altitude performance could meet such a threat. Indeed the Merlin 61 with its two-stage supercharger delivered 600 horsepower at 40,000 feet and a special unit was formed with the modified Mark IXs that could combat the high altitude raiders.

11 DECEMBER 1942

Logbook: Spitfire IX– Experience on type.

> Next I discovered the power of a Spitfire Mark IX. On that short-term attachment to 611 Squadron at Biggin Hill I gained some experience on type and flew not only a later model; one that was full of operational urge. The responses were immediate, the power inspiring and the confidence built up in me, even for a new boy!

12 DECEMBER 1942

Logbook: Spitfire IX – height climb 25,000ft.

During any squadron's stay at Biggin Hill, each squadron had its favourite pub. The pilots of 609 Squadron preferred the Jail at Biggin Hill where the landlady presented them with their own mascot, a goat! Wing Cdr William B. Goat as it became known moved base with them after they were transferred from Biggin Hill. The American Eagle 133 Squadron adopted the Queens Head at Downe as their local and would cycle down the long steep hill to the village. However, the most famous was the White Hart at Brasted that Rodney remembers with fondness to this day and still frequents. There is no confirmation of the rumour that a certain pilot filched 100 octane fuel from Biggin just to get down to the White Hart in 1942, instead today there is just a wry smile!

A regular at the White Hart had been the Biggin Hill station commander in 1940, Gp Capt Richard 'Dickie' Grice who had won his DFC in the 1914/18 war. Every evening during the Battle of Britain the group captain lay on a coach to take his weary pilots to the White Hart to play a game of darts and eat a meal. Apparently he had a loudspeaker fitted to the roof of his car and as he led the coach from Biggin into the hotel's forecourt, he would announce '25 beers!' (or whatever was required) on the speaker!

Grice was an eccentric and was obsessed with the burnt-out shell of a hangar on the airfield. He was convinced that the Germans believed it to be undamaged and would consequently target the airfield with a bombing raid. The bureaucrats at the Air Ministry stubbornly refused to dismantle the large construction, so the intrepid group captain cunningly arranged for the Royal Engineers to dynamite the former hangar during an enemy air raid.

Unfortunately, a subsequent investigation revealed that the Luftwaffe could not have been responsible and Gp Capt. Grice was court martialled. However such was his popularity amongst his immediate superiors that he was acquitted. Nevertheless, as always, bureaucrats (even in wartime) got the last word and Dickie Grice spent the remaining four years of the war posted to Australia.

A tradition was started at the pub one evening after a huge farewell party was staged at the pub for Grice. During the evening Dickie signed his name on a huge blackout screen in the pub and encouraged his colleagues, by then under the influence of copious amounts of alcohol, to do likewise. The signatures of Brian Kingcome, Al Deere, Jamie Rankin, Sailor Malan, Dickie Milne, Tony Bartley, Johnnie Johnson and Bob Stanford Tuck were all added and became the first names on the board. Over the years others were added and the board became known as one of the country's best-known memorials to 'The Few'. Sadly it is no longer at the pub, it does however have pride of place at the Shoreham Aircraft Museum in the nearby village.

Kath Preston, who ran the White Hart at Brasted, said that when pilots came down from Biggin Hill she would often see one or two sitting quietly on their own not wanting to join in the merriment of others. Speak to them and they would often storm out of the pub. It was obvious that they had lost a dear mate. Enjoying a beer was the last thing on their minds. This happened time and time again. The White Hart is still full of memories although the original bar was removed after a refit. There are still many photos and pictures on the walls.

CHAPTER SIX

OPERATION *TORCH* – NORTH AFRICA, 72 SQUADRON

Very soon after the US had entered the war, Winston Churchill met President Roosevelt in Washington in December 1941. Churchill's plans were to continue to aid Russia, to drive the Axis forces out of Cyrenaica and Libya, and to invade Morocco, Algeria and Tunisia.

This would require a combined Anglo-American occupation of French North Africa and enable the Allies to clear the whole of the African coast of the Mediterranean and give the Allies control of the coast from Tunis to Dakar and in due course open up the Mediterranean Sea from Gibraltar to Alexandria. At the planning stage there were differences of opinion as to where and when the landings would take place but eventually it was decided to make the landings on 8 November. At Casablanca on Morocco's Atlantic coast 24,000 American troops were put ashore and at Oran in Western Algeria a further 18,000 American troops were landed. The landings in Algiers, a little further east and closer to the Axis forces, were mainly British and another 18,000 troops were put ashore. The landings in Morocco were the responsibility of the US Navy while those at Oran and Algiers were the responsibility of the Royal Navy. In total the Allied Forces totalled parts of seven divisions, five American and two British, and came under the overall command of an American commander, General Dwight D. Eisenhower.

The air plan for Operation *Torch* as it became known included two separate geographical commands, the Eastern Air Command (EAC) and the Western Air Command (WAC) both of which would be directly responsible to the Supreme Commander. The EAC was made up almost entirely of RAF squadrons and the WAC was made up almost entirely of the US XII Air Force, some of whom had flown with the RAF in Britain after the US had entered the war the previous December. In the EAC and under the command of 242 Group, there would be several RAF wings.

322 WING – COMMANDED BY GP CAPT C. APPLETON AND LED BY WING CDR PETE 'DUTCH' HUGO

81 Squadron – Spitfire V with Sqn Ldr Ronald 'Razz' Berry
154 Squadron – Spitfire V with Sqn Ldr D.C. Carleton
242 Squadron – Spitfire V with Sqn Ldr Denis Secretan

323 WING – COMMANDED BY GP CAPT EDWARD-JONES AND LED BY WING CDR MIKE G.F. PEDLEY

43 Squadron – Hurricane 2C with Sqn Ldr Mickey Rook
253 Squadron – Hurricane 2C with Sqn Ldr Leonard Bartlett

324 WING – COMMANDED BY GP CAPT RONNIE LEES AND LED BY WING CDR D.A.P. MCMULLEN

72 Squadron – Spitfire V with Sqn Ldr Bobbie Oxspring
111 Squadron – Spitfire V with Sqn Ldr Tony Bartley
152 Squadron – Spitfire V with Sqn Ldr John 'Jackie' Sing
93 Squadron – Spitfire V with Sqn Ldr G.H. Nelson – Edwards
225 Squadron – Hurricane 2C Army Cooperation Tactical Reconnaissance with Sqn Ldr E.G.L. Millington

325 WING – COMMANDED BY GROUP CAPAIN DAVID ATCHERLEY

32 Squadron – Hurricane 2C with Sqn Ldr J.T. Shaw
87 Squadron – Hurricane 2C with Sqn Ldr W.E.G. Measures
232 Squadron – Spitfire V with Sqn Ldr Archie Winskill
243 Squadron – Spitfire V with Sqn Ldr Allan E. Johnson

326 Wing were to fly out from England as soon as airfields were available following the landings. They would fly tropical Blenheim bombers known as Bisleys and would be formed from 13, 18, 114 and 614 Squadrons.

Preparations for the invasion had started some months earlier and 72 Squadron had been moved to Ouston in anticipation of its move overseas. No one knew where they were being posted but the Squadron commenced a ground-training programme in mid-October which included route marches, cross-country runs and physical training every day. Sgt Robbie Robertson recalls:

> We were issued with tropical kit and given a lot more injections, everything from a cold in the nose to the bubonic plague, I think, and we were also given lectures on how to survive in the Far East and we were all laying bets that we'd be sent to India or somewhere. It wasn't that we were all that annoyed at being posted abroad, but it seemed to us that we weren't likely to see very much action, but in fact we did manage to see quite a bit eventually.
>
> Finally, with a few bits of our personal gear packed in parachute bags, we embarked at Liverpool on an ancient merchant ship called the Fort Maclaughlin. It was hardly what you could describe as a pleasure cruiser and 12 of us were down in one of the holds in bunk beds next door to what we could understand were coal bunkers and consequently with the rolling and upping and downing of the ship, all we heard were clangings and bangings. In fact on one occasion there such an

almighty bang that we thought we'd been torpedoed and two of the chaps were out of their bunks and up the stairs onto the deck before you could say 'knife!' In actual fact what had happened was that a large chunk of iron from somewhere had clattered along the deck and frightened the life out of us.

We had a large number of crated aircraft on the deck and on each crate, in letters about a foot high, was the word 'Gibraltar', so we thought well that's the last place we were going to land. Anyway, we went up the Clyde to join the rest of the convoy and there were aircraft and ships all over the place. There were little landing craft zipping to and fro and lots of Dakotas trundling around and it really was quite an impressive sight. We disappeared out into the Atlantic at last and the weather wasn't too good. Fortunately none of us were sick, but we had a wing commander with us, a Wing Cdr MacMullen, a strange chap. He had a round face and he looked like one of these cartoon tigers, and he was very upset if he ever heard anyone addressing him as 'Tiger'. As I say, he was a strange enough lad, we'd never come across him before and he thought it would be a great thing if we had a sweep on who was the first chap to be sick. Well, naturally enough, the first person, and the only person to be sick, was Wing Cdr MacMullen.

As I said the sea was a bit rough and we used to go up on deck and watch all the ships in the convoy bouncing up and down. We had a small aircraft-carrier near us and that was followed by a little corvette and we used to stand up on the deck and watch this corvette going up and down and you could almost see the screws at one end and the front sticking up in the air every now and again – I wouldn't have fancied that job at all.

We were supposed to do anti-submarine lookout, so two of us at a time would go up on deck by one of the Oerlikons and stand there and scour the sea for submarines, but fortunately we never saw anything. In fact we weren't troubled by any submarines on the whole trip, but it didn't alter the fact that you always imagined that you were going to be attacked and had visions of sitting on rafts in the middle of the Atlantic for days on end.

Trying to get some idea of where we were going, a couple of us managed to get up into the chart-room and saw our course plotted and from what we could see, we got nearly to New York and turned round and started coming back again and turned round again and all we seemed to be doing were little circles in the middle of the Atlantic. But eventually we got down and we could see Gibraltar and by that time the sun was shining, the weather wasn't too bad and having got land in sight, we all felt an awful lot better.

Sgt Pilot Laurie Frampton also recalls his transfer to the Squadron and the preparations for their posting abroad.

I joined 72 Squadron as a 'Sprog' Sgt. Pilot just out of OTU on 24 August 1942 and made my first flight with 72 Squadron on 27 August on a Mk V Spitfire. The Squadron was then based at Ayr, and had been informed that it was to be sent overseas. Consequently on 25 September 1942 we moved to Ouston where extra personnel e.g. servicing echelon, catering, stores, transport etc. together with their equipment were added in order to make a fully sufficient mobile unit.

As no replacement day fighter squadron had arrived at Ayr F/O Robertson and I were sent back there until another squadron appeared. The only activity in which we were involved was a convoy patrol over the Firth of Clyde. The convoy consisted of one ship, the Queen Mary, loaded with troops, presumably Americans, who seemed to be very pleased to see us – so we 'showed them the flag'. On 11th Oct. we returned to Ouston.

All ranks had to suffer a 'Backers Up' course, which included route marching and weapons training with machine guns, hand grenades etc. to prepare us to defend ourselves against possible enemy attack. We were given refresher injections and additional injections, advice on health precautions for various climates and finally, five days embarkation leave. I was recalled on the fourth day.

The pilots went to West Kirby P.D.C. (Personnel Dispersal Centre) whence we were dispersed in groups of four or five, each group consisting of members of different squadrons. We went to Northern Ireland and after spending a night at RAF Eglinton we were taken the next morning to the RN docks at Londonderry, which was the base for convoy escorts. Each group was allocated a ship, my group to HMS *Erne*, a Black Swan class sloop of 2,000 tons with a main armament of 6 x 4 inch guns and four depth charge launchers. Since she was moored four miles down Lough Foyle we left port on another ship and transferred to *Erne*.

We sailed from the Lough for Liverpool to collect orders and whilst in port we pilots had to remain below decks. On leaving the Mersey we sailed north collecting small groups of merchant ships until we reached the convoy rendezvous somewhere in the region of Lough Linnhe. The convoy having assembled we headed west into the Atlantic Ocean.

The NCOs were berthed in the chief petty officers mess just below A gun, a twin 4 inch mounting. Our hosts made us most welcome even to the point of introducing us to Nelson's Blood (navy rum – neat).

Three of the escorts were in the van of the convoy to ensure that no nasty visitors were waiting for us. HMS Erne's station was on the starboard bow so all we saw of the other ships was an occasional glimpse of a masthead on the horizon astern. The only exception to this was when we went into the convoy to refuel. One evening there was an extremely loud bang, we all dashed up on deck to find that 'A' gun had fired a star shell, as the radar had picked up a blip which fortunately turned out to be harmless.

The voyage continued in bright sunshine with the ship rolling gently in the deep blue Atlantic swell and early in November we were told of the Eighth Army's success at El Alamein and learned that we were headed for Algiers. Seventeen days after sailing we were told that Erne was to escort the convoy to Algiers but we were to go to Gibraltar, therefore we had to transfer to another vessel. Somewhere in the Atlantic whilst steering northeast towards Gibraltar, we climbed down a rope ladder into a whaler to be rowed across to a corvette and climbed aboard. During the night

> we passed through the straits, both shores being brilliantly lit, and the following morning returned to Gibraltar, to disembark on 10 November eighteen days after leaving Britain.

While the Allies were making preparations the situation in North Africa remained complicated. Morocco and Algeria were both French colonial possessions. The German Army, however, had occupied most of France since mid-1940 when France had surrendered. The terms of the surrender meant that three-fifths of France would be turned over to Germany. The French formed a new government at Vichy under Marshal Petain. The colonial possessions of France, however, remained free if only semi-loyal to France.

With this uncertain relationship existing between the Vichy Government and the North African colonies, the Allies had to be cautious. Over 100,000 Vichy troops were stationed in Algeria, Morocco and Tunisia. An unopposed landing would be preferred, but to broker this without the Vichy Government finding out was difficult. To complicate matters further, the French Navy, including several capital ships, occupied ports in North Africa and their potential opposition to the Allied landing posed a grave threat to the success of the operation.

Eisenhower had a secret meeting with General Henri Giraud in Gibraltar. Eisenhower told General Giraud about Operation *Torch* and persuaded him to become commander of French forces in Algeria, Morocco and Tunisia after the invasion of North Africa.

In the meantime 72 Squadron had arrived in Gibraltar. Robbie Robertson:

> We'd left Liverpool on 20 October and we disembarked at Gibraltar on 6 November. We were given our billets, which turned out to be nissen huts on some part of The Rock, quite where we could never find out, but we weren't too enamoured of the food, everything seemed to taste of oil, and you could smell oil for a mile, it was quite a sickly business. One or two of us managed to get down into Gibraltar town, which wasn't too bad. The main street had lots of bars in it, most of them seemed to be up on the first floor and you'd start going up the stairs, to meet some chap hurtling down because he'd been a bit too drunk and had been thrown out by the local bar-tenders.
>
> It was quite often the case, you'd walk along the road and a chap would shoot out from the doorway in front of you and collapse on the pavement. I had a meal with David Cox once, which was sold as steak and it was very, very tasty, but we learnt afterwards it was horse, but it still tasted all right.
>
> We had very little money with us, but what little we had we changed into French Francs and sat around, waiting to hear what we were supposed to do. Well after a little while we learnt that we had invaded North Africa and we were to fly up to Algiers.

On 7 November the Allied forces landed in Casablanca, Oran and Algiers. The French troops fought back at Oran and General Mark Clark immediately began negotiations with Admiral Jean-Francois Darlan, overall C-in-C of Vichy forces, in an attempt to negotiate a ceasefire. Adolf Hitler threatened Marshal Petain that the German Army would invade Vichy if his troops did not resist. When Darlan surrendered on 11 November, Hitler carried out his threat and occupied the rest of France.

French troops in Morocco stopped fighting but some joined the Germans in Tunisia. General Eisenhower now controversially appointed Jean-Francois Darlan as the political head of French North Africa. The decision infuriated General Charles De Gaulle and the French Resistance who claimed that Darlan was a fascist and a Nazi collaborator. However, with the decision endorsed by Churchill and Roosevelt, Eisenhower brokered a deal with Darlan who would assist military operations in the area.

Sgt Robbie Robertson recalls the preparations for the flights to North Africa.

> We spent a few days wandering around Gibraltar, most of the time in bars or going to the local cinema and finally were told to collect some flying gear and get down on the airstrip, which we did. Now none of the aircraft had any registration numbers or lettering of any kind on them and they were also the tropical mod type Spit, which means they had a great big air filter underneath the propeller boss and they were also fitted with long-range tanks. Now none of us had ever flown an aircraft with a long-range tank and we had no idea of how they'd fly or what we had to do to get them off the ground, we were just told to get to the end of the runway and follow your leader. So we undid the armour-plate behind the seat, stuffed our parachute bags in the back, put the armour-plate back, got in the aircraft and sat and waited. Eventually Bobby Oxspring took off and we all followed one after the other. But by this time all sorts of other squadrons were taking off and there were Spitfires right, left, and centre, and as I say, none of them had any markings at all, and it was more by luck than judgement that we managed to get in some sort of formation and head for Algiers.
>
> Now, I must admit, even to this day, I have no idea how a long-range tank works and whether it takes you off and when it finishes you go on to your main tank, or whether you start with your main tank and then transfer to the auxiliary tank. But in any event we flew very gingerly and we all managed to find our way to Algiers, which was like an ants nest. It's a large aerodrome, but it was packed solid with every kind of aircraft you could think of, from B-17s to practically Tiger Moths, little tiny aircraft that the French had been using and the circuit was another mass of aircraft going round and round. Anyway, we all managed to land without too much difficulty and not knowing where to go we just taxied to a spare spot off the runway and sat there. Eventually some character came up and took our details and we were told to find somewhere to eat and sleep.
>
> Well the only thing we could find in the way of a restaurant, was a small sort of café on the edge of the aerodrome, where we all piled in and had a rather greasy meal and then we had to try and find sleeping accommodation and we couldn't, so we finished up, wrapped up in whatever clothes we'd got, on the floor of the hangar

and it wasn't too comfortable, particularly as they used to bomb Algiers, night after night, although fortunately nothing came near you.

In Sicily General Kesselring reacted swiftly to the invasion and flew troops immediately to Tunis, followed closely by further Me109s and Ju 87s from the Luftwaffe. Reinforcements were flown across as quickly as transports could unload them, fly back and collect the next batch. Every available German bomber in Sicily was made ready to attack the Allied shipping and stores at Algiers but they met heavy anti-aircraft fire and the fighters from the three RAF squadrons who claimed 13 shot down.

Sgt Robbie Roberston recalls those first few days in Algiers:

We each took our turn to patrol Algiers and the docks, to keep off any stray Ju-88s or 109s or whatever they sent down, but we never saw anything at all. After a day of this we were told we were being posted to Bone, which is a port about 300-odd miles farther east. So again we took off with our long range tanks, got to Bone where they had a single runway, more or less like a single track road and the ground off the runway was rough, full of stones, holes and what have you and also a lot of dust. No sooner had we landed and got into the dispersal, which in this case was a concrete-block house, than two 109s came over and started shooting up the aerodrome. There was no way we could have got out of dispersal, got to our aircraft and taken off, so we just had to sit there and watch these 109s shoot the place up. There were supposed to be two of our pilots up in the air, looking for things like this, but they didn't see them on this occasion.

We all took our turn at aerodrome patrol and in the evening when it was dark we had to make our way to Bone and try and find somewhere to stay. There was literally no organisation whatsoever while we were at Bone. We had to wander around the town till we came to a hotel and then try and get rooms there. Fortunately we met up with Jimmy Barralldi, and Jimmy could speak French quite well and he managed to find us rooms in this hotel, which was a good thing. Apart from the fact that there were no lights whatsoever, no candles and we had to blunder our way upstairs and into rooms to find out if there was an empty one anywhere. Finally Johnny Lowe and I managed to find a double bed and we crawled in and that was that.

The following day Owen Hardy and I were picked for the first aerodrome patrol and our first job was to get rid of the long-range tanks. We'd had no instruction on this and although we tried pressing every button and switch and lever, there was no way we could get this damn tank off. Eventually one of us sat in the cockpit and pulled the lever and the other one gave the tank a mighty kick and it fell off. So we tried that with the other aircraft and managed to get all of them off without a great deal of further bother.

We'd been doing our usual patrol up and down the aerodrome, seeing if anything was coming our way, flying as usual about 200 yards apart and on the other side of Owen, who happened to be nearer the sea than I was, a 109 came in very, very low and shot across the aerodrome, shooting things up on the way, turned round and belted for home. Owen Hardy and I both turned in to chase the 109, but we hadn't a great deal of height advantage and from what we could gather the Me109 was a lot faster than we were.

Anyway, we chased this Me109 on the deck for quite a way and I had visions of the thing getting away and I was shrieking at Owen to fire as soon as he could. He was quite calm about it. He lined up the 109, gave it a couple of good bursts and the thing burst into flames and hit the deck. That was our first enemy aircraft in North Africa.

From Bougie on 11 November British Troops pushed forward fast towards Tunis along roads through the coastal hills but came under repeated attacks from the reinforcements the Germans had been able to fly into the Tunisian airfields.

On 16 November 1942, one day late owing to bad weather, 1 Para were dropped at Souk el Arba and encountered no opposition in securing the grass airfield there, from which 324 Wing was to operate. By 20 November 72, 93 and 152 Squadrons were operating from Souk el Arba and 111 Squadron joined them on 3 December. Souk el Arba was about 80 miles from Tunis and Bizerte, about 60 miles from Tebourba and 50 miles from Djebel Abiod and was the nearest airfield to the front. At Bone the four squadrons of 322 Wing were kept busy lending support to the Army by protecting the port and the shipping as they were using it to supply the advancing troops. Both the Army and the RAF had to rely on numerous coastal craft and troop carriers for re-enforcements and supplies as larger ships could not get into Bone.

Robbie Roberston recalls the move to Souk el Arba:

The next day we scarcely seemed to have been in bed for more than five minutes when we were all called to get up and get packed. Well getting packed wouldn't normally have taken long because we scarcely had anything with us, but in the pitch dark we had to fumble about the bedroom, finding bits and pieces, stuffing them in our parachute bags and coming down into the cold morning. We were put in trucks and taken back to Bone and told to go off and do a sweep over Beja, which at that time was in enemy hands. We did this, didn't hit anything, didn't see anything and were told to land at a place called Souk el Arba on the way back. We were told that we'd recognise the landing field at Souk el Arba because there was a crashed Potez or some such bomber, smack in the middle of it.

Anyway we found it all right, we all landed but it was like landing on the moon. It was rough, hard mud with the usual dust and potholes and we wondered how long our tyres would last. The town of Souk el Arba, or large village, was at one end of the aerodrome and a road with ditches either side, ran from the town right through the middle of the aerodrome. So we parked our aircraft on one side of the ditch, went to the other and just stood around.

During the day some ground troops arrived, together with supplies of petrol and ammunition, and having nowhere else to store it, we piled all the four-gallon petrol cans in the ditches alongside the road that ran from the little town of Souk el Arba, straight through the aerodrome. The cans were theoretically hidden under the trees, but there was really nowhere else to put the things.

We were given boxes of K Rations but we had nowhere to sleep and no clothes. We managed to dig out some rather poor tents from the French and also managed to scrounge a couple of paper-like blankets. Now although the weather was very nice during the day, pleasantly warm, the minute the sun went down, which was normally about 5 o'clock, everything went completely black. It was freezing, and we crawled to bed and woke up shivering like mad. We managed to scrounge a few more blankets, but even so it wasn't too warm at night and we continued like this for something like a fortnight.

Water was another problem. We'd go into the village and fill our water bottles from the bowser and then put in the little pills we were given to keep us clear of diseases and so on, but there was not enough water to wash in and consequently, after a few days, we were a bit scruffy.

Sgt Laurie Frampton:

On 19th Nov. we flew to Bone and slept that night on the floor of a villa, at least marble tiles were more luxurious than concrete. Next day we flew a reconnaissance to the Beja area in Tunisia and landed on an airstrip at Souk el Arba about 25 miles west of Beja, which we understood to be occupied by the Paratroops. The strip was a level area of hard baked earth with no signs of life, only cans of 100-octane petrol stacked in a ditch on the opposite side of the road. After an hour the first lorry of the RAF servicing commandos arrived, they were wireless mechanics with no gear for refuelling. Using their jack knives they prised the seals out of the cans and together we managed to get fuel into the aircraft. In the meantime contact had been made with the local French army unit who loaned us two elderly bell tents and a few thin blankets. After a hectic drive through the Atlas Mountains the rest of the commandos arrived and a degree of servicing was established.

On our arrival at Souk el Arba we had selected an area on the opposite side of the road for a campsite for when the squadron caught up to us. We erected the bell tents here and dug a slit trench nearby. One night in the small dark hours there was much noise, I woke up and saw a hole in the top of the tent, there was one other person in the tent, we leapt out of bed and headed for the slit trench to be greeted by the other bodies, climbing out. Jerry had dropped a stick of bombs and had now departed – no serious damage done.

Sgt Jack Lancaster:

The following day we were called together and I was told to take a party along with Bill Mann to the airport, to Maison Blanche, and we boarded a C47 crewed by Americans and we took off and flew to Souk el Arba at about 200 feet all the way. There was one of 43 Squadron's Hurricanes on either side of us to give us a bit of protection. We landed at Souk el Arba and the Americans never even stopped the engines, they just turned round at the end of the runway and took off again.

We found our way across this field of sand and mud, and goodness knows what, to where our aircraft were dispersed and we were met by the, I think it was the CO, who told us that the first thing we should do was to dig ourselves a slit trench as quickly as possible because the Germans would be likely to visit us within the next hour and in actual fact this is what they did as six 109s screamed across the airfield and dropped bombs and were strafing. This sort of thing happened quite frequently over the next seven or eight days and the Squadron endeavoured to put up aerodrome patrols to try and catch some of these chaps. Now then, this was before the actual squadron ground crews had arrived, there were just us, about 20 lads, to look after the aircraft and it was a bit difficult sort of keeping the aircraft going because of not having any spares. I remember one aircraft landed and it had a bad gash in one of the tyres. We had a crashed Spit across the airfield near to where the entrance was from the road and I took some lads across to take a wheel off this aircraft so that we could keep our aircraft serviceable.

However, when we got to the crash I got the lads under one wing and they lifted it up and as I was taking the wheel off they suddenly dropped it on me! I wondered what the dear oh me was going on and I said 'Hey where are you going?' and they just ran away. Just then I looked across the airfield and I saw all these sort of flashes on the ground and I, so naïve, I just didn't know what they were. And then one 109 just nipped right over my head and I suddenly realised that once again our German friends were coming to visit us and this chap had obviously been firing at me but he ran out of ammunition before it got to me. So I was very lucky. Anyway, I didn't half give those blokes a bit of a telling-off for leaving me stuck underneath the aircraft because I couldn't get out. Anyway, they lifted the wing up and I managed to get out with the wheel and we went back to the dispersal and got our aircraft serviceable.

At Souk el Arba on the plain, initially conditions were fine. Dust was the main problem. The pilots and ground crew were all in tents with trenches nearby in case of attacks, and these were frequent. The airfield was littered with wrecks of aircraft and among them piles of empty petrol tins. Men lived in their uniforms or what was left of them. They would be dirty for days, with long hair and unshaven but they were excellent in servicing the aircraft and keeping the squadrons flying. During the day conditions were hot and sunny and they would be able to work in shirtsleeves, but it was cold at night. Because conditions were dry, the ground was crumbly and dusty and cracks appeared regularly. The airfield was situated on cultivated land but it was difficult to see how anything could be grown. Surrounded by mountains on each side, there were two rivers situated either side. Tents were pitched on bare earth.

Then came the rain; and how it rained. Day and night, it was relentless. The ground became sodden, they were soaked and then flooded. The earth turned to mud and then a quagmire. Even simple tasks like walking became difficult and the aircraft became bogged down. No transport could move, except the four-wheel-drive 3-ton lorries.

Laurie Frampton recalls:

> During December heavy rains turned the airfield into a quagmire, Summerfeld track (a sort of large heavy duty wire netting held down by steel bars and spikes) was laid to form a runway and taxi track. The mud came up through the mesh and on take-off the radiator would sometimes become so clogged with the stuff that an immediate landing was necessary. The taxi track became very holey and rutted and on occasion everyone would turn out at night to provide human jacks under Spitfire wings to lift an a/c out of a hole and move it onto more solid ground. To stop our tents from falling down we had to drive the pegs into the mud and lay sand bags on the guy ropes.
>
> During this period we were involved with daily sorties involving offensive sweeps over the German-occupied territories from Mateur to Tunis and to the south to the Kairouan area, escort to Hurricanes on bombing and reconnaissance, defensive patrols over base, occasional scramble when air attack was imminent. Whilst on a number of these sorties no contact was made with e/a but the squadron was compiling a not inconsiderable score, personally I was learning what air fighting involved, with very little to show for my efforts. I had a few encounters, e.g. diving after a 109, which was getting away, when I pulled out of the dive the reflector sight had gone blank, the spring clip holding the bulb holder in the base of the sight had been pulled out by the G. When escorting Hurricanes on a recce near Mateur, we were told that the Hurricanes, in the event of enemy action, were to return to base and not get in our way. During the resultant melee an a/c with rounded wing tips was turning to port 150 yds ahead of me, I was about to open fire when it straightened up, it was a Hurricane which should have been back at base by then. One sweep was to cover the army advance through the Sedjenane valley; cloud base was level with the tops of the hills on either side. When we arrived the preceding squadron was still on patrol, imagine 24 Spitfires milling around in a very restricted space. Two a/c did collide, in the circumstances we got off lightly.

They were repeatedly attacked and it became usual practice to have standing patrols over the airfield but the constant interruptions had airmen and ground crew jumping for cover in slit trenches to avoid the strafing attacks and bombs. Almost daily they had to endure raids and the pressure began to tell. Robbie Robertson recalls one such attack:

> If at that time the Germans didn't know where we were, it didn't take them long to find out, because the following day two 109s screeched down the valley, across the aerodrome, up and away, before anyone could take off. So after that we had two aircraft in the air all day long and two on the ground ready to take off. I'd just landed after doing an aerodrome patrol, parked the aircraft and was sitting down, writing a letter to Mum. Now we were expecting another squadron to come and join us at Souk el Arba and no one was particularly surprised when they saw a batch of about

a dozen aircraft in line astern, idling, circling the aerodrome and it looked as though they were coming in to land, until someone suddenly looked up and shouted '109s!'

Well, after that you couldn't see us for dust. There was no way we could get from where we were, across the ditch, into our aircraft and take off, before the 109s came down. In fact they were halfway down before someone started shouting. So we all scattered like mad and I ran as fast as I could, obviously, and then flung myself down on the ground. At that time we had no slit trenches or anywhere else to hide and there were a few of the ground crew who flung themselves into ditches, but unfortunately that's about the first thing the Hun shoots up, apart from aircraft.

We had American anti-aircraft gunners stationed round the aerodrome with their 0.5 machine guns and they were blasting off at everything within sight, but they didn't hit anything, at least no 109s. But the 109s managed to hit the petrol, and some of our ammunition and the petrol went up with a terrific whoosh and although we were, by this time, about 150 yards away, you could feel the blast on the side of your face as though you were sitting near a fire. Anyway, after the first run, I must admit I was scared stiff, and it's no fun lying in the middle of a field where you can hear the bullets hitting the ground and ricochets going right, left and centre and you can't tell from the noise of the bullets, whether they are coming across you, the side of you or through you. Anyway, none of the pilots were hit, so as I say after the first run, we decided to get a little farther away from the action. I got up to run away, and a chap who was some way from me, shouted out 'Give me a hand, Robbie!'

It was Sgt Hussey, who had come across one of our chaps with holes in his stomach and he was trying to drag him along. So I changed my mind and ran back, helped get hold of this shot-up chap. We managed to get him underneath a lorry and there we stayed until all the action had died down. I wasn't madly happy, because I thought they were more likely to shoot up a lorry then they were some chap out on his own in the middle of a field, but fortunately they didn't attack our particular lorry and so we got up afterwards and counted our numbers.

We'd lost several of our ground crew who had taken shelter in the ditches including a couple of Arabs who'd decided to shelter behind the petrol cans but we didn't find those until we started throwing mud and dust onto the fires to put them out, when we came across these two burnt up characters; it wasn't very pleasant.

An hour or so later we were shot up by 190s, but fortunately they did very little damage to our aircraft and none of the personnel, although two of the squadrons which shared the aerodrome with us, 152 and 93, had a fair bit more damage, in fact 152 were pulled out soon after this.

We lost seven or eight aircraft completely destroyed and after that we were never able to put a whole squadron in the air at the same time and consequently we used to join up with 93 and make up a squadron between us. Sometimes Bobby Oxspring would lead and sometimes Nelson-Edwards, the CO of 93 would.

The poor state of the roads in Algeria due to the rain meant that Allied forces in the east of that country and in Tunisia were often short of supplies. Moreover, there were few airfields in the area equipped for all-weather operations, which meant aircraft often became bogged down following periods of heavy rain. These factors imposed severe restrictions on their sortie rates. The Germans by contrast were better placed in the early part of the campaign. Numerically they were the weaker force but their airfields in central Tunisia were better equipped and the arrival of JG2 and its Fw190s gave the Germans a measure of technical superiority. As a result, on occasions the Germans were able to establish air superiority over the battle area, yet for much of the winter, poor weather prevented effective air operations being performed by either side. At times the British were bombed at night. Robbie Roberston:

> We also started getting bombed at night quite regularly and apart from high explosive, a lot of butterfly bombs were dropped, which opened out like little peeled oranges when they hit the ground and scattered shrapnel right, left and centre. But as we were still lying flat on the ground in our little tents, nothing hit us, but the tent had a lot of holes in it. After that we decided to dig slit trenches and these sprung up all over the place and most nights we spent a good part of the night stuck in them. Consequently we were up in the morning a bit on the tired side.
>
> A squadron of Beaufighters had come in and taken over the far side of the aerodrome and they used to keep off the Hun as much as possible at night although we were still bombed, but one night we were in our slit trench as usual and I heard an aircraft go over and then a whistling noise and Danny Daniel, who knew everything, said 'Don't worry chaps, it's a Beaufighter, you can tell by the whistle.'
>
> Well the snag was the whistle was the bomb coming down. So after that Danny had a bit of ribbing to put up with.

The rain continued over Christmas, and the conditions were horrendous. The tents became inundated with mud, aircraft became bogged down and the airmen and ground crew were soaked through. There were no deliveries of mail, no food and no drink so all in all they had a pretty miserable Christmas. Trying to extricate the aircraft from the mud became challenging. The engines were run up to full throttle, with men on the tail and underneath the wings, with the four-wheel-drive lorries laying wire matting down in front of them but the Spitfires just slipped farther and farther into the mud. Even when they were able to take off, landing in the mud caused the Spits to flip over on their backs and the airfield became littered with aircraft wrecks.

CHAPTER SEVEN

NORTH AFRICA, JANUARY 1943

> A two week trip on a transport – HMT Salacia brought us to Gibraltar where we arrived in early January. During our last night on board we had the constant boom of depth charges going off to protect the many ships anchored in Gibraltar Bay. The trip was an opportunity for me to establish a warm friendship with Tom Hughes – something I continue to enjoy to this day. Our time in Gibraltar was spent testing Spit Vs that were being assembled as replacements for the Tunisian Front.

Tom Hughes and Rodney had been together at 58 OTU at Balado Bridge and Grangemouth in Scotland and had been posted for the same operational experience to 611 Squadron at Biggin Hill for the two weeks the previous month. It seemed as though fate was playing a hand in their friendship.

14 JANUARY 1943

Logbook: Spitfire VC Tropical – experience on type.

Prior to Operation *Torch* about 300 fighters had been shipped out to Gibraltar to be assembled and tested and all told when the invasion started there were about 350 aircraft clustered around the runways and hastily built hard standings. In the end rock had to be moved from the north face to make additional hard standings. The airfield was extended into the Mediterranean and was able to accommodate up to 450 fighters, 60 Hudson reconnaissance bombers, 36 Fleet Air Arm aircraft, 15 Photo Reconnaissance aircraft and 10 Catalina Flying Boats. The pressure on the airfield and on the air traffic control was immense with the number of aircraft movements. Gibraltar remained vital when aircraft were flown into and out from England as the first stop en route around the Bay of Biscay and the coasts of Spain and Portugal to avoid German-occupied France. Ultimately, Gibraltar resembled a huge aircraft carrier at sea for all the aircraft that were required for Operation *Torch* and its subsequent reinforcements.

Y SQUADRON NORTH FRONT GIBRALTAR 15 JANUARY 1943

Logbook: Spitfire VC Tropical – sector reconnaissance.

Winston Churchill had flown into Casablanca after a journey of almost 10 hours across the Bay of Biscay and the Mediterranean and stood on the beach there. The purpose of his journey was to meet with his combined Chiefs of Staff and President Roosevelt to hammer out a common strategic policy for the next stages of the war. As the Prime Minister's aircraft had droned across the Mediterranean, General Bernard Montgomery, in charge of the British Eighth Army issued a stirring message to his troops: 'The leading units of the Eighth Army are now only about 200 miles from Tripoli and the Eighth Army is going to Tripoli. Nothing has stopped us since the Battle of El Alamein in October 1942 and nothing will stop us now.'

Montgomery's attack began on the 15th, on schedule, with about 700 tanks. General Rommel could only muster about 90 tanks, two-thirds of which were Italian. The Axis forces fell back and the route was open to Tripoli.

16 JANUARY 1943

Logbook: Spitfire VB Tropical – Ssector reconnaïssance.

At the Casablanca conference Eisenhower reported to the combined Chiefs of Staff on the planned attacks on Sfax. He faced a dilemma: he could either allow the troops in the North of Tunisia to deteriorate by remaining inactive in the appalling conditions in the mud or suffer more losses by pressing ahead despite the conditions. In his opinion, the latter was the lesser of two evils. There was however disagreement at the Conference. General Alexander believed Tripoli could be taken quickly but no further advance east was possible until the port had been cleared and that this would take several weeks. Rommel would thus be given breathing space in which to react to the proposed American move on Sfax in the west. General Brooke stressed that the Allied attacks would be in danger of being defeated by Rommel and he persuaded Eisenhower that the offensive against Sfax could be postponed until the Eighth Army could link up with them after a concerted push in the east. The Casablanca conference also agreed that the Mediterranean theatre would remain top priority rather than being downgraded in preference for a cross-Channel assault into Northern France; that was still some way off. The command structure was also finalised. The conference appointed General Eisenhower as Supreme Commander with General Alexander as his deputy and Air Marshal Tedder as Supreme Air Commander.

18 JANUARY 1943

Logbook: Spitfire VB Tropical – 1. Aerobatics 2. Ferry Gibraltar – Oran – 20 aircraft.

19 JANUARY 1943

Logbook: C47 Dakota – Oran – Gibraltar.

20 JANUARY 1943

Logbook: C47 Dakota – Gibraltar – Algiers – Maison Blanche.

The rains in North Africa had continued into January. Conditions became so horrendous that four new strips were laid down at Souk el Khemis about 12 miles farther east from Souk el Arba. Wire mesh of about 6 inches square and about ¼ inch thick known as Somerfield tracking was laid to make a makeshift runway about 30–40 yards wide and about 400 yards long. The strips were slotted together and laid on the ground in an effort to hold the mud together so the Spitfires could take off without getting bogged down. Conditions were marginally better. The Squadron lived at a farm about two miles from the airstrip. The officers had a mess in a disused railway station, the sergeants mess was in a marquee and the airmen's mess was in a cowshed. Cows and pigs wandered around and Arab children played amongst the aircraft. For a while they were not detected by the Germans, so the number of attacks they had to endure was reduced. The four new airstrips were named after London railway stations Euston, Paddington, Marylebone and Kings Cross. 72 Squadron operated from Euston.

Sgt Jack Lancaster recalls the Squadron move from Souk el Arba to Souk el Khemis:

> We moved from Souk el Arba to Souk el Khemis after the rain got too much for the aircraft, the aircraft were bogged down, we were in a terrible state. We moved to Souk el Khemis which was dryer ground which was very very sandy, but it was much better and they managed to lay down a wire netting runway which helped considerably ... our Sqn was going to be re-equipped with Mk9s and the pilots took the old aircraft away – I don't know where they took them to – but they went back to Gibraltar and came back with some Spit 9s. Now the Mk 5s were fully equipped with filters for the air intake and we didn't suffer a great deal of trouble from spark plug trouble due to sand; however, when we got the 9s every trip we were getting trouble with plugs, and eventually within a few days we had to start changing the front eight plugs, two in each cylinder, of the first two cylinders on each side due to the fact that they were full of sand and obviously the magneto drop was beyond allowance. Not only that, the automatic boost controls got full of sand as well and these had to be removed, cleaned and lubricated and put back and there was nobody on the Sqn able to do this only the NCOs due to the fact that a flight mechanic isn't allowed to or didn't know how to. Only the fitters could do it and the fitters in the maintenance flight were, I believe, at Gare de Mayo about 50 miles back so we had to soldier on as best we could and I think I must have dismantled and cleaned and put back over 50 automatic boost controls in the short time that we were there at Souk el Khemis. I remember one day I was standing on one of the aircraft, had the automatic boost control in bits and I was saying rather nasty things about the people who sent out Spit 9s without filters to a sandy Africa and a voice over my shoulder said, 'Well I can understand your feelings lad, but it was the only thing we could do for the time being and we shall get over it as soon as we can'.

> I turned round to find that he was an Air Vice Marshal and he was the engineer for, not the Mediterranean Allied Command, it was the 242 Group I think. I was careful in the future not to express my feelings without knowing who was around.

Rodney's squadron leader would be Bobby Oxspring. He had taken over the Squadron the previous year whilst they were still based at Biggin Hill and before their posting to Acklington in Northumberland after Brian Kingcome had been promoted to take over the Kenley Wing. Oxspring recalled his original posting to the Squadron.

> I was lucky enough to be plucked from Hawkinge to take Brian Kingcome's place as CO of 72 Squadron. As a measure of his status as a leader he handed over to me what was surely ranked as the best drilled, most experienced and aggressive fighter Squadron in the RAF. He introduced me to this cosmopolitan bunch of tough operators. Within the pilot complement about half were British, two were Australians, a Canadian, a New Zealander, a South African, two Americans and two Norwegians.

This 'cosmopolitan bunch' had then been augmented by half a dozen old sweats when the Squadron was told of their imminent posting overseas the previous November. Oxspring needed experienced pilots who had already completed a tour of operations and were now in instructional roles at operational training units around the UK. After a request had been made to the AOC of the then 13 Group, AVM Jock Andrews, a motley crew arrived for their second tour of operations with No. 72 Squadron. Amongst them were Chas Charnock, Jimmy Corbin, Pete Fowler, Alan Sexton Gear, Jimmy Le Cheminant and D.J. Prytherch. It was into this illustrious company that the four new pilots, including Rodney Scrase and Tom Hughes, would now join.

On the ground Tripoli fell late on 23 January to the advancing British Eighth Army but in the north the British 1st Army and the American Army continued to struggle in the appalling conditions in the mountains. Tunis was re-enforced by Rommel with troops from Italy who even prepared to go on the offensive. Conditions for the Army were appalling, equipment was old and battered including the mercurial 15 cwt trucks, their diet was poor – bully beef and petrol-flavoured water – and their desert sores could not be cured. Many experienced troops or regulars had either been killed or wounded and shipped home or to hospital.

Early in the New Year, two experienced pilots within the Squadron, Derek Forde and Ian Krohn had become tour expired and were posted. Their replacements were from within the Squadron. David Cox – 'Coxy' – took over one flight and dangerous Danny Daniel the other. Both had served on the Squadron with Oxspring since its Biggin Hill days and had enhanced their records considerably since the Squadron's arrival in Tunisia. Oxspring recalled their appointment with fondness:

> In his early days dangerous Danny did not exactly fly a Spitfire, he poled it into positions he wanted by copious use of all the controls. His landings were a series of

> hairy incidents. On more than one occasion he forgot to turn his gun button to safe, which nearly proved disastrous as he pulled back the stick against his massive frame. This final gesture before touch down on squared wheels, spewed forth a hail of cannon fire which galvanised the ground crews and any other passing airmen into a frantic search for cover.

Nevertheless Danny proved more lethal to the Germans than his own side and he was destined to take over the squadron from Bobby Oxspring when he too became tour expired.

David Cox was a Battle of Britain veteran from 19 Squadron in Douglas Bader's wing at Duxford and was a natural leader. Later in the war he would become Rodney's squadron leader with 1 Squadron at Manston in Kent.

28 JANUARY 1943

Logbook: C47 Dakota –1. Algiers Maison Blanche – Tingley 2. Tingley – Souk el Arba. F/Lt Mortimer Rose DFC killed in collision with Wing Cdr G.K. Gilroy DSO, DFC whilst in circuit.

ORB: 6 aircraft, two flown by pilots of 241 Squadron left at 0720 hours to reconnaissance roads and railways between Jefna and Mateur. No movement was seen. Slight flak just east of Jefna and all aircraft landed safely at 0815 hours. 6 aircraft with 2 Tac R Hurricanes left at 1615 hours to reconnaissance area south of Pont du Fahs. About 10 miles south west of Pont du Fahs F/Lt Daniel and Sgt Hussey shot up a heavy tank with a big gun on top which they observed smoking as they flew away. P/O Cheminant fired at 3 lorries, one of which went up in flames. All aircraft landed at 1700 hours. Four new pilots were posted to the Squadron today – F/O Tom Hughes, P/O Rod Scrase, Sgt A.E. Passmore and Sgt J.B. King.

> And it was at the end of the month that Tom and I were ferried by USAAC Dakota to Maison Blanche and then on January 28th to Souk el Arba. So commenced my 15-month stay with 72 Squadron. A short drive in a 15cwt Bedford and we arrived at the new airfield at Souk el Khemis where 72 Squadron were flying from, one of several strips named after London railway stations, ours being Euston. My first day and we were driven down to dispersal to see the Squadron take off as one of a formation in wing strength to escort some Hurricanes. Our first sight was to see on their return a mid-air collision at less than 1,000 feet. The recently appointed Flight Commander to 111 Squadron, F/Lt E.B. Mortimer Rose DFC hit the wing commander's plane. Mortimer Rose lost a wing and went straight into the ground and was killed instantly. The wing commander 'Sheep' Gilroy baled out and landed safely with only minor injuries.

Sqn Ldr Bobby Oxspring remembered the incident too: 'The Wing Leader, Sheep Gilroy and Edward Mortimer Rose rammed into each other over Khemis. Morty spun in and died but Sheep was more fortunate and managed to bale out with only slight injuries.' Greggs 'Spanner' Farish, the Squadron Engineer Officer also recalled the incident:

> Among the many aircraft turning round the sky above the two aerodromes, I saw one spinning down with one wing sliced off. It hit the ground, exploded and when we got to it later the pilot and engine were about 14-feet deep. We thought there were Me109s about but there weren't, looking up again, there was another Spitfire spinning out of control. A blob then separated from it at about 1,000 feet and a parachute opened. It was the wing commander himself, 'Sheep' Gilroy, cut in the face and much shaken from the collision and such a low jump. Mortimer Rose DFC and Bar to be exact, was originally a ferry pilot at Gibraltar chafing his cheeks to get into the fighting. One day he had ferried a replacement Spitfire up to 93 Squadron at Souk el Khemis and refused to go back. He was so persistent that he flew 'arse end Charlie' for 93 Squadron for about two weeks like a sprog Sergeant Pilot. Finally the Group Captain arranged for him to take over a flight in 111 Squadron and the day his official posting came through he was killed in the collision with the Group Captain himself!

He also recalled the arrival of Rodney Scrase and Tom Hughes:

> One day in the little house by the railway line which we used as a mess at Khemis, four new pilots arrived, amongst them one Joe Scrase his name, very young, very talkative and just finished training. Another was Tom Hughes. He was quiet, especially reluctant to mention himself but when he did talk, if only it were a few words, you heard a beautiful voice, speaking pure English. He had a healthy, ordinary, rather spotted face with brown hair. Only the wrinkles on his forehead and his powerful shoulders showed him to be a man.
>
> They looked at his logbook and discovered that he had over a thousand hours flying already, more than any other member of the Squadron. He had been passed as a 'Q' Instructor at the Central Flying School, the highest qualification a pilot can get in the RAF and a rarity in wartime. He had also flown many types. Most new pilots had flown Tiger Moths, Masters and then Spitfires but to this Tom could add Harvards, Hurricanes, Oxfords, Blenheims and Beaufighters. He had only recently come onto fighters having been an instructor at a night fighter Beaufighter and Blenheim twin-engine operational training unit. He had an engineering background and so took on Pete Fowler's place as my test pilot. He would come down after landing and modestly take much trouble to understand what we might be testing and to explain symptoms of what might be wrong. Indeed he was mad on flying, on flight and in the air, he lived for and loved flying and he knew more than anyone I had ever met.

29 JANUARY 1943

ORB: 12 aircraft at 1345 hours were airborne to sweep the Pont du Fahs area. When 23 miles north of Kairouan Blue Section went down and attacked 3 medium sized transports that were left with smoke and flame coming from them. Several motorcyclists were seen approaching a bridge in the same area and were attacked by F/Lt Daniel, P/O Prytherch and Sgt Passmore. Two Macchi 202s were seen flying north but no contact was made. Slight heavy flak, accurate for height but not range was experienced south of Pont du Fahs. All aircraft landed at 1515 hours.

30 JANUARY 1943

Logbook: Spitfire VB – sector reconnaissance W/O Gear showed me around the front.

> On January 30th I did my first flight with 72, a 40-minute sector reconnaissance ably shepherded by Warrant Officer 'Sexton' Gear. Never did know how he got that name, probably a symbol of his extraordinary moustache. And then came confirmation of the news that we were to go back to Gibraltar to collect our Mark IXs.

While with 72 Squadron Warrant Officer Alan Gear was given the nickname 'Sexton', quite why, no one could remember! His name was often abbreviated to the first three letters and then sometimes used with his surname hence 'Sex Gear'. He was also renowned for always wearing his toupee, which presented an interesting sight with his moustache as he had been carefully cultivating the latter, following a wager with an RAF colleague to see who could grow the longest one. He always maintained that he wore it sticking out of his oxygen mask to frighten off any close flying German pilots!

ORB: 5 aircraft (1 flown by a pilot of 241 Squadron) left at 0655 hours to reconnaissance roads south east of Medjez, the Salt Lakes and Pont du Fahs. A gun post situated in a farmyard 2 miles south west of the big lake was shot up. All aircraft landed safely at 0735 hours.

6 aircraft at 1200 hours patrolled area east of Medjez el Bab. 6 aircraft were seen but these turned out to be friendly. No other incidents. 12 aircraft left at 1400 hours to cover army movements. They patrolled over Medjez and Mateur but no aircraft were seen. All landed safely at 1525 hours.

31 JANUARY 1943

ORB: 12 aircraft left at 0920 hours with Hurribombers to attack a Wadi containing motor transport vehicles south west of Pont du Fahs. 2 aircraft returned early with engine trouble and all aircraft landed safely at 1020 hours.

7 aircraft (1 flown by a pilot of 225 squadron) left at 1420 hours to take oblique photos east and south of Medjez el Bab. A lot of smoke and artillery

fire was observed just north of the big lake north west of Pont du Fahs. All aircraft landed safely at 1500 hours.

In February 1943 Axis Troops opposite the British Eighth Army were now positioned in the old French frontier defence at Mareth that had been designed originally to cover Tunisia against an Italian attack from Tripolitania. This line stretched 80 miles from the Mediterranean to the Matmata Hills and offered excellent protection. Rommel was able to re-enforce his troops there by thinning his forces elsewhere. Montgomery on the other hand had to bring up additional supplies and was slowed down and Rommel saw an opportunity to strike against the British and American forces on the other side of Tunisia through the mountains and the Kasserine pass.

1 FEBRUARY 1943

ORB: For the first time since their arrival in North Africa the Squadron was taken off operational flying. The pilots left for Constantine at 1,000 hours by road to rest for a few days before proceeding to Gibraltar to collect new Spitfire IX aircraft. Meanwhile in view of the re-equipping of the Squadron with the new Mark IXs the transfer of the Spitfire Vb's to other units began.

2 FEBRUARY 1943

ORB: The pilots arrived safely at Constantine and went to the RAF aircrew rest home. At Souk el Khemis at approx 0930 hours enemy fighter-bombers attacked Waterloo airstrip causing damage and casualties. Our Squadron AA Flight did not open fire as the enemy aircraft were out of range.

3 FEBRUARY 1943

ORB: Once again at almost the same hour as yesterday enemy fighter-bombers made a further attack on Waterloo airstrip causing further damage and casualties.

4 FEBRUARY 1943

ORB: In the morning enemy aircraft approached the base several times but successfully repelled by our fighters. Many vapour trails were seen and also much cannon and machine gun fire heard.

7 FEBRUARY 1943

Logbook: C47 Dakota Telergma – Maison Blanche.

ORB: Pilots left Constantine by road for Telergma where they were flown by Dakota for Algiers on route for Gibraltar. They had a very comfortable and enjoyable time at the rest house and landed at Maison Blanche after seventy minutes. It was intended to continue the journey that day but all the available Dakotas were being used for supply flights to the Tunisian front so they remained at Algiers.

> A long drive by 3-Tonner and 15-cwt over the mountains to Constantine. There another few days waiting for USAAC Dakotas to fly us back first to Maison Blanche at Algiers and then onto Gibraltar. In our week back in Gibraltar there was some flying the Mark IX to gain experience on type. Most interestingly we had a chance to make a round-the-rock cruise in a submarine. We had got to know some of the navy types and their commanding officer invited us underwater on board HMS *Thames*, a large river class boat in which half a dozen of us watched a different type of handling and peered through the periscope. Sad to think the submarine was to be lost in action soon after our trip.

In fact the pilots had to remain at Algiers for a further week until 13 February when they were able to travel to Gibraltar. Then a further week was spent flying there and getting used to the new Spitfire IXs.

Jimmy Corbin also recalls picking up the new Spitfires.

> The Spit IX was a class above the Spit VB which had served us so well. It was more powerful than its predecessor and the presence of two blowers meant we had the same power at 20,000 feet as we had at ground level. On arrival at Gibraltar the Squadron quickly familiariszed itself with the new Spits, a marvel of modern engineering. They combined a Spitfire V airframe with a Merlin 61 engine and could reach speeds over 400mph and a height of 43,000 feet. Their arsenal included two 20mm cannons. They handled beautifully and would be a formidable addition to our campaign.

On the ground in Tunisia the Germans had decided at a meeting on 9 February on a twin offensive. General von Arnim in the north was to advance through the Faid pass aiming at Sidi Bou Zid while Rommel would advance through Gafsa, Feriana and Kasserine. The offensives began with immediate and startling success on the 14th when von Arnim pushed through the Faid pass. It was the first taste of combat for some American troops who came under dive bomber and fighter bomber attack followed by a German artillery barrage and a tank attack supported by experienced battle hardened troops. Rommels troops entered Gafsa on the 15th and Ferriana on the 17th and captured the important airfield at Thelelpte further north. More inexperienced American troops in the north had fallen back in confusion and lost nearly 3,000 prisoners and 170 tanks. The German troops and Panzers seemed unstoppable in the inhospitable mountain terrain and had seized the initiative. Conditions were poor, it drizzled with rain, it was freezing cold and the interminable mud hampered troop movements.

General Eisenhower tried to reinforce his troops but they were powerless to stop the German offensive through the Kasserine Pass. Enemy probing action had indicated on 18 February that the renewed enemy assault was likely to come through Kasserine about five miles south of the entrance to the Kasserine Pass. The Pass is less than a mile wide at it narrowest point and flanked by mountains from which a strong defence could be mounted and US engineers had laid thousands of mines between the village and the pass before withdrawing through the pass. The engineers dug in, the mines they had laid and the mud in which the German tanks became bogged down bought the first assault launched on 19 February to a swift halt. On the 20th the Germans were re-enforced by tanks from Von Arnim and these pushed through the Pass after a huge artillery barrage. This time the US troops were quickly overrun and suffered heavy casualties and lost vast amounts of equipment that was captured intact. Rommel paused on the push north, as he expected an Allied counter attack but none was forthcoming.

21 FEBRUARY 1943

Logbook: Spitfire IX Gibraltar – Maison Blanche.

ORB: 24 aircraft flown by 72 Squadron pilots and 1 by a ferry pilot left Gibraltar for Maison Blanche where they arrived after a journey of approx 3.5 hours. Due to trouble with his undercarriage P/O H. Lewis had to crash land but he was uninjured.

Already the German push in the mountains had stalled, as Rommel was largely unsupported. Valuable time was wasted, as there appeared to be no unity between Von Arnim and Rommel and Rommel lacked supplies and ammunition, so much so that after the Americans had reinforced the line Rommel had to call off his advance and retreat back through the Kasserine pass.

22 FEBRUARY 1943

ORB: 2 sorties were flown to gain further experience of the Spitfire IXs. It was announced today that P/O R.D. Scrase had been promoted to flying officer w/e/f 1/10/42.

Rommel abandoned the Kasserine area without difficulty and had withdrawn successfully before the Allies realised what had happened. He pulled back to the Mareth Line to prepare his defence against Montgomery there. As he did, Von Arnim launched an offensive in the north to prevent the Allies from regaining the initiative and to cover Rommel's withdrawal. His troops made rapid progress and had the assault been synchronised with Rommel's push through the Kasserine Pass, the outcome might have been very different.

25 FEBRUARY 1943

Logbook: Spitfire IX Maison Blanche – Khemis (Paddington) – Sgt Passmore spun in on approach and was killed.

ORB: 17 aircraft left Maison Blanche for Souk el Khemis (Euston) after lunch. The weather was reported to be cloudy in land but clear along the coast. The aircraft flew along the coast until near the Tunisian border when they turned inland. Here they soon ran into and passed out of a tropical storm. Unfortunately before they could reach base its full force broke over the aerodrome and very soon the runway became flooded while visibility decreased rapidly. Two of our aircraft landed at Tingley while Sgt Hussey made a very good 'wheels down' landing at another airstrip under bad conditions there. The airscrew suffered most damage. P/O Corbin's aircraft tipped on its nose on the runway due to the appalling conditions. All the remaining pilots managed to land successfully except Sgt Passmore who misjudged his landing speed and in trying to correct the aircraft, stalled and spun in. He was thrown about 25 yards from the aircraft and was killed. The aircraft was a complete wreck.

Rodney recalled the trip back and the subsequent tragic landing.

> Our return from Gibraltar was full of incident. First there was a 3 hour and 45 minute trip to Maison Blanche and the next day another of 2 hours and 25 minutes to continue with the rest of the trip. But we made a late take off and faced gradually worsening weather conditions. On arrival at Souk el Khemis we faced a thunderstorm. Landing on a darkened airfield was no fun. No lights but I had the thrill of a safe landing. Such was not to be the case for several of my colleagues. Several of our new planes were damaged on landing and others diverted to Paddington, which had a longer landing strip. One poor chap, Sgt Passmore who spun in on landing was killed and Jimmy Corbin tipped his on its nose and was lucky to survive.

Jimmy Corbin:

> Confusion seemed to set in which was not unusual for the RAF, nevertheless frustrating as we all wanted to get back to Souk el Khemis as quickly as possible. By mid morning we still hadn't received our orders to proceed and were left hanging around until finally after sharing a cigarette with Roy Hussey, Sgt Passmore appeared in the doorway and announced that we had been given the all clear to head back to Souk el Khemis. We took off and headed for base with our route scheduled to take us

over our former base at Souk el Arba. It was there we ran into an enormous electrical storm, the like of which I had never seen before. Hailstones the size of golf balls pelted the cockpit, threatening to smash the Perspex. Lightning flashed and forked across the black clouds and torrential rain teemed down the sides of the aircraft. My Spitfire rocked and bumped through the maelstrom as it battled against the extreme conditions and I had to grip the column hard in an attempt to hold the Spit steady, but it seemed to have little effect. After what seemed an age I spotted Euston runway and a sense of relief swept over me. Visibility was diabolical but I had no choice but to attempt a landing. I could not stay aloft any longer; one lightning strike and I would be dead. I eased back on the throttle and began my descent. The aircraft continued to swing violently as the winds continued to buffet it and rain streamed down the hood distorting my vision. Finally the wheels made contact with the ground with a hard jolt but I knew instantly something was wrong. The Spit's undercarriage seemed to drag in the mud and the aircraft began to career along the runway. I wrestled with the column to keep her straight so she didn't veer off into the quagmire that surrounded us but I need not have bothered. The runway was completely waterlogged and the wheels continued to drag in the mud and slush and I realized that unless I did something quickly I would nose over. I tugged the Spit from side to side to free it from the boggy runway but it made no difference and the Spit was still travelling forward at a speed of about 60mph when the inevitable happened and the wheels trapped themselves in the mud and the aircraft tipped over onto its nose and came to a halt. The wretched rain beating down on the cockpit told me I was still alive and in one piece. The straps had saved me from falling forward and smashing my head on the instrument panel. It was a close shave. Carefully I undid the buckles and straps and slid the hood back and eased myself out of the plane and jumped to the ground. The brief euphoria I experienced on discovering I was still alive turned to anger as we had waited months for these new model Spits and I'd damaged mine, possibly even written it off on its maiden voyage. I was furious with the weather, the whole damn war and myself. An erk was stood with me –'It's totally fucked up isn't it?' He replied 'It's not the worst sir, two made it successfully at Waterloo, five came down at Paddington and four are still missing. We have heard nothing from Sgts Hussey and Passmore.' Word came quickly through that Hussey had crash-landed his Spitfire at Ghardimaou and was unhurt. Two more landed safely at Tingley but Sgt Passmore spun in as he landed and crashed. He was killed instantly. What a waste of a life and all because of the weather, which was rapidly becoming our worst enemy.

The battles of Kasserine Pass and Sidi bou Zid had been close-run things. The American troops had been mauled by the Germans and they had suffered heavy casualties and lost vast amounts of equipment. It was clear they were up against an experienced foe. The training and performance in battle had to be improved dramatically and quickly. Relations between the American Generals Anderson and Fredenhall had also deteriorated and Eisenhower decided to replace Fredenhall with General Patton.

26 FEBRUARY 1943

Logbook: Spitfire IX Khemis (Paddington) – Khemis (Euston).

ORB: The aircraft that landed at Tingley flew in today and Sgt Passmore was buried.

Despite the German retreat back through the Kasserine pass the situation on the ground remained critical. Von Arnim advanced towards the British 5th Corps at the northern end of the 1st Army and managed to pin them down. Rommel moved his retreating units back to the east to strike against the Eighth Army and General Alexander cabled Churchill and was shocked at the critical situation he found. Victory in North Africa was anything but around the corner.

27 FEBRUARY 1943

ORB: The Squadron carried out its first offensive operation with the new Spitfire IXs today. At 1400 hours 6 aircraft with Sqn Ldr Oxspring leading took off on an offensive sweep over the Beja–Medjez el Bab area. At 1420 Red 1 and Red 2 returned owing to RT and engine failure. The rest of the formation flew 8 miles north-east of Beja, then south-west above cloud at 27,000 feet and from there, back to Beja. The Squadron was then ordered to patrol the Teboursouk area as Me109s were reported. Two unidentified aircraft flying line astern were seen and these were reported to have blue and white stripes near the junction of tail and fuselage. Some A.A. fire, probably marker shells for enemy fighters were seen west of Pont du Fahs but the rest of the formation returned at 1520 hours.

Rommel was prepared to push against the British in the east and hoped that Montgomery's forces had been unsettled by the need to reinforce the Americans at Kasserine but again he delayed the attack until unity could be reached in the Axis High Command where opinion was divided as to where the attack should take place.

28 FEBRUARY 1943

Logbook: Spitfire IX – high cover Hurribombers Beja Mateur – Short squirt at head on attack by Me109G.

ORB: 6 aircraft with F/Lt Cox leading took off at noon on an offensive sweep that covered the Medjez el Bab, Bou Arada and Pont du Fahs areas. The aircraft climbed to 22,000 feet but saw no enemy aircraft, though 4 Spitfire IXs of 81 Squadron were seen below. Sgt Frampton returned at 1240 hours because his engine had no oil pressure. All aircraft landed safely by 1315 hours.

At 1515 hours 6 Spitfire IX aircraft took off to act as high cover to Hurribombers and their close escort attacking tanks and transport north-east of Beja. Our

aircraft did not succeed in formatting with the rest of the aircraft involved, but they went over the area, climbing all the time and weaving up sun to the north of Beja where an enemy fighter was seen below. Our aircraft dived and in the ensuing combat, Sqn Ldr Oxspring fired at it and saw pieces flying off the aircraft, an Me109 and claimed 1 e/a damaged. All aircraft landed by 1615 hours.

Acting as high cover for Hurribombers 6 of our aircraft led by F/Lt S.W. Daniel were airborne at 1720 hours. They formatted successfully and went off at 8,000 feet, climbed to 13,000 feet over Beja and zig zagging across sun reached 14,000 feet. The Hurribombers having completed their attack returned but our aircraft continued to patrol the area. After orbiting north-east of Beja, 6 enemy fighters (Me109Fs) were seen slightly below and behind to the north east. The Spitfires turned around but the Me109s did likewise and flew into the sun. They appeared to be operating in pairs for after one complete climbing turn it was observed that as one of each pair flicked over and dived for the ground, the others started to climb. One of the latter was being 'out climbed' by F/Lt Daniel in Red1 when the enemy aircraft went into a vertical dive. F/Lt Daniel also dived at full speed and opened fire at 300 yards closing to 200 yards. Red blobs of fire and a few silvery strikes were seen on the fuselage. Owing to enemy A.A. fire F/Lt Daniel was forced to disengage but claimed the enemy aircraft damaged. Meanwhile Blue 2, P/O F. Malan had employed similar tactics on a second Me109F that was last seen pouring white glycol smoke for about a distance of about 1,000 yards heading at full speed for the Bizerte Lakes. Blue 2 claimed a Me109 damaged.

Today it became known that F/Lt Forde who left the Squadron in January to command 152 Squadron had been awarded the DFC as well as being mentioned in dispatches. W/O Charnock DFM now back attached to the Squadron in a non-flying capacity pending the next medical board was also awarded the DFC A third recipient of the DFC was P/O R.J.H. Robertson, now on his way home after losing an eye as a result of his crash landing after an engagement with the enemy on 20 December 1942. The promotion of P/O J. Le Cheminant and W.J. Corbin to flying officers also became known today.

Spanner Farish recalled W/O Charles Charnock – 'Chaz' to everyone on 72 Squadron – with fondness.

> If ever you saw a dissolute looking fellow, here was one. W/O Charnock DFM who even in his worn flying clothing would have been better placed propping up a nightclub bar. At least he contrived to have a bottle of whisky in his hand when on the ground. He was over 30, by far the oldest pilot in the Squadron. He was a regular and before the war had been a substantive flight lieutenant until he pushed a senior officer into a fishpond. He had flown everything and had broken Spitfires up in the air with aerobatics and was the maddest fighter pilot I ever met, completely round the bend and yet one felt he had seen the whole world.

Rodney first operational flight was on the last day of the month.

> I flew my first operational sortie as yellow two. We were giving high cover to Hurricane-bombers in the Beja-Mateur area. There was lots of activity both on the ground and in the air. I managed a short squirt at a Me109 as we passed each other head to head!

During March the delays caused by the friction in the Axis High Command enabled Montgomery to prepare his troops.

1 MARCH 1943

Logbook: Spitfire IX. Independent high cover sweep Cape Serrat. Saw 2 Me109s over Beja but they dived away from us.

ORB: The month opened with the Germans trying desperately to reach Beja from about three different directions. Stiff resistance by our forces was offered and much air support by 324 Wing was provided. The Squadron with its new Mark IXs appears to have arrived at an opportune moment because there was now an aircraft available to compete with the enemy at high levels. This was vividly shown soon after mid-day when Sqn Ldr Oxspring and W/O Hunter together destroyed one Me109 near base. The two pilots each stated that the German seemed to rely purely and simply on speed to escape them and did not take any evasive action whatsoever. The pilot baled out at 18,000 feet but some link in the Luftwaffe maintenance service had not in this case done its job properly, because the parachute after opening up momentarily fell away from the pilot who fell like a stone to the ground. His remains were found and afterwards interred by the Army. P/O Le Cheminant at the same time damaged another Me109 in the same area. In all 22 sorties were flown at various heights from 16,000 feet to 23,000 feet. Enemy aircraft were fairly active throughout the day but as usual did not willingly 'mix' it with our pilots.

2 MARCH 1943

ORB: A maximum effort in support of Army operations was made today by the Squadron. In all 4 missions totaling 24 sorties were flown. One of these was to provide high cover for Fortresses bombing Bizerte. At 1100 hours 8 aircraft climbed to 28,000 feet and flew with the bombers all the way to the target and as far as Beja on their return. About 20+ enemy aircraft were seen below and once again the Spitfire IXs proved a match for the Me109s when they out-climbed them to 34,000 feet at which the bandits went whence they came. Returning at 18,000 feet over Medjez el Bab 4 Me109s were seen and engaged. F/O Jupp and Sgt Hussey chased a Me109 down to ground level and their

combined efforts resulted in the Me109 being destroyed near Pont du Fahs. The B17s were escorted by P38s that for the second time in the campaign attacked the Squadron. This time P/O D.J. Prytherch was fired on by 3 of these friendly aircraft, luckily without any effect. Flak over the target area was on a fairly large scale but aimed mostly at the bombers. Pilots reported that on the road, parachutes could be seen.

In the last operation of the day that commenced at 1600 hours 6 aircraft were engaged and just as the formation was at 12,000 feet over Beja, A.A. fire began and 4 Me109s suddenly appeared. A melee followed and the enemy went at high speed for home. F/O Le Cheminant however managed to get in some rounds at one Me109G that he chased down to the ground. Near Pont du Fahs the enemy aircraft whose approx speed was 380mph crashed headlong into a hill. The other 3 enemy aircraft were inconclusively engaged. After the fight whilst patrolling Teboursouk, on the orders of the Controller, F/O Tom Hughes reported that his engine had cut and that he was crash landing. This he did, but the spot was unfortunately very isolated and inaccessible. The Engineer Officer F/O H.G. Farish at once tried to get to the scene of the accident across the hills but his first attempt was unsuccessful. Later in the evening with one airman he set out on foot across the hills.

Greggs Farish:

> We had our first crash due to technical failure. Tom Hughes had to force land south of the here and over the mountains and near the German lines, I went out to look for him in case he was hurt and to find the cause of the crash. I looked for him with Mike McCaul from the Orderly room. He could read the stars and we spent all night in the hills, finally getting three hours sleep in an Arab tent 15 miles away on the floor. Our Arab hosts were very courteous and knew where the aircraft was and guided us to it in the morning. It only took a few seconds to see that the throttle control had parted for lack of a locking split pin. As we were examining the aircraft to see whether it could be salvaged Danny Daniels flew over and dropped a message that told us we were in friendly territory and there was a road to the aircraft from a town called Teboursouk that was also friendly. He was going to send a lorry from Souk el Khemis to pick us up which was duly dispatched and we returned to Khemis. Tom Hughes meanwhile had disappeared into the hills and arrived back at Khemis about half an hour ahead of us, exhausted and delirious and the Doctor had put him to bed. When he saw me all he said was 'thanks for looking for me all night, Spanner, it was the throttle control wasn't it?' So I suppose there was nothing I could have done about it. I went looking for Sgt North who had been doing the re-connection job, He somewhat shamefacedly admitted that the coffee truck had come around while he was in the middle of the job and must have forgotten to put the split pin back in after the interruption. Of such small errors are crashes made. It had taken Tom 20 hours of struggling over the mountains in the dark to get back and he had nearly lost his life.

Tom Hughes described his adventure:

On 2 March 1943, 72 Squadron had taken delivery of its Spitfire IX aircraft in Gibraltar and returned to the Tunisian front at its landing strip, Souk el Khemis – Euston. Six of the Squadron were escorting a late afternoon Hurribomber attack between Beja and Medjex el Bab. I was flying No. 2 to Plt Off. Prytherch DFM who came from Liverpool and was, later, sadly to go into the sea between Sicily and Malta when his engine failed.

We suddenly met six Me109s head-on at 15,000 feet. They pulled up straight ahead of us and I fired at one's belly as it climbed. Eventually, I seemed to be shooting vertically upwards. I did not see a single strike; I had not allowed enough deflection. Then my engine failed. It simply throttled back to a tick-over speed with the throttle lever linkage loose in my hand. I put on some steep gliding turns. Fortunately 'Pryth' saw something was wrong and followed me down. I had no idea where we were in relation to the 'bomb line'. I felt we were over the lines on the German side. I seemed quite clear of all the other Spitfires and Me109s, except for Prytherch who was circling watching 500 feet above me, good chap that he was.

I stretched my glide westwards towards home, looking for somewhere to land. Then I saw a green valley and picked on that. I saw smoke from a fire somewhere and checked the wind direction. I made a good wheels-up landing and stepped out unhurt. The Spit looked sad with its Rotol prop snapped off on all four blades, but it would fly again. I wondered whether to blow it up or not. There was not a sound of gunfire from the battle on the ground.

I ran across the field to the hillside, which was covered with sand and scrub. In no time I was well buried with just my face showing. I thought I would watch and wait. Suddenly an Arab appeared and walked around the aeroplane, which was a hundred yards from my hiding place. He may have been the farmer for all I knew. There was still no clue as to whether I was on the German side of the lines.

It soon got dark and I thought I would head off to the west towards Souk el Khemis or at least – friendly troops. The stars were out and there was no moon. There was not a distant shot to be heard. The ground underfoot was very rough. Sand, rocks, thorn, scrub and endless foothills were all very hard to see by starlight. I stumbled once and put out my hand; there was a stout stick with a curved top almost like an overgrown walking stick. It was quite miraculous for it was suddenly there in my hand. The North Star steered me westwards all that night. It was amazing how I could always see hills ahead of me against the night sky. My flying boots were warm and sloppy and hell to walk in as they did not fit well around the ankle. As the night wore in I made good progress, although scratched by thorns, I had not fallen thanks to my stout stick. I thought that by dawn I should get up on a hilltop to see what I could. It was freezing cold and my teeth chattered as I waited – wondering.

As the new day dawned I could see some Spitfires circling one of the airstrips in the valley near Souk el Khemis. I thought I only had about ten more miles to go. I walked down into another valley past a sleeping shack where Arabs lived. A few chickens scattered and a dog barked. I climbed more foothills and realised how thirsty I was. I dropped into a little gorge where an Arab was loading a little donkey with sticks for a fire from the scrub and bushes. I asked him if he had any water and he took me round a rock where there was a crystal spring. I had my RAF issue sunglasses on and its tin with the strange domed lid was in my pocket. I had water purifying tablets and dropped one in as I scooped up the welcome drink. The Arab thought me more than fussy and drank with one hand to show me how. He looked at my revolver and wondered if he could win it from me but we parted friends, and I was refreshed by his cool spring water.

The heat of the day was terrible. I took off my thin jersey and hooked it over my forehead like a nurse's cap. By three in the afternoon I looked out over the wide valley with its five airfields and its muddy river. I saw two Spitfires, Dan and Pry Maybe, searching through the hills. I had two red flares, but why waste them if my legs were still working? I came to another Arab's hut and he proudly showed me his First War Croix de Guerre and a photograph when he served with the French against the Boche. He offered me his donkey but I proudly refused it for I was in sight of home.

I got back to the Mess by dusk, pretty dehydrated, and told Greggs Farish, the engineer, that the throttle linkage had let me down. A split pin was left out and a cotter pin vibrated out. The aircraft thus had crashed but was subsequently salvaged. I was right in my diagnosis of the fault, but the important thing was that the pilot had returned to base – with a little help on the way.

3 MARCH 1943

Logbook: Spitfire IX. High cover (28,000ft) sweep Mateur Tebourba.

ORB: The search for F/O Hughes by the Engineer Officer was unsuccessful. He returned at 0800 hours having to report that after searching for about 6 hours he was forced to abandon the search. Happily later in the day F/O Hughes returned. He was semi-delirious but soon recovered. It then became clear that the search party and the pilot must at one point have been within about half a mile of each other, because F/O Hughes admitted to striking matches to light his path. The Engineer Officer saw one of these.

F/Lt Daniel and P/O Prytherch found the crashed aircraft later in the day following an air search. It was necessary to travel as far as Tebersouk before getting on the road to the scene of the crash. It was not considered that any purpose could be served by the complete salvage of the aircraft. After all valuable spares had been salvaged, the wreck was left.

The first mission of the day, a hundred-mile offensive sweep, which began at 1000 hours and in which the Squadron provided top cover did not produce any enemy reaction. F/Lt D.G. Cox DFC reported on return that several bomb holes were visible in the north-west corner of an otherwise vacant airfield at Bel Aid (Mateur). In the afternoon a rather abortive high cover operation to Fortresses attacking Bizerte that arrived an hour late, left several pilots short of

fuel. The enemy did not react to our presence and one pilot counted at least 30 ships in Lac Bizerte. All of the aircraft despite the fuel shortage landed safely by 1545 hours after being airborne for 90 minutes.

4 MARCH 1943

ORB: The Army today was engaged in moving up troops to stop the enemy thrust westwards from Sedjenane to Djebel Abiod and to cover this move the Squadron made 10 sorties. P/O Malan owing to R/T failure had to return early from the mission. Enemy aircraft were reported but not seen and a low haze over the area aided the move. In the afternoon 10 aircraft took off at 1315 hours to act once again as high cover to Fortresses bombing Bizerte. It was arranged that the rendezvous should be over Le Kef but no Fortresses appeared. The Bizerte area was covered and although there was about 8/10ths cloud generally, the target area was clear, enabling our pilots to count about 17 Transports in Lac Bizerte. P/O Malan and P/O Le Cheminant returned early due to R/T and engine trouble respectively but the remaining aircraft all landed safely at 1445 hours.

An up-to-date copy of the 324 Wing victories today showed that the Squadron still headed the list with 31 destroyed, 8 and 2/3 probably destroyed and 21 damaged. An example of the unreliability of the Arabs was shown in an Intelligence Report received today that said that the enemy had armed Arabs in the Gafsa area and that they were hostile.

5 MARCH 1943

ORB: After the intensive efforts of previous days the Squadron did not make any operational sorties. The problem of sand getting into the No. 61 Merlin engines is a real issue. The Vokes air filter applied to a Spitfire VB is unsuitable for use on a Spitfire IX. If the Squadron is to continue to fly, the sand must be kept out of the engines. One method to date has been to lay the dust by throwing scavenged oil on the runways with a fair amount of success.

6 MARCH 1943

Logbook: Spitfire IX. High cover Hurribombers NW Medjez.

ORB: At 1100 hours the Squadron provided 6 aircraft as top cover to 24,000 feet for Hurri- bombers. The controller reported enemy aircraft but none were seen and all aircraft had landed by 1150 hours after an uneventful operation. Later at 1300 hours the Army required a photographic reconnaissance of the Medjez el Bab area. The Squadron provided top cover again and a patrol at about 23,000 feet was carried out. Some black Bofors flak was seen, accurate for height but not range bursting behind our aircraft. A state of readiness continued until

1800 hours because 20+ bandits were reported towards the base so 6 aircraft were scrambled. They patrolled the Tebersouk area at 16,000 feet and then 7,000 feet but no enemy aircraft were encountered. The dusk comes very quickly in North Africa and it was necessary for the Squadron to perform dusk landings at 1840 hours but all landed safely.

The German attacks began with an advance by the 10th Panzer Division between Metameur and Medenine supported by the Afrika Corps; but they came up against a carefully prepared British defence who were dug in with excellent emplacements, about 350 field and medium guns and about 300 tanks. The Eighth Army also had doughty support from the Desert Air Force and the tanks of the Germans suffered mercilessly in a shattering demonstration of combined firepower from the artillery and the air. The German infantry fared little better against the Eighth Army. By dusk the battle had finished and British patrols pushed forward into the Matmata foothills and only experienced minimal contact with the enemy.

7 MARCH 1943

Logbook: Spitfire IX. Practice flying line astern and ranging.

ORB: The weather was not very much better today but at 1205 hours it was possible for 6 aircraft to take off as high cover for the elusive Fortresses bombing Bizerte. Once again the operation turned into a sweep over the area because no Fortresses were seen nor were any results of bombing observed. The cloud stretched up to 22,000 feet. After lunch conditions became worse and no further operations could be carried out. The Army authorities today commenced the issue of an Intelligence Summary on the ground situation in Tunisia. A report of the Beja battle came to hand and it was gratifying to see that the assault had been held and then repelled. More gratifying was the comment that said 'RAF support did much to thwart the enemy's plan and had been greatly appreciated by the Army.' This appreciation was expressed in a message from the G.O.C. 46 Division and highlighted one instance of Army/RAF co operation which had been reported during the battle was of an Artillery Officer who utilized his V.H.F. set to inform a Hurribomber formation the location of an enemy tank concentration that was promptly and successfully attacked.

Repeated German attacks were launched but achieved little success. Rommel himself later admitted that:

> It soon became clear that the attacks had failed and there was nothing more to be done about it. The attack had bogged down in the break-in stage and never had a chance to become fluid. The British commander had grouped his forces well. In fact the attack had been launched about a week too late and a great gloom settled over us, as we had

to prepare for the inevitable Eighth Army attack which was now imminent and which we would have to face. For the Army Group to remain in Africa was now plain suicide.

8 MARCH 1943

ORB: The weather at first light indicated that little change had taken place overnight. There was low cloud over the airfield once again. At 1145 hours 6 aircraft provided high cover for Fortresses but Sgt Frampton returned at 1155 hours with engine trouble. The other aircraft flew at 25,000 feet to Bizerte and out to sea returning to the east of Bizerte. Near Mateur on the outward sweep some flak was encountered but this was behind the Squadron formation. 2 unidentified aircraft were seen going eastwards at Bizerte but the whole operation was rendered abortive again by the nonappearance of the bombers. Pilots who landed at 1320 hours reported the presence of a flak ship off Cani and an enemy Cruiser off Cap Zebib. After lunch and at 1530 hours F/O Hardy led a formation acting as escort to Hurribombers whose target was in the Bedjenane area. They reached 23,000 feet over the area and then dived to 13,000 feet over Lake Achkel. The operation was in support of the attempt to hold the eastward advance of Von Arnim's forces in the north.

Two new pilots Sgt Keith E. Clarkson (Aus) and P/O George Keith (Can) arrived today.

9 MARCH 1943

ORB: No flying but news received today very pleasing in that the Eighth Army had defeated the Axis tank attack on 7–8 March.

General Rommel left North Africa on 9 March, having decided to fly to see the Führer and explain the situation there to him direct.

10 MARCH 1943

Logbook: Spitfire IX. Scramble and patrol Tebourba area. Heard a great deal but saw nothing but Spitfires!

ORB: 4 offensive patrols carried out today. In the course of one of these patrols, the CO and a second pilot fired at some enemy aircraft without visible results. The question of sand penetrating into the engine of the Spitfire IX has been energetically considered recently. F/O G. Farish and P/O P. Fowler have between them designed a form of shield filter that is jettisoned after take off. At first a parachute was used but this has now been dispensed with. The actual filter is collected after jettisoning and is replaced on the end of the runway after landing. So far it has only been an experiment but it is to be 'mass produced'.

Hitler's reaction to Rommel was that Africa must be held at all costs but Rommel was adamant that he could see no future in delaying the inevitable and was not prepared to see his Afrika Corps destroyed. Hitler ordered him to go on sick leave and refused Rommel's request to return for a few more days so Von Arnim took over for the final struggle. Von Arnim was not prepared to withdraw from the Mareth line and felt confident in the old French defensive positions. To the north lay the sea and to the south lay the Matmata Mountains, which stretched to the inhospitable Dahar sands. Montgomery however had other ideas and had discovered chinks in the German shield. He had already sent the Long Range Desert Group forward on a reconnaissance mission to locate a gap in the Mountains at Foum Tatahouine and planned to dispatch a force through this gap and then through the vital Tebaga Pass that would open a way to the plains of El Hamma and Gabes and behind the Germans in the Mareth line. This left hook consisted of the New Zealand Corps under Major General Freyberg and amounted to 25,000 troops and about 150 tanks.

12 MARCH 1943

ORB: Area of operations switched temporarily. At 1015 hours 93 Squadron with 6 aircraft from 72 Squadron as top cover ground strafed in the Pichon-Fondouk area. No enemy aircraft were seen but Kairouan airfield was reconnoitred and except for an obstruction at the north east of the runway, no further signs of occupation were seen. At night it was possible to hear and plainly see the guns firing at the front. At 1530 hours Hurribombers with 6 aircraft from No. 72 Squadron acting as top cover took off to attack targets near Sedjenane. There was nothing of incidence to report.

13 MARCH 1943

ORB: The Squadron was inactive until later afternoon when at 1710 hours, 2 squadrons of which No. 72 was top cover again took off and went out at 0 feet in an attempt to interrupt enemy operations supply dropping their troops. They flew slowly around Sedjenane area at 10,000 feet but returned to base without seeing any enemy aircraft.

14 MARCH 1943

Logbook: Spitfire IX cannon test.

ORB: A little practice flying and filter trials but the weather closed down for the day and with it all flying. It was pleasing to hear that Bone had provided such a hot welcome for the Luftwaffe last night destroying 2 and damaging 3 enemy aircraft.

15 MARCH 1943

ORB: The only operational mission was a second unsuccessful attempt to stop the supply planes to enemy troops in the northern sector. 8 aircraft were airborne at 1710 hours with 93 Squadron and climbed to 22,000 feet to patrol the area. No enemy aircraft were seen. One aircraft of the close escort crash-landed.

16 MARCH 1943

ORB: Today saw the first attack on the airfield here since the 3 February when 5–6 Fw190s dropped bombs from 9,000 feet at approx 1740 hours. At 1630 hours we had scrambled 6 aircraft to intercept bandits reported in the Mateur area. At 21,000 feet no enemy aircraft were seen. On their return having been told to land by control, just as one of our aircraft was about to touch down, the A.A. opened up and the bombs fell. The pilot, F/Lt Daniel, at once opened up and took evasive action. Meanwhile at 1715 hours, 6 more aircraft were dispatched on the now routine attempt to intercept enemy supply planes in the north. They had reached Tabarka at 12,000 feet when enemy aircraft were reported at 15,000 feet. The formation turned and saw 4 enemy aircraft diving towards Souk el Arba. Pursuit followed but owing to cloud cover the enemy aircraft were lost. Almost at once the A.A. over base opened up and the aircraft then made for Beja to either intercept the Fw190s or their escort. No enemy aircraft were seen however, despite several reports. F/Lt Cox and W/O Gear had been separated and flying at about 2,000 feet near Sidi Naceur, encountered light flak. After going as far as Tabarka they returned southwards by flying down the road Cap Serrat–Sedjenane and saw between 18–20 enemy transports that they overshot in view of their speed. The actual damage caused by the raid at the airfield was negligible and the raid was not pressed home as on previous occasions. One gunner was killed and the telephone line from the Dispersal to the Orderly Room was temporarily severed.

Units of the 30th Corps began attacks against the Mareth line as a diversion from the main attacks by the New Zealand forces in the mountains.

17 MARCH 1943

Logbook: Spitfire IX. Patrol Cape Serrat–Medjez. Damaged pitot head in a very ropey landing!

ORB: Activity was most marked in the northern battle area and the Squadron carried out 24 sorties in the course of the day. The first mission led by the CO and which lasted for 100 minutes was uneventful but the second operation, a sweep of the Sedjenane–Cap Serrat area resulted in a visual on 4 enemy aircraft being obtained, but cloud cover enabled them to escape to the north east of Souk el

Arba. To the south west of Cap Serrat some more aircraft, not unlike Stukas with a fighter escort were seen a long way off. The Stukas were flying in a V formation. Our aircraft being short of fuel could not pursue them. The last of the operations for the day commenced at 1530 hours proved to be of more than usual interest. From the start of the campaign in this theatre it was known that the enemy had in his possession and was actually using some of our Spitfires. This afternoon F/Lt Cox reported a very strange occurrence that cannot easily be explained. Over Mateur at 22,000 feet after Me109s had been reported at 20,000 feet a single aircraft was seen and at once investigated and was seen to have American markings without any identification letters. It was later found to be a Spitfire. It insisted on carrying out German-like tactics and gradually drew our aircraft closer to Bizerte. When one of our machines was actually in firing position a voice was heard to say 'OK – American' but the general consensus from our pilots was that its position and behaviour made it very doubtful to believe that it was actually friendly.

W/O C.W. Charnock DFC and DFM returned to the Squadron just three months after his memorable day and a new pilot Sgt Shaw from New Zealand was posted to the Squadron today. Following on from the Malaria lecture a survey of the area has been completed by the S.M.O. and from this it would appear that the actual living site area is not very suitable for the spring period. The A.O.C. has given orders that all squadrons living in farms have to be moved by the end of March. The supply of tents will, however, be a big problem.

Chas Charnock's return to the Squadron was celebrated, as he was a popular member of the Squadron even if a little unorthodox. Greggs Farish recalled:

> In the early days at Algiers and Bone and Souk he had knocked down three in no time at all but he got himself shot down twice. It was one of his first bar stories that he persuaded the RAF that he had baled out with all his kit in a kit bag so that he could get compensation. Twice he had pocketed the gold sovereigns of the pilot's emergency wallet. The second time he had descended into no man's land and met an Arab with a donkey and tried to borrow the said animal. The Arab refused so Chas pulled out his revolver and shot a stray passing dog dead. He then had no problem with borrowing the Arab's donkey! The last time Chas had been posted missing, this time presumed killed, he had broken away from Bobby Oxspring's formation straight into a gaggle of Germans above. There had been no news for a couple of days then a signal came in from an army clearing station – 'Credit me with two! Chas.' He got the DFC after that but had been seriously injured in the crash and did not fly again for two months and turned up from Algiers with a medical certificate that pronounced him fit to fly.

It later transpired that the medical certificate was forged after Charnock passed out at 5,000 feet over Souk el Khemis and although he landed safely further examinations resulted in the forgery being discovered and Charnock was promptly dispatched back to UK.

18 MARCH 1943

ORB: At 1125 hours 6 aircraft provided an escort for Hurribombers over a target in the northern area but no results of the bombing could be seen because of cloud cover.

The New Zealand troops had cleared the mountains and begun to move round the edge of Dahar and by the 20th the Germans were well aware of the threat they faced. At the same time attacks began against the east of the Mareth line itself but came up against strong German resistance and counter attacks, which gained valuable time in preventing the Eighth Army encircling movement around the Mareth line. The American army under Patton began its advance through Gafsa to the north east of Von Arnim. Maknassy was taken on the 21st to threaten the German rear.

22 MARCH 1943

Logbook: Spitfire IX Scramble Souk el Arba, Teboursouk.

ORB: No operations in the morning but a sweep lasting a hundred minutes in the afternoon at 1650 hours in the Mateur–Tunis area. 6 boats were observed in Bizerte as well as transport on the Tebourba–Medjez road. At 1730 hours 4 aircraft were scrambled as 4 Me109s were reported over Souk el Khemis at 14,000 feet. No visual contact was made and the plot faded so the aircraft landed at 1810 hours.

23 MARCH 1943

Logbook: Spitfire IX Scramble Souk el Arba, Teboursouk. Fired at by our own flak 28,000 ft!

ORB: For the first time since the Beja battle the Squadron carried out 4 missions and a total of 30 sorties. The first was a sweep over the Pont du Fahs–Kairouan area that proved fruitless. At 1445 hours 6 aircraft were scrambled because enemy aircraft were reported near the base. When the aircraft had reached 27,000 feet near base about 8 bursts of flak came close to our aircraft, but they were undamaged and managed to continue the patrol. At 1600 hours high cover was provided for a Tac R sortie to the Depiene area by 6 aircraft. Enemy transport was seen and all aircraft landed safely. To finish the day at 1730 hours 6 aircraft patrolled at 23,000 feet in the Medjez el Bab–Tebourba area without incident.

We continued to receive unwelcome visits from the Germans. Their Fw190s used our airfield as a regular spot for dropping bombs. On one occasion as we came back from a sortie, bombs dropped around us. An old schoolfriend had driven up to see

> me. He was serving with a LAA Essex Regiment nearby. I had written to Laurie at his home address in South London and the letter was forwarded to him in North Africa. Surprise, surprise, he found that we were only three miles from each other. Laurie and his driver were astonished to find that we showed so little concern for the German attacks.

On the ground after the scare when everyone but Rodney dived for cover, he met his good friend Laurie Little who had travelled up with his driver from the camp nearby to meet him. Laurie also recalled that meeting years later.

> I remember your insouciant landing on a Tunisian airfield at Souk El Khemis where I had gone to meet you, when all hell broke loose as one of theirs followed you in. I cowered under a table in a tent; the driver who'd brought me ran for the distant foothills and you acted like someone in a Noel Coward play!

The other unwelcome visitors were the flies, thousands and thousands of them. Life under canvas which Rodney was to experience for the most part for the next year or so was bearable at best and horrendous at its worst. The tents had three cots to each tent, each with a mosquito net under which all of their personal belongings and flying gear had to be kept. The mess tent was a large marquee and this too was enclosed by a huge mosquito net and sprayed with DDT before each meal. This did not prevent the flies getting in. Although the food was not too bad if they could beat the flies to it, they became used to sharing their meals with them and having to brush them off their knives and forks or spoons between plate and mouth, and even then some made it through. Disgusting! Olive trees surrounded the airstrip and there were invariably urchin beggars sitting in whatever shade they could find with flies crawling all over their bare arms and legs and probing the corners of their eyes in search of whatever food they could find. The children had become so used to them that did not even bother brushing them away. The heat was terrible. In the daytime, even in shade, it would frequently reach 120 degrees. They all wore short-sleeved shirts and shorts with sand boots. They also had to be careful about bare skin touching metal on the aircraft, which could result in a nasty burn. Sitting in the cockpit for an hour on 'readiness' was torture in the heat and they often wanted to get into the air just to cool off.

24 MARCH 1943

Logbook: Spitfire IX Scramble Kairouan, Pont du Fahs 29,000ft. No joy though we stopped 109s from attacking forts.

ORB: One of the biggest explosions ever seen by our pilots was at Ferryville dockyard when American B-17 Fortresses being escorted by the Squadron hit the target. The Fortresses were met at 26,500 feet over Souk el Arba and as

usual the Germans sent up their fighters to attack the B-17s but our aircraft prevented them from reaching the bombers. The explosion at Ferryville sent up a column of smoke 12,000 feet that could be see from the base quite easily. The Squadron became involved in a dogfight but F/Lt Cox cannons jammed and prevented an almost certain kill on his part. The aircraft made use of the bombers' smoke trails in an attempt to reach them and there seemed to be more spirit in their attacks.

Von Arnim urged his superiors that withdrawal should begin in view of the American threat to his rear and the Eighth Army outflanking offensive.

25 MARCH 1943

ORB: W/O Charnock and Sgt Mitchard returned to Algiers this morning as they had become unwell following their practice flying on 20 March. At about 1830 hours a message from Operations to the CO that ordered the Squadron to move to Thelepte tomorrow and to operate from there by day, returning at night to base. A skeleton ground personnel was necessary and hurried plans were at once made to provide a convoy of 6 lorries with all the necessary men and equipment and this was on the road by 2200 hours.

26 MARCH 1943

ORB: The route taken was Souk el Arba, Le Kef, Tadjerouine, Kalan, Djerda, Thala and Kasserine. A brief halt was made to the south of Thala to inspect the area where the German thrust in February was checked. Several tanks and much debris lined the roads in and around the Kasserine gap. At the side of the road a dead donkey was lying, and out of curiosity one of the party went up to it. It was obviously a clever trap because the airmen concerned, A.C. Hitt, trod on a concealed land mine. He and seven other airmen were wounded and first aid had to be administered at once. An American Aid Post was called and their timely arrival and expert attention undoubtedly saved Hitt's life. He had lost a lot of blood and was transferred to Feriana General Hospital while the remainder of the party continued to Thelepte airfield and arrived there at the same time as our aircraft. The airfield at Thelepte is much larger than ours and it is possible for the whole squadron to take off at the same time. It is stony and sandy and as filters were not used, quite a lot of sand was collected.

Greggs Farish recalled the trip.

> Recently got back from a rush trip to Thelepte servicing the Squadron on a day's attachment with the USAF. The trip was most interesting and adventurous in that we had three mishaps. We arrived back with 8 less men and one less lorry than we

started with though no one was killed. After a normal day's flying one evening the CO called me in at about 8 p.m. from trying to get a Bedford truck out of the mud. He had a job for me – bags of work now. He showed me Thelepte on the map which was about 200 miles away and said that we needed to be there for tomorrow morning with a servicing party for about three days or less. The men were rounded up and we arranged to meet outside the cookhouse at 9.30 p.m. We would take about 40 men and seven 3-ton lorries after they had been loaded with armament, signals, flight equipment, petrol and oil. We were finally ready to move out at about 12 p.m. after a briefing on a map laid out on the ground by torchlight. As we moved farther south it gradually became lighter until we could see all around. At about 7.30 a.m. having passed through Kasserine and only about 8 miles from Thelepte, we stopped for a breather as we were ahead of schedule. The guys got out to stretch their legs and check the fuel and oil. There was a dead donkey off to the side of the road that attracted the attention of the men. While they were around it, kicking it, an explosion went off and five or six of them collapsed to the ground. Everyone else dived to the ground thinking they were under bombing attack, but there was no aircraft noise. Landon came to his senses first and realised it was a landmine left from the German retreat. He told Sgt Cousins to return to the Red Cross at Kasserine for help. In the meantime he wrapped the other men that had been hit in blankets to help against the shock. A.C. Hitt had a piece of shrapnel in his leg, which must have cut a main artery as he was losing a lot of blood but with the help of an armourer A.C. Foot applied a tourniquet and succeeded in stopping the flow of blood. By now an American doctor had arrived and proceeded to arrange to get the wounded off to hospital at Feriana. There A.C. Hitt was given a blood transfusion so the immediate first aid administered at the scene and the blood transfusion undoubtedly saved his life. When we returned to the aerodrome the pilots were about to take off on a sweep. We saw them off and set about making a temporary camp.

ORB: At 1115 hours 12 aircraft took off to act as withdrawal cover to some twenty A–20s attacking an airfield at Djebel Tebagan. At 17,000 feet our pilots saw the close escort in contact with about 15 bandits.

Two sections bounced the enemy aircraft and in the combats, F/Lt Daniel destroyed one Me109 and damaged another while F/O Hardy destroyed a Me109 and F/Lt Cox damaged a further Me109. P/O Fowler thought he had been hit and flew back to Soul el Khemis while Sgt Hussey landed short of fuel at Sbeitla. The bombers were last seen over their base. The American 31st Fighter Group provided some excellent food for both pilots and ground crew. A second operation was carried out at 1600 hours when 10 aircraft carried out a sweep over the Maknassy area that proved uneventful and the aircraft returned afterwards directly to Euston and landed safely at 1715 hours. The Americans were very much impressed with our Spitfire IX that had supplied the key to their problem of being able to deal with the Me109 at height. News arrived that confirmed the award of the DFC to F/Lt S.W. Daniel today.

Farish continued:

> All the kites got back and the pilots and the Americans when they heard were very excited for they had shot down at least two Germans. Tired out though we were this news kept us going for the rest of the day and made us feel the whole effort was worthwhile. There was one more sweep that day after which the Squadron flew straight home.

27 MARCH 1943

ORB: No flying at Souk el Khemis and the ground crews left Thelepte for Souk el Khemis at 1500 hours but this time the route taken was via Tebessa.

Next morning after a good night's sleep and visiting A.C. Hitt in hospital Farish gave orders for the return to Khemis.

> After lunch I spent some time with the American Group Engineer for whom I had promised I would re-set the engine controls of their slowest Spitfire, which I did. After instructing several of their very fine technical men in the controls of the Merlin, which are so important but not taught even in RAF text books. The aircraft on test then out-climbed the fastest kite they had. I also showed him our home-made jettisonable air filter, which we demonstrated and which he took drawings of. Although it was home-made it worked and was all we could do against the sand in the field.
>
> The lads enjoyed themselves at Thelepte. It was an airfield set almost in the desert but you could not see across it for a rise in the middle. The food was marvellous, varied rich and sweet and we had peanut butter, honey, sweet corn and fruit juices to drink. We were sorry to leave and hoped to return to see our American friends again.

Another diversion was their wine collection run. Some 8 miles away was the village of Thibar administered from Souk El Khemis and across the Medjjerda valley. Olives, vegetables and sheep and cattle were sold in the market at Souk El Khemis that translated from the Arabic means 'Market Wednesdays'. During the latter part of the nineteenth century the White Fathers had come out from France and had chosen Thibar as the finest spot in the whole country. The Fathers soon set about cultivating the land in that area, which benefited from the waters of the ever-flowing Medjerda River. The rich red soil was cultivated to produce wheat, fruit, vegetables and vines; and as well as the Church, a seminary, a hospital and a school were set up in the village. Houses were built for the local population. To find more work for the locals they also began the production of fine carpets – but for the Squadron there was the opportunity to buy wine and also the thick and sticky liqueur, Thibarene. Soon at the end of most days there was a queue of Army and RAF vehicles waiting to purchase wine and also to collect supplies of beer. On many occasions Rodney was called on to make the purchases for 72 Squadron and perhaps that's how he got nicknamed Joe!

30 MARCH 1943

Logbook: Spitfire 9 – Patrol Sedjenane area below cloud 9/10ths at 500ft. Saw First Army advance towards Mateur.

ORB: The Squadron, despite low cloud and very heavy rain, gave support to the Army in their push to Sedjenane today. The first patrol began at 10.25 hours with 6 aircraft flying at 500 feet over the Sedjenane area to the west. Troop movements were seen and reported to 5 Corps who were grateful for the information passed by our pilots. West of Sedjenane, French troops (identified by their primitive transport) were seen moving up, as were British Infantry on either side of the road. In Sedjenane itself there was little movement and few tanks were seen. Light flak was encountered to the east and south of the town but all our aircraft landed safely at 1140 hours.

At 1105 hours 6 more aircraft took off to carry out a further patrol. On their return at approx 1230 hours they reported that infantry were now in action to the north and south of Sedjenane. A bridge that had been destroyed temporarily held up our troops as transport at the western side had to be dispersed.

By his admission Rodney's contribution in March was just nine operational flights but this was because their campsite had suffered from the theft of parachutes by some of the locals.

> When the local police came on camp they were able to converse only in French. Silly Scrase started to talk to them in their own language and soon enough I was designated as the Squadron interpreter! Not only that, but a few days later and with great daring I chased some young lads who were wandering around our camp site who were carrying stolen goods. I pulled out my .38 revolver and fired into the air. This had a resounding effect as the boys dropped everything they were carrying and stopped. I was able to hand them over to the burly gendarmes for appropriate attention.

By the end of the month British units in the 5th Corps in North Tunisia ended a four-week slogging match by restoring the position in the coastal sector and the American armour had pushed down the Gafsa–Gabes road and presented a threat to the German positions at Wadi Akarit.

3 APRIL 1943

ORB: Today the Squadron was engaged for them in a new area acting as high cover to Mitchell bombers attacking enemy aerodromes in the Tunis area and north of Enfidaville. The Squadron had their first successes in Northern Tunisia since the beginning of March. The use of medium bombers on such an operation forced the enemy to put up his fighters. On returning from the

target area Me109s were found in the Medjez el Bab area. F/Lt Cox destroyed one Me109 and damaged a second while P/O Keith scored his first success since joining the Squadron by destroying a further Me109. Sgt Clarkson was hit by an enemy aircraft and said he was bailing out, he is thought to be safe.

General Alexander issued his orders for the final campaign in Tunisia, coordinating the efforts of both the US 1st Army in the west and the British Eighth Army in the east.

4 APRIL 1943

Logbook: Airborne 05.40 before sunrise. High cover to Hurribombers.

ORB: Ju88s have been very active in the battle area lately making use of cloud cover. Their hit and run tactics have been very difficult to intercept so their base was the target for Hurribombers just after 6am. 72 Squadron came to readiness at 0500 hours and at 0550 hours 12 aircraft were airborne to act as top cover for the Hurribombers. The attacks were pressed home but as the Squadron was at 13,000 feet no results were seen. News that Sgt Clarkson was safe was received early this morning and he returned none the worse for his adventures after breakfast. He damaged a Me109 before himself being hit.

Yellow jaundice or hepatitis was the other major health problem. At any one time there could be several personnel suffering from the disease. First the corneas of the eyes turned yellow, then the skin took on a sickly hue and their bowels began to erupt. The officers had three latrines, one for those lucky enough to escape, two for those stricken by the disease. At times it was awful and they could not move more than a few yards from the safety of the latrines before the terrible cramps started. The medical officers did not know much about the treatment of jaundice to start with, so the worst cases were confined to a couple of tents and treated in isolation. Then they were fed as much sugar as they could eat. If any of the pilots were not released from flying duties and suffered an embarrassing accident during the flight they were simply hosed down when they had landed by an unsympathetic ground crew! As the ground crew wised up to the problems faced by the pilots, they began to bore a few holes in the bottom of the Spits just below the pilots' seats just in case. It avoided any further mishaps.

6 APRIL 1943

Logbook: High cover Mitchells- Enfidaville.

ORB: Level of flying increased today but the Squadron only flew one mission when they provided top cover to B25s attacking Enfidaville. The target was attacked continually throughout the day and the long columns of enemy transport fleeing from the Eighth Army were severely hammered.

Eventually, on 7 March, advancing Eighth Army units coming from Alamein originally in the east linked up with US 2nd Corps landed under Operation *Torch* in the west.

9 APRIL 1943

Logbook: High cover patrol – Medjez el Bab area.

ORB: Squadron took off at 0740 hours to act as top cover for Tac R in the Medjez el Bab area. There was little activity and after patrolling over Tebourba at 21,000 feet for a time, all aircraft returned safely. Later the Squadron acted as close escort for 241 Squadron attacking enemy troops at Enfidaville. It seems that the enemy is now really on the run from the Eighth Army.

10 APRIL 1943

Logbook: Close escort Spit bombers near Enfidaville. Ended up as R3 due to 'fall outs'. Hardy and Hussey each damaged 1 Me109.

ORB: No flying in the morning but in the afternoon two missions providing top cover to the Enfidaville area. On the first nothing of interest was reported but on the second the Spit bombers attacked transport on the Pont du Fahs road with fair success. Just as the bombs were falling 7 Me109s were seen to the north about 7,000 feet below. These were at once attacked and F/O Hardy and Sgt Hussey each damaged a Me109. We suffered no casualties but 4 aircraft returned due to technical reasons.

Sfax fell to the Allied armies.

11 APRIL 1943

Logbook: Escort at 28,000ft Fortresses Tunis Docks. Lot of flak over the target but very good bombing.

ORB: The day that had been eagerly awaited has arrived as P/O Malan had the honour to destroy the Squadron's 150th enemy aircraft in the course of the Squadron's mission to provide high cover to 12 Hurribombers of 241 Squadron with 12 aircraft from 111 Squadron in close support. On the return from the target area, flying at 20,000 feet the Squadron was directed to Medjez el Bab where Me109s had been reported. They were well and truly bounced by the Squadron and in a dogfight lasting several minutes at heights from 20,000 feet to ground level P/O F. Malan destroyed a Me109 and Sqn Ldr Oxspring, Sgt Shaw and W/O Gear each damaged a further Me109 each. Our only loss

was Sgt Sollitt who was last seen with 2 Me109s on his tail at about 1,000 feet. 241 Squadron lost 3 aircraft all to flak during the attack.

At 1100 hours 6 aircraft led by P/O Prytherch took off to act as high cover to Hurribombers attacking the famous 'Longstop Hill'. Apart from a little flak little was seen as our aircraft were flying at 15,000 feet. A section went down to search for Sgt Sollitt but no trace was seen.

At 1315 hours 10 aircraft led by F/Lt Cox took off to act as high cover at 27,000 feet to 18 B17s bombing Tunis docks. The attack appeared to be very successful. It was possible to see 8–10 aircraft on El Aouina airfield. It also appeared that the A.A. defence around Tunis as the Squadron encountered accurate flak as far west as Moranghea.

The fourth operation was to act as high cover at 17,000 feet to 12 aircraft of 241 Squadron with 111 as close escort. Although there were several reports of enemy aircraft around, the Squadron did not see any.

Sgt Sollitt who was shot down at 0840 hours this morning has been reported safe by the Army. He is in hospital but not badly hurt.

12 APRIL 1943

Logbook: 1. Escort at 13,000ft Mitchells Oudna. No resistance but bombing bad. 2. Sweep Kairouan area in our hands. 1 Me109G damaged. No. 2 to P/O Lewis, quite hectic. F/O Walker, Sgt Griffiths Me109s damaged and F/Lt Cox Me109 probable.

ORB: Today heavy attacks are being made on enemy aerodromes in the remaining parts of the country still occupied by them. In these attacks, medium, light and fighter-bombers are being used.

At 1145 hours 12 aircraft took off acting as high cover to 18 Mitchells attacking Oudna with 93 Squadron as close escort. They flew at 15,000 feet and saw the bombs fall in the area. On the return the Squadron was diverted to Le Kef where 6 enemy aircraft at 17,000 feet were reported. These were seen but were too far away to engage. More were reported north-west of Pont du Fahs but these could not be pursued due to a lack of fuel.

At 1445 hours 12 aircraft took off acting as high cover with 111 Squadron as medium cover and 93 Squadron as close escort to rendezvous with 12 Bostons at Souk el Arba. The target was again to be Oudna airfield. After the bombing when our aircraft were north east of Medjez el Bab at about 10,000 feet bandits in the area were reported. A little later 3 Me109s were seen flying towards our formation at 10,000 feet. Blue section at once turned and climbed. F/Lt Daniel engaged one Me109 and it was last seen at 1,000 feet over the Goubellat Plain belching black and white smoke with the airscrew just ticking over. This was allowed as destroyed. P/O Prytherch also attacked a Me109 causing white smoke to appear and claimed one Me109 damaged.

At 1730 hours Wing Cdr Gilroy led a 3 Squadron sweep to the Kairouan area. 12 aircraft of 72 Squadron with F/Lt Cox were top cover and when south of Djebiona 25 Me109s and Fw190s acting as escort to 6 Ju88s were seen. Wing Cdr Gilroy at once engaged and then called 72 Squadron down from 19,000 feet. A dogfight was at once joined and the following claims were made. F/Lt Cox – one Fw190 probably destroyed, F/O Scrase – one Me109 damaged, F/O Walker – one Fw190 damaged and Sgt Griffiths – one Me109 damaged. The Me109s had yellow crescents and white wing tips and was last encountered by the Squadron at Maknassy in March. The attacks on the enemy aerodromes had been heavy and had forced him to fight.

Rodney recalls the moment: 'In a sweep of the Kairouan area I fired at a Me109G which I claimed as damaged. It was my first.'

Sousse was seized but the Italian German forces opposing Montgomery were established in their last stronghold at Enfidaville. The Eighth Army that had seen General Montgomery so successful since El Alamein now appeared to be pushed to one side. Montgomery expected to lead his troops in the final push to oust the Germans from North Africa but instead General Alexander realised that the offensive against Tunis needed to be driven by the 1st Army in better tank country inland and farther north than the Eighth Army positions. The 1st Army had easier terrain in front of it and towards the natural gateway to Tunis and Bizerte. Preparations were well in hand for the attacks but with an earliest possible start later in the month, on 22 April.

13 APRIL 1943

Logbook: Escort at 16,000ft Mitchells to the Oudna area.

ORB: Together with 12 aircraft from 93 Squadron 12 aircraft took off at 0945 hours on a sweep of the Kairouan–Cape Bon area. The Squadron flew at 21,000 feet but the sweep was uneventful. All landed at 1105 hours safely and then were released to fit extra fuel tanks. The next operation took place at 1655 hours when 12 aircraft acted as high cover with 243 Squadron as close escort to B25s attacking Oudna. Heavy flak was encountered and a fleeting engagement with 1 Me109 but no claims were made. 243 Squadron lost 2 pilots.

14 APRIL 1943

ORB: Together with 12 aircraft from 93 Squadron 12 aircraft took off with long-range tanks acting as high cover to a sweep of the Tunis–Cape Bon area. Sweep was uneventful. Later at 1405 hours a further 12 aircraft were airborne on an independent sweep of the Medjez el Bab area at 21,000 feet. Immediately the Squadron became airborne a vector was given to the west of Beja where

bandits were reported between 14,000 and 17,000 feet. Visual contact was made and an engagement at long range but the bandits used the cloud cover and dived and got away. A further 12 aircraft were scrambled at 1655 hours and climbed to 17,000 feet to intercept bandits reported in the Medjez el Bab area again. No contact was made but the Squadron remained on patrol at 27,000 feet and returned safely without incident. All Allied aircraft operating in the area now have red spinners.

15 APRIL 1943

Logbook: 1. Ferry to Montesquieu (Souk Ahras) 2. Montesquieu to Khemis Euston.

ORB: 6 aircraft led by F/O Le Cheminant were airborne at 1135 hours to act as high cover to 243 Squadron in the Medjez el Bab area. After patrolling at 13,000 feet for a few minutes 4 enemy aircraft were seen. Blue 1, P/O Prytherch chased one Me109 to Mateur where heavy flak forced him to break off. No claims were made.

The report of 50 enemy aircraft in the Medjez area resulted in 12 aircraft from each of 72, 81 and 111 Squadrons being scrambled at 1340 hours. The area was patrolled at 25,000 feet and fleeting glimpses were seen of the enemy. F/Lt Cox attacked one Me109 that was about to attack No. 81 Squadron but made no claims. All aircraft returned safely at 1510 hours.

16 APRIL 1943

Logbook: Sweep to Bizerte 24,000ft. Returned early with F/O Walker to find the fields being bombed.

ORB: 6 aircraft from 72 Squadron and 12 from 243 Squadron took off at 1030 hours to act as high cover and close escort respectively to 6 Boston bombing Bizerte. We flew at 24,000 feet and bombs successfully dropped on target area. On the return the Squadron were diverted to Medjez el Bab where 9 Me109s were encountered. In the ensuing dogfight Sgt Hussey damaged 2 Me109s (he attacked 5 altogether) P/O Lewis also claimed one Me109 damaged. All our aircraft returned safely to base.

Later 12 aircraft led by F/Lt Daniel took part as high cover to 2 aircraft from 225 Squadron on a combined shipping reconnaissance and fighter sweep. This proved uneventful until on the return 12 enemy aircraft were encountered in the Beja area. These were at once attacked and several pilots fired. F/O Hardy claimed one Me109 probably destroyed. The enemy aircraft were evidently returning from an abortive raid on our aerodrome, where little damage was caused. At the time of the raid F/Lt Cox was testing an aircraft and on sighting 3 Fw190s lagging behind near Beja pursued them and opened fire at 200 yards. Bits came off the starboard wing of one but as there were more enemy aircraft

above, F/Lt Cox had to break off the engagement. All our aircraft returned safely at 1845 hours. Sgt Jacobs (RAAF) was posted to the Squadron today.

In the intensity of the operations, some pilots on their first tour took their lead from some of the old sweats and more experienced pilots. Rodney, Tom Hughes and another good friend Roy Hussey fell into this category. 'Roy seemed to have a sensitive nose for trouble and a natural instinct to do the right thing. He would go onto shoot down six enemy aircraft in the Tunisian campaign and was deservedly awarded the DFM.'

General Alexander changed his plan of attack. Instead of relying on the 1st Army alone, the Eighth Army would now push forward, advancing against Enfidaville, Hammamet and Tunis to prevent the Germans from withdrawing to the Cape Bon peninsula.

17 APRIL 1943

ORB: 6 aircraft acted as high cover to 6 A20s who successfully bombed targets at Grieh el Cued. Nothing of incident to report other than Sgt Hussey could not take off due to mechanical trouble and had to fly a second aircraft that also became unserviceable on take off. The Squadron on return was released in order to fit long-range tanks. After lunch at 1425 hours 12 aircraft, 3 of which returned early, took off on a sweep of the Cape Bon peninsula but nothing of incident was reported. A further raid by Me109 and Fw190s was made on the aerodrome. Bombs fell near to the 243 Squadron dispersal but caused only slight damage.

At 1745 hours a further 6 aircraft took off to act as escort to Boston attacking Army targets. This was uneventful also. Obviously the large scale attacks being made by medium and light bombers of the last week have forced the enemy to try reprisal raids against our airfields. For the first time since January, the enemy sent over Ju88s to attack our airfields. Flares were dropped over Kings Cross and a bomb fell near to one of our aircraft rendering it completely unserviceable.

18 APRIL 1943

Logbook: 1. Patrol Medjez el Bab area 24,000ft. 2 air test.

ORB: 12 aircraft from 72 Squadron, with 6 aircraft from 111 Squadron took off to act as high cover to 2 aircraft from 225 Squadron on a TacR sortie in the Medjez area but there was little of interest to report.

19 APRIL 1943

Logbook: Offensive patrol 10,000 ft Tunis Bizerte Road. 5 freelance squadrons,, 48 bombers with 3 squadrons close escort bombing La Sebala, Protville. Very hectic, Danny shot down but safe after getting a probable (later a Me109 destroyed). Jimmy one Me109 damaged and Wing Cdr Gilroy a Me109 destroyed.

ORB: Today a heavy offensive programme against enemy aerodromes was carried out. In the morning with Wing Cdr Gilroy leading 48 aircraft from 72, 81, 93 and 154 Squadrons took off to carry out a freelance sweep of the Tunis area. The Squadron provided high cover with 81 Squadron. Over Tunis 9 Me109s were encountered and at once engaged by the Squadron. F/Lt Daniel destroyed 1 Me109, F/Lt Cox, F/O Corbin and F/O Hardy each damaged Me109s. In the course of the same combat F/Lt Daniel collided with a further Me109 but he managed to crash land successfully at Oued Zarga and returned later in the day. The next operation was a fighter sweep to Tunis to cover B17s bombing the docks area. Unlike the morning no enemy aircraft were encountered.

We were one of five squadrons providing freelance cover to 48 Bostons and Mitchells with a further three squadrons as close escort. We ran into some Me109s and 72 Squadron claimed two destroyed and one damaged. This was the biggest show in which I had taken part so far.

The Eighth Army offensive against Enfidaville began with the Germans and Italians refusing to withdraw. The fighting was savage and hand-to-hand. The Indian troops and Gurkhas in particular came into their own. Both sides refused to give an inch.

20 APRIL 1943

Logbook: Freelance striking force 12,000ft Tunis. Similar to previous show, little opposition.

ORB: Two missions today, the first was a freelance sweep over Tunis by 12 aircraft that was uneventful and later in the afternoon with Wing Cdr Gilroy leading and Wing Cdr Dundas flying as Yellow 1, a further 12 aircraft took off at 1625 hours on a similar mission that again proved uneventful. Today on the roads leading from Central and Southern Tunisia to Medjez el Bab towards the north, streams of the Eighth Army and US armoured transport were seen. No doubt the final push cannot be long now. Rivalry to be the first Squadron in 322 or 324 Wing to destroy 50 aircraft in this campaign is growing. The Squadron has had its rather comfortable margin reduced with 81 Squadron now very close and 111 Squadron a little further behind.

There was a similar operation the following day but we met with much less enemy opposition. Close on 100 Spitfires in the air in one operation! The drier weather, the better flying conditions and improved serviceability of our aircraft meant we were really getting on better against the enemy. We could sense that the end was in sight in North Africa.

21 APRIL 1943

Logbook: 1 air test 2 high cover 18,000 ft 'Hurribombers' Mateur–Ferryville Road. Dusk landing!

ORB: The third day of the offensive against the Luftwaffe bases but the Squadron activities were limited to 2 missions. 12 aircraft were airborne at 1350 hours and carried out a sweep of the Tunis/ Bizerte area at 12,000 feet. One Fw190 was encountered but inconclusively engaged. The flak encountered over Mateur at 4,000 feet by Yellow section when chasing the Fw190 was terrific. Our own A.A. was firing at us regularly from the Medjez el Bab area. The second mission carried out produced no reaction but the Squadron acted as top cover to 241 Squadron. One Me109 was seen but not engaged. Today is D-1 and at dawn tomorrow the reinforced 1st Army will launch large scale attacks in all sectors. In anticipation of this, the enemy made strong counter attacks, but these were repelled. The weather however does not appear to be very promising.

22 APRIL 1943

Logbook: 1. Sweep Medjez Bou Arada 10,000ft. Large scale tank battle between Bou Arada and Medjez. 2. Sweep Mateur-Tebourba 22,000ft. Huns below. Yellow section went down and W/O Gear Me109 destroyed but W/O Hunter missing.

ORB: It was clear that the battle was in full swing and it was quite obvious from the pilot reports when they returned from the freelance sweep in the Medejz el Bab area. They observed clouds of dust, burning tanks and shellfire all clearly seen on the Goubellat plain from 10,000 feet. Later 12 aircraft including Sqn Ldr Forde together with 12 aircraft from 111 Squadron escorted 12 B25s bombing Mateur. The attack appeared successful and on the return 111 Squadron met 8 Ju52s, 20 Me202s and Me109s. They destroyed 3 aircraft (1 Ju52 and 2 Me202s) and damaged 3 Me202s. They lost one pilot. The Squadron did not encounter the same aircraft as they returned with the B25s.

In a freelance fighter sweep to the Tunis area by 12 aircraft that were airborne at 1600 hours the Squadron suffered its first loss to enemy action since 5/1/43. The Squadron flew at 22,000 feet and met 12 Me109s near Djedeida. W/O Gear destroyed 1 Me109 but W/O W.H. (Red) Hunter RCAF who was last seen chasing 1 Me109 with 2 Me109s on his tail, did not return. W/O Hunter was one of the original Squadron party to come to North Africa. The battle reported earlier today seemed to have moved more to the east.

The US 1st Army launched its offensive towards Medjez and Tebourba. Farther north US troops were making slow progress against difficult positions in the valley of the Sedjenane and the hills around Mateur.

23 APRIL 1943

Logbook: Sweep Mateur–Medjez 22,000ft. Artillery duel on the ground north of Teukabeur.

ORB: No show was planned for the morning, but at 0955 hours 12 aircraft were scrambled to intercept 9 bandits over Medjez. With the exception of 1 unidentified aircraft at 28,000 feet nothing was seen.

10 aircraft took off at 1300 hours on a freelance sweep of the whole battle area at 22,000 feet. No enemy aircraft were encountered and little was seen. All aircraft landed safely at 1420 hours.

Today we heard with regret that the squadron commander, Sqn Ldr R.W. Oxspring DFC and Bars and the Officer Commanding 'A' Flight F/Lt Cox DFC are leaving us. Their operational tours have expired. The simultaneous loss of these two distinguished pilots and personalities at this time and at the height of the battle will be hard to bear. We wish them both goodbye and good luck.

By now Sqn Ldr Bobby Oxspring was out on his feet and tour expired. He had been sat in his Spitfire cockpit and had to vacate rapidly before being ill. Maybe the bully beef and fag diet had taken hold, but he looked worse than normal and had the misfortune also of being ill in front of the Squadron Doctor, Paddy Griffin, who ordered him off to bed and left him there retching. Paddy was a good doctor and recognised the signs easily, although Bobby was reluctant to leave the Squadron, especially as it appeared that the campaign in Tunisia was on its final lap.

> Bobby Oxspring was a marvellous man and nobody could quite believe it when he suffered from twitch sickness and needed a rest. However a battle-fatigued squadron leader could have been a liability to the Squadron and so it was that Bobby was stood down for a well-earned rest.

Before he left, Oxspring totted up some statistics. In the five months since its arrival in Africa, 72 Squadron was the top-scoring fighter Squadron of the campaign with a total of 53 enemy aircraft destroyed, 20 probable and 50 damaged. To add to this were the many enemy aircraft and transport vehicles destroyed on the ground.

Conversely, the Squadron casualties, although distressing, had been light. Three had been killed in action, three had been posted as missing, four had been wounded and two had been killed by a mid-air collision.

All of the pilots, including the departing Oxspring and Rodney appreciated the efforts of the ground crews. Their dedicated efforts ensured a high level of aircraft serviceability. Maintenance was achieved in the open despite the extremes of weather, the torrential rain and the dust storms and the dive bombing and strafing attacks by the Luftwaffe. There was an overriding sense of camaraderie and it was a close-knit unit.

24 APRIL 1943

Logbook: 1. Sweep Salt Lakes near Pont du Fahs. Plenty of ground observation and tanks we frightened. 2. One Me109 damaged. F/O Le Cheminant and Sgt Hussey Me109 destroyed and Sgt Griffiths One Me109 damaged and W. C. Gilroy One Me109 destroyed in fantastic 'doggers' ho.

ORB: There was no operational flying before lunch. At 1425 hours 6 aircraft were airborne on a sweep of the Pont du Fahs area at a height of just 1,500 feet due to the adverse weather conditions. The area was patrolled without incident for a time and then 4 Me109s dived down in front of our aircraft to ground strafe our troops. As they were strafing F/Lt Daniel and Sqn Ldr Forde attacked and each damaged 1 Me109 and rendered the attack abortive. All our aircraft returned safely.

A second mission of 6 aircraft took off at 1510 hours and carried out a similar operation and in this Sqn Ldr Forde damaged a further Me109 with machine gun fire. The third operation was a similar sweep and heavy flak was experienced. Once again Me109s were met. F/O Le Cheminant blew one in half and described afterwards how the enemy aircraft aft of the cockpit fell away and the engine and wing continued to climb momentarily. Sgt Hussey destroyed one Me109 while F/O Scrase and Sgt Griffiths damaged one each. Wing Cdr Gilroy also destroyed 1 Me109. P/O Keith's aircraft was slightly damaged by a Me109 but he returned safely. We were very pleased to hear that F/Lt S.W. Daniel DFC is to be our new squadron commander and that his successor as Officer Commanding 'B' Flight is P/O Prytherch DFM.

Sgts H.B. Smith and J.T. Connolly were posted to the Squadron today.

> Flying as Red Two I got another Me109G damaged. Really a fantastic doggers-ho and was the perspiration flowing over me!

New arrivals arrived with newly issued tropical kit that had now also been issued to the other Squadron personnel. All pilots were issued calf length, suede, lightweight sand boots, khaki knee-length socks, shirts and shorts, topees and a canvas flying helmet with a flap in the back to prevent sun burn. It led to a multitude of different styles in uniforms! The new arrivals also had what became known as a camp kit that consisted of a collapsible canvas chair, washstand, bathtub and a sleeping cot rolled up in a woollen blanket. This was wrapped in a heavy canvas cover held together by two straps with a handle to carry it all. The whole thing weighed about sixty pounds but it proved useful when set up on site in tents.

25 APRIL 1943

Logbook: 1. Sweep Salt Lakes near Pont du Fahs 19,000ft. 2. Sweep Salt Lakes near Pont du Fahs 19,000ft.

ORB: An early sweep when 12 aircraft were airborne at 0625 hours and swept the Medjez el Bab and Bou Arada area at 20,000 feet but no enemy action was encountered. At 0920 F/Lt Cox carried out his last operation with 72 Squadron when he led 6 aircraft on a further patrol in the Medjez el Bab area. Again there was nothing much to report. At 1005 hours Wing Cdr Dundas led a further 6 aircraft on a similar patrol at 10,000 feet just below cloud and all aircraft returned safely at 1130 hours. A further 12 aircraft were up at 1335 hours to act as high cover on a freelance sweep to 6 aircraft of 152 Squadron. 152 Squadron met 5 Me109s and 1 Fw190 and damaged 2 Me109s. We met 3 Me109s 2,000 above at 20,000 feet and F/Lt Prytherch attacked but made no claim.

The enemy dived away towards Tunis. 12 aircraft that were up at 1655 hours to carry out a freelance sweep at 20,000 feet over Pont du Fahs and provide cover to A20s bombing the area carried out the last mission of this strenuous day.

Today was a record-breaking day for the Wing. 455 sorties have been flown. The score is 3 Me109s destroyed, 8 Me109s damaged for the loss of 3 Spitfires and 2 Hurricanes with one of the pilots safe.

F/O Le Cheminant is leaving the Squadron today to become a Flight Commander with No. 232 Squadron.

26 APRIL 1943

Logbook: 1. Sweep Salt Lakes near Pont du Fahs 8,000ft. Met about 8 Ju 88s and 8 Me109s escorted by Me109s and Fw190s. Everyone fired with no results. P/O Malan missing.

ORB: At 1120 hours 12 aircraft led by Wing Cdr Dundas took off on a fighter sweep at 8,000 feet over the Pont du Fahs battle area. When flying north about 10 miles from Bon Arrada 12 bandits were reported coming southwest towards Bon Arrada at about 12,000 feet. The Squadron did a climbing turn. Almost at once about 6 Me110s, 6 Ju88s escorted by Me109s and Fw190s were seen diving out of A.A. at Bou Arada.

They flew head on at the Squadron and it was only possible to fire very short bursts at them. F/Lt Prytherch fired and hit 1 Me110 already damaged by flak but made no claim. By the time the Squadron could turn the enemy aircraft were going very fast in a gentle dive and were out of range. P/O Malan and F/O Hughes did however chase 1 Me110 down to 1,000 feet. P/O Malan was last seen weaving frantically to avoid flak at about 1,000 feet and was then lost to F/O Hughes who had to break away to avoid the flak. P/O Malan did not return from the operation. The remaining 11 aircraft landed at 1245 hours.

Later a further 12 aircraft from 72 Squadron provided top cover to 12 aircraft from 232 Squadron at 16,000 feet who in turn were providing close escort to 24 A 20s. We saw no enemy aircraft and with the exception of very intense flak over the target area nothing of incident was reported.

F/Lt R.A. Hagger arrived today to become Officer Commanding 'A' Flight in succession to F/Lt Cox. News of the battle that has been in progress for 4 days has been very scarce. Only limited successes have apparently been gained and the enemy has put up very strong resistance everywhere.

Laurie Frampton recalls:

> On 26 April the army were advancing and being attacked by enemy aircraft, so all Spitfires were scrambled to go to their aid. Over the target area the e/a had departed and the sky was full of Spits, all trying to avoid each other. It was by this time dusk and on returning to base the ground staff had set out two rows of gooseneck flares to mark the runway. The landing area was approximately 900 yards long and 20 yards wide with a taxi strip of 15 yards wide alongside. The other squadron sharing Euston had Mk.V a/c, the exhaust ports of which were grouped in pairs so there was three stubs each side directly at eye level. Our Mk IXs had individual stubs, i.e. six per side. At night the flare from the exhausts cut off all forward view. In the failing light our CO asked the other squadron leader to allow 72 to land first, in view of the greater restricted view with our a/c, with which he agreed. When it was my turn to land one of the Mk Vs cut in front of me as I was levelling off for the touch down. At about twenty feet I hit his slipstream, my right wing dropped, I picked it up and landed, out of the corner of my eye I saw two rows of flares, I was on the taxi strip. Kick the rudder hard left, hard right, a quick chicane between the two flares, lined up on the runway as the boss taxied past.

27 APRIL 1943

Logbook: Escort Bostons west of Salt Lakes 10,000ft. Just saw 3 Fw190s in distance.

ORB: 12 aircraft led by Wing Cdr Gilroy acted as top cover to 111 Squadron on a fighter sweep of the Medjez el Bab–Tebourba area. Over Djedeida 3 Fw190s were seen and engaged at extreme range but no claims were made and all aircraft landed at 1345 hours. Later a further 12 aircraft led by Sqn Ldr Daniel acted as high cover to 152 Squadron at 10,000 feet over the Medjez el Bab area which is well inside our forward positions. Our pilots saw at least 12 aircraft drop bombs and fly away north-east towards Tunis. It was thought that because of the hostile actions that the aircraft were Me109s. The Squadron gave chase and closed to 200 yards and one pilot fired a short burst. They were then seen to be American P 40s. Fortunately no serious harm was done but by their actions and appearance from astern they looked hostile.

28 APRIL 1943

Logbook: 1. Sweep Medjez–Pont du Fahs 13,000ft. 2. Sweep Medjez–Tebourba 8000 ft. Some excitement, saw Me109s and Fw190s. Sgt Smith crashed south of Tebourba – PoW.

ORB: 12 aircraft led by Sqn Ldr Forde took off on a sweep in the battle area at Pont du Fahs at 18,000 feet. No enemy aircraft were seen and all aircraft landed safely. At 1050 hours with Wing Cdr Gilroy leading, 12 aircraft took off on a sweep of the Tunis area at 10,000 feet. 2 Me109s were seen diving towards Tunis. F/Lt Hagger and Wing Cdr Gilroy turned and chased the enemy aircraft. F/Lt Hagger shot one of these Me109s down but Wing Cdr Gilroy had some bad luck to have something come loose just as he was about to fire and he had to break away. The rest of the Squadron had climbed to engage about 15 Me109s above at 16,000 feet but these did not fight and dived away.

Later a further 12 aircraft led by Sqn Ldr Daniel on a sweep over the Pont du Fahs–Tebourba area. At about 10,000 feet and east of Pont du Fahs 6 Me109s were seen 'cloud hopping'. Just afterwards 1 Me109 came out of cloud and Sqn Ldr Daniel rolled away and chased and damaged it. As the rest of the Squadron dived, a Spitfire was seen streaming glycol in a vertical dive and crashed south of Tebourba. This was presumably Sgt H.B. Smith who did not return. All remaining aircraft landed at 1600 hours.

Both the British Eighth Army and US 1st Army had found their ways blocked by stiff German resistance so Generals Alexander and Montgomery reached a decision independently but almost simultaneously that would provide a solution as to how the final push against Tunis was to be organised. The 4th Indian Division and the 7th Armoured Division plus the Guards Brigade were to reinforce the 1st Army in the west for the renewed thrust.

29 APRIL 1943

Logbook: Tactical reconnaissance St Cyprien–Bin Meherga 9,000ft.

ORB: 6 aircraft led by F/Lt Prytherch acted as escort to 2 aircraft of 225 Squadron carrying out a TacR in the Bin Meherga area. No enemy aircraft were reported or seen.

The British forces under General Anderson continued to push in force along the road from Medjez el Bab with overwhelming strength against the Germans who were running low on fuel and ammunition.

30 APRIL 1943

Logbook: Sweep Sidi Nsir–Ksar Tye 8,000ft.

ORB: The month ended rather quietly and with a little anti-climax. The Army attacks seem to have diminished, and whilst all of their objectives have not been gained, some progress has been made. The only operation today was at 1135 hours when Sqn Ldr Forde led 11 aircraft on a freelance patrol north of Medjez el Bab. No enemy aircraft were reported.

And so April ends. It has seemed a very long month and much has happened. The most notable feature of the air war has been the introduction of the medium and light bombers to help the hard-working 241 Squadron. 152 Squadron with their Spit-bombers have also added weight to attacks.

The 2nd Corps of US Army continued to battle through the hills in the north and threatened to encircle the Germans in the Sedjenane valley. Though the Germans managed to pull back it meant that Bizerte was in reach of the Americans and they too were prepared for the final push against Tunis.

1 MAY 1943

Logbook: Sweep to 20,000ft over Tebourba. Very hazy.

ORB: Overnight the Squadron aircraft had been fitted with long-range tanks. The idea of this was to enable a sweep in the Gulf of Tunis for the usual Ju52 and Me323 ferry service between Italy and Africa to be carried out. 12 aircraft took off and patrolled off the shore between Bizerte and Tunis at 3,000 feet. No troop or supply aircraft were seen but a He111 escorted by 6 Me109s was intercepted as it flew towards Italy. 111 Squadron led by Wing Cdr Gilroy shot down the He111 while 72 Squadron turned on the Me109s which promptly fled. The Squadron returned via Cap Serrat as all long- range tanks had been jettisoned when the Me109s were seen.

Mention has already been made of the race for the 50th victory. Up to date our closest rival has been 81 Squadron and their Spitfire IXs. Today however, by destroying 6 Me109s and a Me110, 111 Squadron has leapt into the lead for the first time. The attacks of the 1st Army appear to be diminishing in intensity. There is now apparently a lull whilst certain dispositions are made. The intense air effort is however not being reduced as the total number of sorties for the Wing – 239 – clearly shows.

The Germans and Italians left were by and large shell-shocked, short of supplies, fuel and ammunition, yet had still been ordered by Hitler to fight to the end. About 135,000 German and 200,000 Italian soldiers were left to try and repel the final onslaught.

2 MAY 1943

Logbook: Escort Spit bombers to Cape Bon Peninsula 17,000ft. Target a beached destroyer. Only 1 bomb was a near miss!

ORB: Squadron at readiness at 0800 hours but it was not until 1215 hours that 12 aircraft took off to act as high cover to 152 Squadron Spit-bombers attacking a beached enemy destroyer. The attack was made at 4,000 feet while the Squadron maintained cover at 16,000 feet. Heavy and light flak came from Solinen and the destroyer. No enemy aircraft were seen or reported.

All day the Squadron was also at readiness to move to Djebel Abiod but the move for the Squadron has been cancelled. Nos 111 and 93 Squadrons proceeded this afternoon.

3 MAY 1943

Logbook: Escort Fortresses (36) to Bizerte 25,000ft but 10/10 cloud over target.

ORB: The lull in the battle continues apparently on both sides except north east of Medjez el Bab where the enemy has tried a local attack with some success. It appears the lull is being used to obtain the most up-to-date information of the enemy's movements. This is being done by numerous Tactical Reconnaissance and Photographic Reconnaissance sorties. At 1005 hours this morning Sqn Ldr Daniel led 6 aircraft as top cover to one of these photographic missions in the Medjez area. They flew at 9,000 feet and covered the area but encountered no enemy aircraft until they were about to land. A.A. was also conspicuous by its absence. There appeared to be quite a bit of ground movement in the Mateur area that has apparently been captured by the Americans. All aircraft landed safely at 1125 hours. To complete a very stormy day with thunder in the offing, 12 aircraft took off as high cover to 36 B17s attacking Bizerte. The Squadron flew at 27,000 feet but conditions for bombing were not good and the heavy and medium bombers encountered inaccurate flak.

4 MAY 1943

Logbook: Patrol Tunis–Bizerte 24,000ft.

ORB: The lull before the storm. It is now we have been told, only a few days before the main offensive is to start, that will hopefully bring this war which has lasted for over 3 years on this continent to an end. Today there were no operations before lunch but at 1445 hours 6 aircraft took off as escort to a further Tac R sortie. At 1510 hours a further 6 aircraft provided escort to a PR Mustang in the battle area. Both missions were carried out uneventfully. Later 12 aircraft were

airborne at 1820 hours on a patrol of the Tunis area at 20,000 feet in support of P 40s bombing targets in the area. Weather today very warm but rain is threatening. Tropical dress is now being worn and is welcomed by all and it is remarkable that very few mosquitoes have been seen since the opening of the malaria season.

5 MAY 1943

Logbook: 1. Escort Tactical Reconnaissance Tunis- Bizerte area.2. Scramble and Patrol Tunis, Mateur, Medjez 25,000ft. W/O Gilroy, F./O Hardy Me109 damaged. I saw F.A!

ORB: The Squadron provided 12 aircraft as high cover for 2 Mustangs of 225 Squadron on a photographic mission in the Tunis–Bizerte area. The Mustangs flew at 8,000 feet with 8/10 cloud cover and the Squadron role was to stay in the area without maintaining visual contact until the mission was completed. The Mustangs encountered 2 Fw190s damaging one over Lake Bizerte but the Squadron did not encounter any enemy aircraft.

At 1105 hours with Wing Cdr Gilroy leading, 12 aircraft took off on a freelance sweep of Tunis and Bizerte at 25,000 feet. South-east of Mateur 8 Me109s were encountered and Wing Cdr Gilroy and F/O Hardy each damaged one a piece. Heavy and intense accurate flak was encountered north west of Tebourba and caused damage to Sgt Jacob's aircraft and injured him in the eye. F/Lt Hagger landed at Marylebone with undercarriage problems, as did Sgt Clarkson with a burst tyre.

This evening the plan for the main attack was unfolded to the commanding officer who then addressed the pilots in the officers mess. 'The final big assault will begin at dawn tomorrow, the programme has been amended, the bombers with their fighter escort – us – are to blast a way for the army. F/O G. Sharp (RAAF) and F/O R.R. Barnfather were posted to the Squadron today.

The final push against Tunis was scheduled for the next day.

6 MAY 1943

Logbook: 1. Patrol Djedeida-Tebourba area 18,000ft. 2. Patrol Djedeida–Tunis area at 10,000ft. A glorious mix-up with 20 Me109s and Fw190s. I fired but cannons jammed. Little to show although was within 25 yards. F/Lt Hagger one Me109 destroyed and one Me109 damaged. P/O Keith two Me109s destroyed and one probable and F/Lt Prytherch and P/O Shaw each claimed a Me109 damaged.

ORB: Flying commenced again on 6 May, the day of the final push to defeat the combined German and Italian armies in North Africa. In the afternoon 12 Spits from 72 Squadron swept over the battle area at 14.00 hours flying at

14,000 feet. Bad weather over Tunis prevented much from being seen there, but north of Bizerte, 16 Me109s were encountered. Wing Cdr Gilroy led a section down on them from 10,000 feet but they fled. The rest of the Squadron climbed rapidly after them, got amongst them and a terrific battle ensued during which F/Lt Hagger claimed one and one damaged, P/O Keith claimed two and a probable and F/Lt Pytherch and P/O Shaw claimed one each. Two more were damaged.

Jimmy Corbin also remembered the big day.

> We were put on readiness. The skies were filled with the menacing drone of Allied bombers as they headed towards Tunis and Bizerte. I estimated that by 8 o'clock in the morning somewhere in the region of 150 bombers had passed overhead. As I wrote in my diary, that many bombers were going to leave a hell of a mess when they hit Tunis and the surrounding area.
>
> It turned out to be a busy day for 72 Squadron too. We began by escorting a group of bombers on their operation to attack Tunis, the final stronghold of the Germans. It had been a beautiful city surrounded by orange groves. The air was thick with the smell of their blossom. It was here that our intelligence led us to believe that the Germans hid their tanks and aircraft so it was here we dived down onto their orchards and strafed the long lines of trees. The resulting explosions revealed our information had been spot on and we had been successful in wiping out numerous enemy aircraft and armour. Resistance from the Germans was waning.

It was the Air Force that started the battle and at dawn the Squadron was at readiness and watched the sunrise – a beautiful morning and the Squadron's task was to escort the medium bomber Bostons all day. It was a tribute to the number of sorties flown and the Allied air superiority that no aircraft were lost and over 1,000 sorties were flown. The Germans had gone to ground, heavily camouflaged and dug in and from the air the ground looked dead and deserted. On the ground in the early hours of the morning the infantry divisions advanced against their objectives behind a massive rolling artillery bombardment reinforced by heavy bombing when daylight came. By 10.00am that morning the advancing armies were ahead of schedule. Every objective had been taken and the advance units had to slow down to allow the flanks to catch up. The pilots of 72 Squadron returned to base to refuel and take off again. Their second sortie only encountered some minor flak but the third sortie they ran into about 20 Me109s at about 7,000 feet over Tunis. The enemy had been a formidable one but their pilots were now largely inexperienced and between them the Squadron recorded four destroyed and three damaged. After the fourth mission of the day for most of the pilots, many of them were exhausted and were relieved that the end was in sight. At the same time, they had spent long days doing very little that in turn had led to boredom and frustration.

The Germans and Italians continued to fight, often to the last man and by dusk the British tanks and armour still remained about 15 miles from Tunis.

7 MAY 1943

Logbook: 1. Sweep North Tunis area 8,000ft.

ORB: Tunis orbited up to 8,000 feet with 12 aircraft including Wing Cdr Gilroy and Sqn Ldr Boddington. Took off at 09.05 but no aircraft encountered. There were between a dozen to 20 motor transports on the Protville–Tunis road. All aircraft landed safely at 10.25.

Logbook: Sweep La Goulette pranged barges. Destroyed 2 barges and one motor torpedo boat full of men. Damaged a tug. Port wing dented by a large piece of the motor torpedo boat!

> A lot of strafing and little opposition. Always a price to pay for low level attacks so when attacking some barges off the port of Tunis I was hit in the port wing by part of one of the barges on which I had been firing.

ORB: 8/10 cloud at 10,000 feet when Sqn Ldr Daniel and 11 other pilots took off at 18.05. Tunis patrolled at 8,000 feet and there was much small shipping to the north of Tunis. Our aircraft went down and attacked off the mouth of the River Medjerda. 4 barges left smoking and a destroyer and 3 smaller craft also attacked. Destroyer left on fire and two of the smaller craft sank. Light flak encountered. P/O D.N. Keith was hit and crash-landed at Medjez el Bab but was unhurt.

The speed of the advance had taken the Germans by surprise and opposition began to crumble. Tanks moved on relatively unhindered and news filtered through that Tunis had fallen. In the late afternoon American tanks entered and took Bizerte and the noose around the German forces was drawing tighter. Most of the remaining German fighters were ordered to fly out of Tunisia.

8 MAY 1943

Logbook: 1. Strafing transport north of Tunis and destroyed one lorry with others damaged. 2. Strafing Korba airfield, one SM79 destroyed (flamer) and one Me109 damaged. Strikes on Macchi 202s with 6 others destroyed.

ORB: Squadron flew at 10,000 feet in the Cape Bon area, weather and visibility good. Motor transport seen moving between Hammet–Kelibia and Kerda al Medzel and were attacked. Came across 20 Me109s and one He 111 left on the ground. F/Lt Hagger destroyed two, Sgt Clarkson damaged two and F/O Hughes damaged a third. Squadron later flew again around Cape Bon area and though no enemy aircraft reported, 50+ motor transport seen at and observed north-east of Soliman. Heavy flak encountered at Soliman.

Both Tunis and Bizerte were in Allied hands and subdued. It came as no surprise to many of the pilots that Tunis had been captured. The Squadron's role was to shoot up the road between Tunis and Bizerte to try and prevent the Germans evacuating the area.

9 MAY 1943

Logbook: 1. Strafing Cape Bon Peninsula. Back noughters ho! Interesting trip! 2. Sweep Cape Bon again.

ORB: Flying at 12,000 feet in fine weather, both coasts could be seen, but no enemy aircraft reported or seen. Heavy flak encountered. Shipping seen at Korbous and Cap de Forbas.

The Squadron was briefed to attack enemy lorries at Zaghouen and columns of vehicles were attacked. There was little flak around and a couple of trucks were left smoking. From there they flew onto Carthage where enemy ships were waiting to collect the retreating troops. Motor torpedo boats in the harbour were attacked and one exploded in an enormous ball of flame that shot up into the air. Sgt Griffiths 'Griff' picked up a hole from the flak but managed to nurse his Spitfire back to Souk el Khemis. The rest of the Squadron returned unscathed.

The Germans were doomed and they knew it and were forced into the confines of the Cap Bon peninsula, whilst in the La Sebala area, they hung on for another few days only to be wiped out eventually, few escaping. There were some remnants in the Enfidaville area, they were totally surrounded yet continued to fight on valiantly. Realising the hopelessness of the situation they finally surrendered in vast numbers and it was here that General von Armin was taken prisoner.

10 MAY 1943

Logbook: Sweep Cape Bon, the end in sight. Cooks Tour.

Losses were very low and they continued to harass the evacuating troops right up to the next day when it was considered that the North African campaign was ended. Freelance patrols continued and for a few days the odd fighter was encountered but after this our only concern was flak that was still heavy and accurate.

They were flying over Tunisia at 10,000 feet now whereas a week before it had only been safe to fly at 25,000 feet – a mark of the quickly changing circumstances. They continued to strafe shipping, parked aircraft, transports and troops but this was stopped because the Allied troops were advancing so rapidly that it was difficult to identify targets accurately. To their knowledge they never made the mistake of attacking their own forces but this was as much down to good luck as good management.

11 MAY 1943

On the ground the roads were packed with tanks and troops following the advance and there were constant traffic jams. An advance party was sent through and reported back that the smell was awful, flies and bodies were everywhere.

General Alexander was able to cable Winston Churchill who was in Washington on 13 May. 'Sir it is my duty to report that the Tunisian campaign is over. All enemy resistance has ceased. We are masters of the North African shores.'

> The Squadron moved away from their base at Souk el Khemis. Remaining flights that month were few. Just bringing repaired kites back to our new location at La Sebala just north of Tunis. The Axis forces surrendered on May 13th. Next day I was one of a group of chaps who drove out in a 15-cwt truck to the Cape Bon peninsula where the enemy troops, now disarmed, were marching back towards their PoW camps. Revolvers and binoculars were being thrown into the bushes and available for one to pick up. I got a super pair of binoculars but unfortunately these were lost many years later on Epsom Derby day!
>
> I still regarded myself as the new boy. I had learnt something of operational flying but I felt my shooting had to improve. At the same time I had fitted into the team, had been accepted and could be relied upon to carry out my orders and instructions.

17 MAY 1943

Logbook: To La Sebala and Patrol Bizerte harbour.

The sweep over Tunis and El Aoinna airfield showed large numbers of damaged enemy aircraft and enemy activity in the skies above Tunis was scant. There was now a strong sense it was all over bar some sporadic gunfights in the city as some Germans decided to make a brave last stand. In the afternoon some of the pilots treated themselves and travelled to Tebourba where they were able to swim and get clean in the sea. The warm water felt glorious and for a time they were able to relax.

Over the next few days life in the Squadron became pretty routine. A number of uneventful patrols were carried out after the Squadron moved from Souk-El-Khemis to La Sebala, an airfield about eight miles north west of Tunis. La Sebala was still under construction. It was from here only five days before that Me109s had taken on the Spitfires from 81 squadron. La Sebala was an excellent aerodrome, wide and flat, completely grass-covered with no litter or useless material left lying around; but it was not the same on all captured airfields. Many others were littered with shells, grenades dead men and animals. On the aerodrome itself there were 10 burned out Ju 52 transport planes which lay crippled at the edge of the airfield but several Me109s stood intact and untouched in their bays, hidden in the orange groves at the southern edge of the airfield. They dared not touch anything since there was the chance that material had been rigged with explosive set to go off with the slightest touch fromy an unwary trophy hunter or scrounger. Often the most innocent appearing object would be wired so they had to be extremely careful.

The journey by the advance party had solved one problem and that was how the Germans had kept flying after most of his airfields had been bombed; it was because they had used long, straight stretches of roads with parking bays built by the roadside. These had camouflage nets to hide the aircraft. The Germans had also left a parting gift at the airfield other than the booby traps and mines – most of the Squadron went down with dysentery. While the water bowser had filled the wells, on examination they contained dead animals.

Despite this and to observe the victory a number of pilots were dispatched with four-gallon tanks with orders to fill them with local wine. Several hours later they re-assembled to drink and revel, they drank and drank for an age without anything happening! Eventually, somewhat disgusted, they retired still apparently sober. By morning however they were all drunk and the slow acting date wine finally revealed its potency and they were drunk for most of the day. Nothing else ever compared to that slow acting but potent Tunisian wine! 'Lunatic's Broth' it was called, and they had access to gallons of the stuff, so they made full use of it. Jimmy Corbin:

> With fighting now confined to Zaghouan, some 60 miles south of Tunis we pilots had time on our hands. Joe Scrase, Chem and a few others decided to investigate the city that we had patrolled for so many months. We managed to 'borrow' a jeep and began our own victory tour of Tunis. Joe Scrase had scrounged a bottle of whisky that we took in turns to swig from. It didn't quench our thirst but it made us merry enough. As we drove through the streets of Tunis the sun was beating down and the temperature reached 100 degrees. The damage to the city was immense and it was incredible to see what the bombers had done. There was very little left, entire streets had disappeared completely leaving behind piles of rubble. Elsewhere buildings were pockmarked with bullet and shrapnel holes revealing the scars of battle. Despite the devastation and undoubtedly the deaths that had occurred the Tunisians turned out in their droves to wave and cheer us on. Their spirit seemed indomitable. As we rounded a corner of a street on the outskirts of the city a sight that stopped us in our tracks confronted us. Joe Scrase stopped the jeep and we all got out. In front of us was a prisoner of war camp that stretched as far as we could see. Inside, row upon row of German soldiers sat cross-legged and in eerie silence. Some looked up at us but most faces were expressionless. They were filthy and ragged looking and a far cry from a once-proud German army. We stared at them and realised that this was what it was all about. This was the enemy, and these were the people who had been killing us and we had been killing. I didn't know whether to hate them or feel pity.
>
> We drove away from the camp and continued our tour of Tunis. Joe Scrase was a young pilot officer who joined the Air Force after the Battle of Britain. He spoke fluent French and this was now put to the test as he pulled up next to a couple of

schoolgirls and fell into easy conversation with them. They invited us to their house to have a meal with them and their parents by way of thanks for what we had done. It was a remarkable act of generosity. The Tunisians had suffered a great deal themselves but still wanted to prove they were excellent hosts and insisted on sharing what little food they had with us.

20 MAY 1943

Logbook: Patrol Bizerte Harbour.

ORB: F/O Hardy led the squadron of 12 Spitfires on a patrol at 18–20,000 feet in the Gulf of Tunis to intercept any enemy aircraft that might attempt to attack Tunis during the Victory Parade. None seen or reported and all landed safely.

Tunis played host to an official victory parade. While one of the other squadrons provided the spectacle of a low fly past, 72 Squadron remained on readiness and carried out a couple of patrols over Tunis to make sure the Germans did not gatecrash the party. By now it was clear the main job in hand had been done and a sense of boredom began to creep into the camp while they waited to move onto the next stage of the war.

21 MAY 1943

Logbook: 1. Patrol Convoy 'Hemingway' off Bizerte. 2. Scrambled to Tebourba. Sex got Me210 destroyed.

ORB: 2 aircraft Sgt L.A. Frampton and P/O R.R. Barnfather scrambled to intercept enemy aircraft 25 miles north-west of Bizerte but no contact made. 4 aircraft led by W/O A.H. Gear scrambled at 17.15 hours to intercept enemy aircraft 10 miles north-east of Bizerte going west at 23,000 feet. Section climbed to 26,000 feet and a visual was obtained but soon lost. This was regained and enemy aircraft identified as a Me210. W/O Gear fired two bursts from above and the port engine caught fire and it spun and crashed into the sea off Tebourba leaving only a patch of oil. All aircraft returned safely.

22 MAY–31 MAY 1943

ORB: No operational flying but squadron moved from La Sebala to Mateur.

There was a liberty run into Tunis that day for most of the Squadron. According to the operations book, cars and motorcycles in various states of repair began to appear around the campsite. Trophies of the campaign were eagerly sought after by many and German helmets; rifles and badges became popular trophies. A few managed to get hold of transport and with wheels they were able to explore further afield far more quickly. Approaches to any of the towns were littered with the carcasses of horses and bodies of soldiers and were surrounded by hordes of flies in the intense heat. The stench of decaying flesh was overwhelming.

Tunis, however, was marvellous and a popular retreat with wide streets and lined boulevards and the pilots were able to shop in the stores. The Army had managed to drink the two breweries dry in the week following its capture before Monty had instructed the Redcaps to move in to restore some sort of order. The pilots and ground crew drank wine and champagne around the bars and clubs near the docks and harbour, which only weeks beforehand they had flown over when the medium bombers had struck the very same targets. The medium bombers had also succeeded in destroying a large amount of shipping as was apparent from the masts, funnels, debris and keels protruding above the waterline. Even though the harbour was in close proximity to the city itself, very few bombs had gone astray.

The pilots were able to relax in the warm water and on the beaches and quite quickly wore a tan. The ancient city of Carthage with the temple of Apollo became a regular haunt. The sunshine, mountains and brilliant blue of the sea and sky and the areas of historical interest enabled the pilots almost to forget that there was a war. Happy days.

The success of both 322 and 324 Wings in the months of March, April and May was even more spectacular when one considers the opposition they were up against and the conditions under which they had to operate. Their opponents had principally been JG 51 and JG 53 flying the latest Me109s and JG 2 flying Fw190s. These units had been based on the permanent all-weather aerodromes around Tunis and Bizerte and their pilots were amongst the most experienced in the Luftwaffe. The Allied squadrons had operated under much worse ground conditions and were frequently unable to fly because their airfields were under water. This made living conditions intolerable and it was also evident that the German communication and warning systems were much better than the Allies. In addition, the Germans could use the main highways as emergency landing grounds whereas the Allies frequently had to deal with quagmires. The Allied squadrons had no hangars and there was always a shortage of spares for the aircraft when they were damaged or unserviceable. Ground crew had to be ingenious and resilient and along with pilots had to endure bombing raids and ground strafing attacks in the open. The ground crews, unlike the pilots, had little opportunity to rest or take a holiday but their commitment and efficiency was undoubted and without them the pilots would have been helpless.

Despite this, there is no question that Allied air superiority meant the campaign ended swiftly and without further loss of life. The Germans later admitted that they could not fight against the tremendous concentrations of aircraft that the Allies were able to bring to bear exactly where and when they were needed and this accounted for the sudden collapse of the enemy in the Cap Bon peninsula. Under such superior air cover it was clear that the Germans were not prepared to try and evacuate their trapped troops. In short, some of the Germans best and most experienced troops were sacrificed. Had they been saved, they could have been used effectively later. Along with the troops, some 290,000 of them, were 26 generals and masses of equipment, machinery and supplies, food and ammunition. The amounts captured were staggering and must have had some effect on the German's ability to fight and later counter attack when the Allies landed in Sicily and Italy. Most of the German prisoners were detained in open sites around Carthage.

Relaxing times came to an end as the pilots became bored with the excess of spare time. Reading, writing, swimming and seeing the sights were a far cry from ops in almost impossible conditions. Disease was becoming rife as the diet was so limited and they were constantly reminded of the precautions to take to avoid contamination. Sanitation was very basic, a spade for digging a hole in the ground. At one stage they had some large-lidded galvanized buckets with a tented screen but the Arabs pinched the lot so they had to return to the spade. They also used petrol cans cut in half with holes bored in the bottom and filled with sand. Jerry cans had not been invented then and the cans they used were thinner and leaked all over the place but when empty were extremely useful. The Arabs treasured the cans as well, called them 'be days' and used them for a whole host of reasons, even to build shacks from. They became valuable because they could be traded for eggs and fruit or used as a stove (bottom filled with water, top filled with sand and petrol) that could be used for cooking and laundry.

One thing the pilots and Rodney in particular never forgot was that the success of their operations against the Germans was in every way just as much due to the ground crews that provided the back up as to themselves. Sgt Jack Lancaster also recalls the team spirit and camaraderie.

> The personnel of the Squadron obviously was quite different to what it had been in England. We now had our own transport and transport department, we had our own mechanics and fitters and we also had our own equipment people like Sgt Horner. In the transport section there was F/Sgt Carver and Sgt Arthur the Sgt Fitter, but he was a grand chap and much older than we were, obviously been in the Service quite some time. However, there were of course a lot of drivers who we'd not had before and this obviously made the Squadron a different organisation altogether to what it had been before. The Squadron now had three flights again of course, A, B and maintenance flight and A flight was Chiefy, F/Sgt Hogg, Sgt Coussens and Sgt Johnny Waite. B flight of course there was Chiefy Landon, there was myself and Sgt Mann – Bill Mann. And in maintenance flight there was F/Sgt Dawes and with F/Sgt Dawes I think there was Sgt Blackie and Cpl Punter was Fitter 2.
>
> Now 60 years on it's very difficult to remember all the names of the lads, I still remember Nobby Clarke and Ben Hades and Bence, Cpl Spencer, Chick Fowler. They were a good bunch of lads altogether and we got on very well. I don't remember anybody every being hauled over the coals, I cannot remember anybody being put on a charge at all and we never had any trouble. People just got on with the job and it was a great Squadron.

They were not to know but the Squadron was being prepared to move again at short notice.

CHAPTER EIGHT

INVASION SICILY, OPERATION HUSKY, JUNE–AUGUST 1943 – 72 SQUADRON

1 JUNE 1943

ORB: After spending a few days rest at either Tebourba or Tunis all the pilots returned to Mateur today. Included in the party were 4 new pilots posted to the Squadron, F/O J.F. King, Sgt C.R. Piper (NZ) Sgt L.C.R. Morris (Australian) and Sgt K.C. Weller.

Ground personnel working at full pressure today in preparation for the Squadron movement. All aircraft are being re-camouflaged from the desert colours to a dark green colour similar to that employed at home. The difficulty is that no proper spray paint is obtainable and at the moment it is a matter of trial and error. All the Squadron's motor transport is being prepared and marked with the Squadron's numbers and letters. A definitive scale of kit to be taken has been laid down by 242 Group, which only allows one kit bag per man to be taken.

Signal received at 08.30, 'as many members of the Squadron as possible were to proceed to Carthage to be addressed by an important person between 11.00 and 12.00 hours'. As time was short and there was such pressure of work only a few airman attended. It was guessed that the important person would be the Prime Minister and this proved to be correct. At about 13.10 the familiar figure of Winston Churchill appeared from the cabin door of an Avro York at El Aouina. His aircraft had been escorted in by 6 P38s. As he stepped from the aircraft he was given a rousing welcome and seemed in great spirits.

Churchill left later for Carthage where in the famous amphitheatre overlooking the Mediterranean he made a further speech to the 1st Army. He said that he had come on behalf of the King and the Nation to thank the members of the 1st Army for their glorious victory in Tunisia. Many more victories would fall to the lot of the 1st Army but none would be so glorious and significant as that accomplished in Tunisia.

Following the surrender of the Axis forces in Tunisia the next stage of the Allies plan was put into action, the aerial assault against and the ultimate capture of Pantelleria. Preliminary bombing had begun on 9 May and each day saw a step up in the aerial and naval bombardment. Houses were pounded into dust, jetties smashed, roads blocked and with the water distilling plant destroyed, it became more and more difficult to distribute. About 15,000 enemy troops were left on the island and had to spend most of their time crowded into tunnels and trenches and huge hangers built into the rock on the island.

3 JUNE 1943

Work continued on very hot days with conditions at Mateur not ideal. All ground personnel were living in tents on a very dusty plain, beside the landing ground and miles from the sea. Pilots remained in Tunis where similarly no adequate arrangements had been made – they were cooking and eating their own food in the passages of the hotel where they stayed. General opinion was that all personnel could have camped by the sea and arrangements could have been made for the guarding of the aircraft. Lack of organisation led to considerable unrest. It was perhaps fortunate that the Squadron was resting and off operations. The ground crew continued to have to work hard on the grounded kites and the overhaul of the ground equipment and motor transport. Little work was done in the heat of the afternoon, so after a light lunch, many would jump in whatever transport was available and drive to Ferryville, where at the blue lake they would swim and sunbathe all afternoon. There were spring boards, high boards and a water polo pitch and most of the squadrons mingled. They would return to the aerodrome in time for tea, and then if necessary, the ground crews, would work in the cool of the evening.

Options for entertainment in the evening included the 'flea pit ' cinema in Mateur or dancing or watching a film, held on the side of a hill, with a screen set at the bottom. It was invariably watched by thousands including the troops who would sit or stand around on the grass or try and get a better view by gaining a vantage point on one of the lorry transports. These were warm and peaceful nights.

4 JUNE 1943

First elements of 322 Wing began arriving in Malta, also from Tunisia. 81 Squadron landed at Takali led by Wing Cdr Colin Gray, the new Wing leader, while 322 Wing's former Wing Leader, Gp Capt Piet Hugo, was appointed OC Wing. 81 Squadron were joined by four other squadrons: 152 Squadron led by Sqn Ldr F. Lister, 154 Squadron led by A. Wiseman, 232 Squadron led by Sqn Ldr C. Arthur known as 'Duke' and 242 Squadron led by F/Lt G. Sylvester. Advance elements of another Spitfire wing, 244 Wing, also began to arrive led by Wing Cdr Peter Olver DFC with 145 Squadron led by Sqn Ldr L. Wade, 601 Squadron led by J. Taylor. They went into Luqa from where they were to operate for the forthcoming invasion. The arrival of the other squadrons was imminent, with 92 Squadron and 417 RCAF and SAAF due. With so many Spitfires at Takali and Luqa, the squadrons already resident there moved to a new strip at Safi and became the Safi Wing commanded by Wing Cdr Duncan Smith.

Most of the squadrons on Malta were being re-equipped with brand-new Spitfire IXs. For the last couple of years, the defence of the island had been in the hands of the older Spitfire Vs but the Germans had introduced the Me109G and the Fw190 which were superior in performance to the older Spitfires. The Spit IX was slightly heavier because of the larger engine but it had the same airframe, lovely loose ailerions, an additional 250bp, a four-bladed propeller and a supercharger that came in with a tremendous kick at about 21,000 feet. Its introduction would give the Allied air forces the advantage over the Me109Gs and Fw190s once more.

5 JUNE 1943

ORB: At 07.00 hours 324 wing units including 43, 72, 93, 111 and 242 Squadrons began to move off to Sfax. 140 vehicles were involved and very good time was made. Convoy camped for the night en route.

6 JUNE 1943

Arrived in Sfax.

7 JUNE 1943

Vehicles of wing and squadron embarked on transport. Axis fighters beginning to put in an appearance against the American bombers relentlessly targeting Pantelleria.

8 JUNE 1943

ORB: Embarked. All possible motor transport was loaded onto LST 403 and this was to be their home for the voyage. These mass produced craft have a very shallow draft and a retractable bow to enable transport to be loaded and unloaded on beaches where no proper docking facilities exist. The convoy of LST's with a corvette escort HMS *Roxina* sailed at noon. Conditions at sea were ideal, with very little swell or wind. After a quiet night land came into view at 06.30, the destination, Malta.

With the island of Malta in the background, Wing Cdr Brooke, Senior Padre of 324 Wing conducted a short religious service on the upper deck. Ship's captain Lt Cdr J D Row RNR was asked to say a few words at the end and he expressed his satisfaction with the conduct of all troops on board and expressed the opinion that the stay on Malta would be short for they had a major part to play in the forthcoming offensive. By 13.00 hours all personnel had disembarked and reached Hal Far camp.

For the first time in seven months the Squadron would not be required to live and sleep under canvas as the billets were empty houses in a small but picturesque village. By evening most of the airmen were installed and spent most of the time bathing in the sea.

9 JUNE 1943

The build-up of aircraft and how Malta managed to handle and sustain so many extra units preceding the invasion of Sicily was an astonishing example of efficiency in supply and organisation. The island had been turned into a gigantic aircraft carrier supporting 23 Spitfire squadrons, five night fighter squadrons and a large number of bomber, strike and reconnaissance squadrons. The two Spitfire wings had now left Cross's 242 Group and transferred to the Desert Air Force under Air Marshal Harry Broadhurst, who besides being experienced in tactical operations, had led the Western Desert Air Force in support of the Eighth Army through the Libyan and Tunisian campaigns.

Many of the pilots and ground crew appreciated the newly acquired comforts of Malta. Conditions had only recently improved following the ending of the siege of the island at the beginning of 1943. Before then conditions had been as primitive, if not worse than North Africa, and food was in such short supply that the island's occupants were slowly being starved. After Tunisia – the extreme heat, dust, flies and lack of a suitable diet – Malta with its cool buildings, fresh water, and reasonable food now that the supply lines had been kept open, was positively palatial. It was a pleasure to sit down in a Mess and be served dinner by the Maltese staff. It was a pleasure simply to eat without being hounded by flies!

With the build-up of Allied aircraft in Malta, the German air raids that had been almost a daily feature of Malta life for the previous two years became less frequent. The battle scars remained however. Malta, had been, after all, the most bombed place on earth. (For the full extraordinary story, see *UXB Malta* by S.A.M. Hudson.) The harbour at Sliema Creek and Valetta were covered with masts of sunken ships and whilst food remained in relatively short supply with rationing still in place, beer and wine were plentiful again as it was made on the island. The girls were lovely and they were friendly. Most were half English anyway with soldier fathers, were bilingual and all wanted an English husband to be able to get off the island. Dances were held in Valetta most nights and at weekends at the other stations such as Hal Far, Luqa and Kalafrana. Valetta also had a notorious street called the Straight, known to servicemen as 'The Gut'. Every building was either a pub, cafe, doss house or brothel. There were no officers allowed but for a small fee hats could be exchanged so that they too could enjoy the delights of Malta's nightlife.

Flying from Malta would bring about a change in tactics, not only because they would be flying over enemy territory; the large distance over water between Sicily and Malta was a difficult enough barrier to overcome in itself. Sir Keith Park lost no time in briefing his pilots on arrival at Malta – in approaching Sicily they might be at 25,000 to 30,000 feet in the hope of catching the enemy either coming up towards them or be in a position to see them below. He also stressed to all ground staff that maintenance was vital for this long haul over water.

10 JUNE 1943

Logbook: Mateur to Hal Far Malta – Pantelleria surrendered today.

ORB: For everyone a very busy day, at noon the aircraft had arrived from Mateur and the rest of the day was spent in servicing the aircraft and completing checks and unpacking stores.

Malta was our next base. We flew to Hal Far on the 10th June one of five squadrons in 324 Wing led by 'Sheep' Gilroy.

11–14 JUNE 1943

Logbook: Practice flying tail chasing.

ORB: There was no operational flying. Sqn Ldr H.S.L. Dundas DFC posted from HQ – NATAF for Wing Commander Flying Post. Aircraft of 43 and 243 Squadrons also arrived.

15 JUNE 1943

Logbook: Cannon test.

ORB: 324 Wing including 12 aircraft from 72 Squadron carried out a sweep over Sicily flying at 26,000 feet. Some flak over Comiso but there was nothing else to report. New 'Wingco', Wing Cdr Hugh Dundas of 324 Wing succeeded Wing Cdr Gilroy who has been promoted to Group Captain, flew with the Squadron this morning but had to return early due to engine trouble.

16 JUNE 1943

Logbook: Sweep to Southern Sicily, Comiso area.

ORB: Further sweep over Sicily, again flak over Comiso. Total of 35 Spitfires up from 324 Wing over Ragusa, Comiso and Gela in late morning.

17 JUNE 1943

ORB: It appears that the enemy is using the same tactics as he used in Tunisia and that he refuses to react to purely fighter sorties and will only use his fighters when bombers are operating. Only 6 Me109s seen by the whole of 324 Wing (37 Spitfires from 72, 93 and 111 Squadrons and led by Wing Cdr Dundas) and they all avoided combat. Sweep was a prelude to bombing of Comiso and Biscari by US Liberators, the bombing force themselves covered by a force of about 70 Spitfires drawn from 322 Wing and the Krendi and Safi Wings.

18 JUNE 1943

Logbook: Sweep to Comiso 27,000ft. 20+ Me109s in three groups below. Nothing much done, F/O Keith Me109 destroyed. F/Lt Prytherch baled out. In dinghy but posted missing.

Not a happy day for the Squadron. Despite the fact that the Squadron opened the Wing score when P/O Keith destroyed his fourth Me109 with the Squadron over Sicily in the morning the Squadron lost F/Lt Dalton Prytherch, who baled out because of engine failure off the Sicilian coast. The engine failure was not due to enemy action. He was seen to bale out successfully but was then dragged along by his parachute in the water. W/O Gear flew at 50 feet immediately after the parachute was seen in the water but no trace of the pilot was seen. A search was carried out with no results. F/O George Keith RCAF, a Canadian from Alberta with three victories already in Tuisia, was separated from the rest of the Squadron and as he was crossing the coast on his return, spotted the two Spitfires of Clarkson and Gear circling looking for Prytherch but with an Me109 poised to attack them both. He attacked the Me109 from above, closed to within 300 yards, fired a short burst, observed strikes on the wing root and glycol pouring from its radiator. He fired another burst and saw the cockpit hood and other pieces fall off and the pilot then baled out. F/Lt Prytherch was an experienced pilot and a valuable leader and his loss was a heavy blow to the Squadron.

> We flew at 27,000 feet as top cover in a wing sweep over Comiso, the major Italian airbase in south east Sicily. We saw some 20 Me109s in three Groups but did not engage. Meanwhile, one of our team, F/Lt Prytherch, reported engine failure and that he would have to bale out. This was about 10 miles south of Ragusa. Two of the Squadron went down to observe and give a fix on the spot. His parachute was seen to be dragging him along in the sea. Sadly he drowned. In a separate incident George Keith was returning to base by himself when he saw and engaged an Me109G. The enemy aircraft was hit and the pilot, none other than the commander of II/JG 53 Major Michalski, baled out over land with a wounded leg and a broken ankle. He was picked up quickly and taken to hospital.

19 JUNE 1943

Offensive sweeps over south eastern corner of Sicily continued but no enemy aircraft encountered even when escorting 9 US Liberators that bombed Reggio de Calabria and San Giovanni.

20 JUNE 1943

Logbook: 1. Scramble local patrol 20,000ft. 2. Scramble over Grand Harbour with Yellow section vectored on 2 Me109s out to Sicily. F/O Sharp shot down by Me109 later destroyed by W/O Gear.

That day for the first time the people of Malta saw their King. He arrived on HMS *Aurora* escorted by four destroyers at Valetta early in the morning and spent the whole day inspecting the island. The squadrons at Hal Far only caught a fleeting glimpse of him as he drove along the perimeter track towards Kalafrana. He was dressed in the uniform of Admiral of the Fleet and was accompanied by Lord Gort.

ORB: It has been the turn of the Squadron to be at readiness from dawn until dusk. Five scrambles were ordered but only one produced any results. At 18.30 hours Wingco and 3 other pilots, F/O Gordon Sharp, W/O Alan 'Sex' Gear and Sgt Keith Clarkson were scrambled to investigate hostile plots over the Malta channel. They climbed to 26,000 feet and flew towards the Sicilian coast and found two enemy aircraft flying south-west towards Gela. The formation split up, two aircraft going in pursuit whilst the remaining two provided top cover for them. The enemy aircraft crossed the coast and then saw our aircraft between them and the coast. They turned away and were about 600 yards in front. The enemy leader then did a slight left hand turn and with a wide deflection shot hit the aircraft flown by P/O Sharp, who had in turn been warned by W/O Gear to take evasive action. The Spitfire turned on its back and dived into the ground near Biscari. W/O Gear at once turned onto the enemy leader and with a 3-second burst blew the cockpit hood off and the enemy aircraft also turned on its back and dived into the ground at Biscari. Operation therefore ended on equal terms.

It became known today that the Squadron was to lose some of its Spitfire IXs and be partially equipped with Spitfire Vs. This move brought both 322 and 324 Wings into line with the fighter wings of the Desert Air Force formerly operating with the Eighth Army. The idea was to allow the most experienced pilots in the Squadron to benefit from the superior performance of the newer Merlin engine.

21 JUNE 1943

Logbook: 1. air test. 2. Ferry to Safi. We lost our '9s', 6 in each squadron now. 3. Ferry Safi to Hal Far.

ORB: W.C. Dundas leading, the Squadron carried out a further uneventful sweep over Sicily. The transfer of 10 Spitfire IXs to other squadrons in the Wing took place this evening and at the same time 10 Spitfire Vs were received as replacements. Four Spitfire IXs took part in a fighter sweep over Comiso and again no enemy reaction was seen. This serves as confirmation of the fact that the enemy is employing the same tactics as in Tunisia by conserving his aircraft to deal with bomber raids and to ignore the fighter operations.

We had been one of the first squadrons in Tunisia to be equipped with the Spitfire IX. Now in what we saw as a retrograde step we were to give up our exclusive use of that fine model to share the planes we had with the other squadrons in the Wing. It was to be six Mark IXs for each and we collected our clapped out Mark Vs to make up our establishment.

23 JUNE 1943

ORB: Four Spitfire IXs acted as top cover to Spitbombers who intended to attack aerodrome at Comiso but target was obscured by cloud so an alternative target was attacked. 2 Me109s seen and F/O Hughes attacked one without results.

24 JUNE 1943

ORB: Readiness dawn to dusk – 2 small missions carried out without incident. Visits by the 'top brass' were not over and airmen of 243 and 72 Squadron assembled near the windsock on Hal Far to hear an address by Sir Archibald Sinclair, the Secretary of State for Air, who on behalf of His Majesty's Government, thanked the squadrons for their services in North Africa.

25 JUNE 1943

ORB: For the first time since the Squadron had arrived on Malta, the Squadron was totally released for the day. A rare day of pleasure visiting Valetta. Large quantity of mail arrived. The effect of the mail was noticeable, spirits rose, conversation became animated and a general feeling of satisfaction was apparent as soon as the mail was distributed. There was no doubt it had a tremendous effect on morale and any news from home lifted spirits even more. The more they got the better, as far as the pilots were concerned.

Large formation of B17s from North Africa had raided Messina in the morning and inflicted much damage.

During the six weeks we spent in Malta our non-flying activity was limited to looking at historic buildings, drinking plenty of beer, joining the evening throng in Main Street and swimming and sailing. One challenging swim was out to Kalafrana Bay where the remains of one of our Merchant ships, the *Breconshire* lay. She had been in a convoy in the summer of 1942 and was so badly damaged she had been beached there. It was a good half an hour swim out to the rusting sides of the ship where we would rest and sunbathe and then race back to the shore.

Farrish recalled:

Tom Hughes however was worried about his contribution to the Squadron. He had not shot any down, he had a damaged back in the Tunisian campaign and although he had flown many operational hours he showed none of the common signs of pilots being tired, never came back early for imaginary reasons, was always keen and his flying did not deteriorate. He became most popular and sincerely respected by everyone and would go far out of his way to do anything, big or mean, for anyone.

We moved to Malta and we used to go out sailing, Tom and I found a common interest in the red-sailed Sharpe dingy. Sailing across Birzebbuga Bay in the bright sunshine or swimming from the boat in turns we used to talk. Once we talked of shooting down Huns. We discussed it intently; fighting in the air was a science to him, deeply thought out. He said that some people like Danny Daniel and George Keith were fitted by character to be fighter pilots. Even Joe Scrase with his boyish ways, would fight like a demon in a tight corner. There seemed to be a certain absoluteness or concentration about it, besides the ability to shoot straight, to watch your own tail, to avoid tactical enemy traps and not to follow a German down. Tom was worried about it, he pointed out that he couldn't seem to shoot them down, perhaps he was so good a flyer that he could not throw a plane around like Chas Charnock did and he could not purposely side slip to get his gun sights on the enemy.

27 JUNE 1943

Logbook: Sweep to Southern Sicily, Comiso 20,000ft. Pleasant Squadron practice.

ORB: Since arriving on Malta, there have been 17 cases of Malaria reported so the use of Alabrine will be resumed. It is thought that the use of the drug will keep the disease under control. Offensive sweep by 10 Spits of 72 Squadron in morning but brought no reaction from Axis fighters.

28 JUNE 1943

Logbook: Patrol Grand Harbour 26,000ft. Milk train turned back.

ORB: ASR Wellington sent out to search for missing Wellington bomber that had crashed into the sea off the Sicilian coast during the night. Escort provided by 24 Spits from 324 Wing. Dead body in flying clothes, empty dinghy and debris found over a wide area but no survivors.

29 JUNE 1943

ORB: Further large amount of mail arrived. News arrived of P/O F. Malan (missing since 26/4/43) regarding his fate. It appears that his aircraft disintegrated in mid-air and he died a few minutes after being rescued by the 15th Light Field Ambulance.

30 JUNE 1943

ORB: Further day of release for the Squadron again spent in Valetta. This ends the month of flaming June. On the whole it has been a trying month for the Squadron and its difficulties have been increased by the loss of F/Lt Prytherch. Despite this however, the Squadron at once has taken its place as the top scoring squadron in the Wing.

Operation *Husky*, the planned Allied invasion of Sicily had been the subject of intensive planning by the American General Dwight Eisenhower and the British commanders in the Mediterranean theatre, Air Chief Marshal Tedder, General Alexander and Admiral Cunningham.

The Allies had had some success in subduing the small island of Pantelleria, midway between Malta and Sicily, solely by naval and aerial bombardment. The Allied leaders had hoped to knock out the Luftwaffe and Regia Aeronautica on their Sicilian airfields and achieve air superiority before the beach landings. Attacks on the Sicilian airfields had begun almost a month earlier on 15 June and continued on an almost daily basis with raids by heavy bombers. The build-up to the planned invasion was to see intensive action erupting in the skies above and around Sicily for the whole of July – in contrast to the relative quiet of June.

There were to be three main phases in the air plan. The first had begun as soon as Tunisia had fallen and comprised the systematic bombing of Italian industry and Axis airfields, with care taken to distribute the attacks so as to give no hint of where the amphibious landings would be. RAF bombers from England would attack Italy and Germany while more bombers from the Middle East would attack the Dodecanese and Aegean Islands. Until 3 July, a week before D-Day, strategic bombing attacks were made against the principal enemy airfields in Sardinia, Sicily and Southern Italy. The second phase for a whole week before D-Day was aimed at destroying enemy fighters and communications in Sicily and Sardinia, but in order to maintain surprise, no beach defences were attacked. The third phase was to be the all-out attack on local airfields coordinated with the attacks made by the land forces. It was considered that the day after D-Day would be the most hazardous for ships approaching or lying off the beaches, since by then, the main Allied concentration points would have been revealed. The fighters would then be needed to transfer from their offensive roles to the task of protecting the shipping from enemy bombers and this would be needed day and night from the Spitfire squadrons within range on Malta.

Now assembled on Malta and on the neighbouring island of Gozo in readiness for the impending invasion of Sicily were no fewer than 23 Spitfire squadrons, one photo-reconnaissance squadron, and one TacR squadron, comprising about 400 Spitfires.

> July brought us back into a full operational state. There were now six wings of Spitfires in Malta, a total of 23 fighter squadrons of which three were USAAC. Numerically this force was substantially in excess of the Luftwaffe and the Regia

Aeronautica but in terms of individual performance the Me109G remained superior to the Spitfire V.

1 JULY 1943

ORB: Sweep over Sicily to escort 8 Spitbombers of 1435 Squadron bombing Biscari aerodrome. Squadron engaged 12 Me109s and allthough they quickly dived away, Sdn Ldr Daniel damaged one Me109 after firing a 3 second burst and seeing strikes before it dived away. Squadron sufferred no losses. Judging from reports from the Strategic Bomber Force and the reports of the Malta pilots it would seem that the tempo of the battle over Sicily is now being stepped up quickly and a tremendous amount of damage is being inflicted both night and day.

2 JULY 1943

Logbook: Patrol Grand Harbour 26,000ft.

ORB: F/O R.R. Barnfather and W/O A.H. Gear admitted to station sick quarters today.

4 JULY 1943

ORB: Wing co-operated, on American Independence Day with American elements of the Strategic Air Force by acting as top cover to B17s attacking Catania in Sicily. Long-range tanks were used. Fleeting contact with Me109s and Mc202s but no claims were made. 3 B17s attempted to land Malta on their return, 2 landed at Hal Far but one crashed into the sea, the crew having baled out. Sadly a member of the crew was mortally wounded. One B17 that landed claimed they had destroyed a Me109 and had seen at least 50 enemy aircraft.

For the first time the Medium bombers of the Tactical Air Force, which had played such an important part in the Tunisian campaign and the capture of Pantelleria, were in action over Sicily.

5 JULY 1943

Logbook: Escort Fortresses Gerbini 23,000ft. Me109s up in strength. A turning game.

ORB: Squadron transferred to Middle East Command. US bombers again pounded the airfields. Escort to B17s heading for Gerbini were met near Ragusa by more than 100 Me109s. F/O Tom Hughes claimed 1 Me109 as damaged.

6 JULY 1943

ORB: Acted as cover for 3 squadrons of P40s of the Tactical Air Force, the target being Biscari. No enemy reaction apparent. No doubt that the full Allied bomber strength being used to batter Sicily with the Malta Wings, including 72 Squadron providing fighter cover for the bombers.

7 JULY 1943

Logbook: Escort Mitchells to Comiso and Biscari 15,000ft.

ORB: Squadron escort to Mitchells bombing Biscari, again no opposition. The weight of the attacks now appear to be having an effect.

8 JULY 1943

ORB: Tremendous pounding being meted out on Sicily and it is clear that air superiority is now clearly in our hands. The softening process seems well under way and the ground offensive cannot long be delayed. The Squadron was successful when acting as withdrawal cover to B17s over Comiso aerodrome.

P/O Roy Hussey at 14,000 feet saw enemy fighters circling to land which he at once attacked and destroyed an Me109 with white tips. Sqn Ldr Daniel also destroyed an Me109 and a third crashed without being attacked. F/Sgt Hermiston and Sgt Scott also damaged 2 Me109s. The airfield at Comiso was then attacked and a Ju 52, Fw190 and Hs129 were damaged together with admin buildings and wireless operations.

9 JULY 1943

Logbook: 1. Patrol invasion convoys – a truly wonderful sight. 2. Patrol invasion convoys again. The invasion starts tonight.

A large numbers of invasion barges arrived in Malta and the plan was unfolded that day. Two conferences, one of squadron commanders and one of intelligence officers, were held where the broad strategic and technical plans were outlined. The intention was to attack Sicily and capture it by use of air- and sea-borne troops, the assault to be divided between British and American forces. The British troops would force the south east coast and the American troops would attack from the south west. Parachute and airborne troops would be landed at key positions in advance of the sea landings. Enemy dispositions showed that the assault was expected in the west and the only German units in Sicily were located in that area. Airborne troops were to land soon after 22.00 hours and the sea-borne troops would land the following morning. For the rest of the day the vast armada of landing craft proceeded to their objectives provided with continuous air cover from Malta. The long-awaited day was about to dawn. In a few hours, British and American troops would be fighting for a foothold on Hitler's Europe.

For the Axis forces the first warning that Sicily was about to be invaded came after reconnaissance aircraft on a routine patrol in the Mediterranean spotted five convoys in the sea south of Malta heading towards Sicily, each with about 150–180 landing craft. Later convoys joined with two battleships, one aircraft carrier, four cruisers, together with the considerable Allied air power. The carriers were HMS *Formidable* and HMS *Indomitable*. All Axis garrisons on Sicily were put on full alert. At nightfall on 9 July the water off Sicily seemed deserted, yet despite the windy weather and rough sea, the Axis forces on the island were aware of the presence of a huge fleet of ships and vessels somewhere in the darkness moving towards the island. The Axis forces could do little except wait for the resumption of the Allied air bombardment that would signal the start of the invasion.

In fact the start of the invasion was heralded by British Glider-borne troops of the 1st Airborne Division which had been tasked to attack and hold positions south of Syracuse –the operation was to go horribly and tragically wrong. The majority of the gliders were towed by C 47s of the US 51st Troop Carrier Wing and the remainder by RAF Albemarles and Halifaxes. Winds of up to 35 mph buffeted and blew the gliders and heavy flak forced many of the pilots of the towing aircraft to take evasive action that dispersed the formation and some pilots then released their gliders early. Confusion reigned and some planes opened fire on each other to add to the chaos. Others turned around and headed back towards Tunisia. Of the 136 gliders that had set off, about half ditched in the sea, many paratroopers were drowned and the remainder were spread over a 25-mile area between Cape Passero and Cape Murro di Poosco.

At the same time as the ill-fated 1st Airborne Division assault on the area around Syracuse, the Americans planned a similar airborne assault to the east of Gela. About 200 C 47s were to transport 3,500 men of the US 82nd Airborne Division from airfields in Tunisia. Again, the high winds and inexperienced pilots meant that the paratroopers were dropped along 50 miles of coast. Both airborne operations were disastrous failures, though the few airborne troops and paratroopers who landed in the right place at the right time contributed to the success of the landings. The harsh lesson from the British perspective was not to rely on American transport aircraft with inexperienced pilots because the troops were too valuable to be wasted.

> A truly wonderful sight, the Invasion starts tonight. For the next few days we were patrolling Acid Beaches.

10 JULY 1943

Logbook: Escort Mitchells, diverted to 'Acid' Beach Patrol. First sight of landings, thrilling!

ORB: Sicily invaded. Operations appear to be proceeding to plan and penetrations made inland after an intense naval barrage. Comiso already in our hands. Squadron stood by from dawn but were not called upon until late afternoon when they provided bomber escort, completed without incident.

Despite the battering that Sicilian airfields had taken in the build-up to the invasion and the toll of aircraft destroyed in the air and on the ground, the Axis forces still presented a major barrier to the invasion forces. Montgomery later reflected however that 'Allied air forces had definitely won the air battle and this was quite apparent from the first moment the troops landed on the shores of Sicily because the enemy air force was swept from the skies and were not allowed to inconvenience them.'

The Western Naval Task Force carried the US 7th Army and made landings at three designated areas, codenamed CENT near Marpina, DIME near Gela and JOSS near Licata, with the first troops landing at 02.45 hours. Some resistance was seen, small formations of Fw190s, Me109s and Ju88s and Italian fighter bombers began dropping flares and attacked the troops and USS *Philadelphia* and USS *Jefferson*. Spits based on Malta covered the landings all day, in turn. The first sorties over the landings were flown by 242 Squadron between 05.00 hours and 05.30 but were met by indiscriminate fire from American gunners who were later to riddle Wing Cdr Warburton's PR Spit who was photographing the landings. His plane was severely damaged and he only just managed to get back to Malta.

The British landings were further east and the Eastern Naval Task Force beached on the Sicilian coast at around 05.00 hours on five designated areas, codenamed ACID North near Cape Murro di Porco, ACID South near Avola, Bark East near Marzameni, Bark Middle near Cape Passero and Bark West from Pozzallo to Pachino. The British Eighth Army met a few elements of an Italian division, which did not put up much resistance. Some troops remembered seeing that they had fighter cover from first light, and the Spits from 324 Wing were over the landings at about 05.30 hours led by the OC 324 Wing, Grp Captain 'Sheep ' Gilroy and came across a Ju88 south of Syracuse. The next patrol was led by Wing Cdr Dundas and its job was to maintain air cover over the Syracuse area throughout the day, in Squadron strength, with each Squadron due to spend about 35 minutes on patrol over the beaches. This timing was critical for fuel conservation and depended on formation leaders heading back promptly for Malta once their time was up, provided that they had been relieved by the next Squadron and they were not engaged by the enemy. From the first patrol led by 'Sheep' Gilroy the Spitfires were delayed before returning to Malta, so much so that F/O Leslie Connors had to ditch his aircraft about a quarter of a mile from Hal Far and though he was seen swimming for the shore, by the time a launch had arrived, he had disappeared, presumed drowned. Three other Spits landed short of fuel at Safi rather than at Hal Far, which indicates the critical fuel tolererances because Safi was less than two miles from Hal Far!

Patrols were maintained throughout the day; 12 Spits from 92 Squadron encountered Me109s near Cape Murro di Porca. On duty that day with 92 Squadron was

F/O Milton Jowsey RCAF. After encountering the Me109s, where no claims were made, they came across six Ju88s attacking shipping. F/Lt Tom Savage shot one down but he was then believed to have been hit by gunfire from the warships and, unable to bale out, lost with his aircraft. Milton Jowsey recalled:

> Over the landing craft we found six Ju88s, numerous Mc202s, Me109s and Ju87s. We came in too fast and overshot the Ju87s. I saw F/Lt Savage shoot down one Ju88 and while in pursuit of another, at about 10,000 feet, he was shot down by Royal Navy flak. We were very loath to pursue enemy aircraft near RN ships as they only seemed to get close to us.

Another Ju88 was claimed by F/O John Gasson but a second Spit was also shot down with F/Lt Dicks Sherwood having to bale out into the sea. He was picked up and taken back to Malta.

The problem with friendly fire continued when the Spits of 93 Squadron led by Wing Cdr Duncan Smith were back over the beach head in the afternoon. They sighted six Ju88s bombing shipping with some Mc202s as escort and were chased away withou any claims being made. As the Spits swept down over the beach the A.A. gunners put up a heavy and accurate barrage, which hit two of them. Wing Cdr Duncan Smith managed to nurse his damaged aircraft back to Malta but F/Lt Raoul Daddo-Langlois crash-landed on the beach and suffered a severe fractured skull in the crash. He was carefully removed and placed aboard a small lighter to take him aboard a hospital ship. Another bombing raid came in and the lighter was sunk. Daddo-Langlois, or 'Daddy Longlegs' as he was affectionately known, a veteran of the air battles in Malta a year before, was lost.

Further sweeps and more claims and successes followed though 72 Squadron were not required until the late afternoon and did not encounter any Axis aircraft. US bombers and fighter-bombers from North Africa continued to pound the Axis airfields and defences and with the onset of darkness further raids were carried out against Trapani, Milo and Gerbini. Allied forces had by the end of the day captured Syracuse, Pachino, Gela and Licata.

11 JULY 1943

Logbook: 1. Patrol Acid Beaches up to Syracuse. 2. Patrol Acid Beaches but weather duff and recalled.

ORB: First operation of the day was 14 Spits led by Gp Capt Gilroy and Sqn Ldr Daniel who together with 12 Spits from 43 Squadron patrolled the beaches south of Syracuse but failed to locate any aircraft. Second operation of the day was more successful when Sqn Ldr Daniel led the Squadron and in the course of the mission encountered some 20 Mc200s which were being very roughly handled. The CO shared a Mc200 destroyed with F/Lt Christopherson and two

others were claimed as damaged by Sgt Hermiston and P/O Roy 'Jack' Hussey. With the Squadron fairly short of fuel, south of Syracuse, F/O Keith became detached and did not return with the other pilots. It was thought that he had crash-landed short of petrol. Later he returned, complete with serviceable Spitfire, and explained that before he had made a forced landing at Pachino in Sicily he had also destroyed a Mc 200 and a Ju88.

News of the landings appeared to continue to be good and with the exception of Gela and Comiso, enemy opposition appeared to be steadily reducing. There was another Squadron sweep over the Noto beaches in the evening but this was again uneventful.

During the night the main attacks on Sicily were delivered against air and supply bases in the west of the island. Mitchells bombed Bo Rizzo airfield and Wellingtons did likewise against Trapani, Marsala and Mazzaro de Vallo. More Wellingtons bombed Porto Corvino Ravella airfield near Salerno on the Italian mainland where German bombers were stationed. Liberators and Halifaxes from Cyrenaica attacked Reggio di Calabria airfield and pressure on the Axis defending forces continued. Allied land forces were also on the move. US 7th Army troops occupied the important airfield at Comiso where repairs started immediately. In addition, the US 82nd Airborne Division dropped its second paratroop wave in front of the Allied landings at Gela. Again, it proved disastrous and of the 144 C47s, 23 failed to return and 37 were severely damaged. It turned out that many had been hit by friendly fire from Allied shipping offshore that had not received instructions that the air armada carrying the paratroops was friendly and the ships had been instructed to fire on any aircraft flying at low level over them. It seemed incredible that the Air Force would lay on such a hazardous low level flight over the assault area, over Allied shipping that was committed in combat and which had been subjected to enemy raids for the previous two days, without any warning.

12 JULY 1943

Logbook: 1. Patrol Acid Beach x 2 10,000 ft. 3. Pachino to Hal Far. Sgt Morris flying 'K' crash landed but picked up by Navy. 1 Mc200 destroyed and 1 damaged in slaughter. 8 destroyed, 1 probable and 7 damaged. Tremendous 'Doggers' Ho with Me109s squirted a little. Squadron destroyed 3, 1 probable and 2 damaged. Sgt King missing.

ORB: A record day for the Squadron. In 3 sorties to the Syracuse–Augusta area in Sicily the Squadron destroyed 13 enemy aircraft (8 Mc200s, 4 Me109s and 1 Ju 52) probably destroyed 3 Me109s and damaged a further 10 (4 Mc200s and 6 Me109s) The Squadron losses were 2 aircraft missing (Sgts King and Morris) and 2 slightly damaged. Sgt Morris later reported to have been picked up from the sea by the Royal Navy.

Move of the Wing from Malta to Sicily began today with the departure of the Wing HQ party. Squadron attitude at the end 'of a hell of a day' was 'let them all come'. 72 Squadron big show had already caught the eye of the 'high-ups' hence receipt of the following signal from the A.O.C. Malta 'Well done 72. Congratulations on your magnificent combat this morning when you destroyed eight enemy aircraft without loss to yourselves.'

The main effort for the day was still the provision of fighter cover for the landing beaches and Allied shipping in the occupied harbours. Near the end of the first patrol, south of Syracuse, a number of pilots saw two aircraft go down in flames, victims of 72 Squadron that had encountered about six Me109s and a few Mc 202s near Augusta. F/Lt Arthur Jupp claimed one Me109 probably destroyed and Sgt Keith Clarkson claimed a second, which dived into the sea. F/O Keith then shot down a Mc 202 but Sgt J. Morris was forced to land his Spit near Malta. It was badly damaged and he was given a lift back to Malta on a LST and arrived back two days later.

On the second patrol of the day just before mid-day, the Squadron led by Sqn Ldr Daniel came across a large force of 30 Me109s, 6 Mc 202s and more fighter bombers escorting a single Ju52 in the Augusta area. The Ju52 was rapidly shot down by P/O B. Ingalls RCAF who also damaged a Me109. Sqn Ldr Daniel also claimed a Me109 shot down and aother was damaged by F/O Cameron. In addition five fighter bombers were shot down by F/O Tom Hughes, F/O John King, Sgt A. Griffiths (two) and F/O Rodney Scrase who also claimed a damaged. One probable was claimed by F/Lt M. Johnston and Sgt Scott. All this for no losses!

On the third patrol of the day at about 17.00 hours 12 Spits led by F/Lt Arthur Jupp engaged a large number of Me109s and Mc 202s north east of Carlentini between 9,000 and 12,000 feet, which had been attacking Allied tanks and motor transport advancing over the Catania plain. The Squadron tore into the enemy fighters and two Me109s were claimed by P/O Roy 'Jack' Hussey and Sgt Scott, while P/O Eric Shaw RNZAF claimed a Mc 202. F/Lt Jupp and F/O George Keith each claimed a Me109 and three more were claimed as damaged by Sgt Keith Clarkson, Sgt Pearson and F/O J. King. Another Spit flown by Sgt King failed to return and he later became a PoW. Sgt Griffths returned to Malta with his aircraft badly damaged and P/O Roy Hussey landed despite damage to his tail.

For its successes during the day the AOC Malta sent a letter of congratulations to Squadron leader Daniel and pilots of 72 Squadron.

> On 12 July occurred one of those extraordinary clashes. 72 Squadron at full strength encountered what we took to be Macchi 200s. The Squadron claimed a total of seven destroyed, one probable and seven damaged. My personal bag was one destroyed and one damaged. I chased two aircraft from the Italian formation. They kept flying in echelon; a spick and span air show formation. My two guys just kept on flying straight and level. I lined up behind the No. 2 and fired. He fell away smoke billowing from his fuselage.

> His leader continued and in my excitement I kept my finger on the gun button for much longer than necessary. The plane was damaged with bits flying off the wing. All I could do was watch and hope he would have to bale out. No such luck, he flew on back to his base. I returned to our base to be greeted by our ground crew and had to confess to them that 12 or 13 seconds worth of ammunition was nowhere near long enough for me! It was only later that we learnt that our opponents were Fiat G 50 fighter bombers and were probably on a non-operational move out of the immediate combat area.

Tom Hughes also recalls the action that day:

> I was leading eight aircraft over Sicily in the Syracuse area. Suddenly I spotted a tight formation at the same height to the west and they looked hostile. Opening up I gained a little height and the 'bandits' started to dive to the northwards. The ten-mile gap closed quickly and they appeared to be the slow but very manoeuverable Macchi 200 of the Regia Aeronautica. There were just six of them. I saw my seven Spitfires were nicely spaced astern but there seemed nothing hostile above or behind. [Fifty years later the Italians confirmed that they had been Fiat G50s.]
>
> I closed extraordinarily quickly now and had to throttle right back. It seemed amazing that they had not seen me and had taken no evasive action. I gave one long burst from line astern but saw no hits. I was now two hundred yards behind another and I fired again. No luck. I dived below them and turned. My friends were in line abreast having good shooting practice above me. Suddenly the Italians broke formation. An amazing wheeling melee followed. Cameron, the Canadian, was turning tightly with an aerobatic Wop. I joined him and in two turns was right on the tail of the Fiat. A one-second burst from my cannons set him ablaze. It was fearful to see. But there was a parachute near Melilli so I think the pilot got out. I hope he wasn't scorched too much.
>
> I climbed up and all seven other Spitfires soon joined up on me. I set course for the southern tip of Sicily and then home to Malta. On the way we were attacked by a Macchi 202 and two Me109s but they dived away, although I shot at the Macchi, without success.
>
> We got back to Hal Far in good spirits. I knew that there were only six Fiats in that formation because I had counted them carefully – we got the lot. My bag was just the ONE DESTROYED. Cameron was disappointed, I offered to credit him with half of mine, he would not hear of it. Two months later he was killed in the Straits of Messina by 'flak'. I still have his 'wings'. Cameron's wings were leather backed and small 'full dress' size; they looked smart on his tropical shirts and later on mine. Roy Hussey said he would have them from my gear if I was shot down but he must have forgotten or changed his mind for I had them returned from the Air Ministry with my kit when I came back from my prison camp. By then Roy had been killed in a Mustang.

13 JULY 1943

Logbook: 1. Patrol Acid Beaches x 3 10,000ft. P/O Hussey 1.5 destroyed and Sgt Griffiths 0.5 destroyed.

ORB: Squadron flew four sorties/sweeps over Sicily. During the second P/O Hussey destroyed a Mc 200 and shared a Me109 with Sgt Griffiths. News of the Squadron move to Sicily arrived in the evening and arrangements for the move were started with an advance party leaving Hal Far early the following morning.

This was the last day that the enemy was able to put up any effective aerial resistance over Sicily. Coastal radar installations had been lost to the invasion forces and other key installations including airfields at Catania, Milo and Trapani were attacked by B17s and Marauders. 72 Squadron relieved 111 Squadron on the patrol line over the beaches between Augusta and Noto at around 10.00 am and came across a group of Axis fighters that included Me109s and Mc 202s.

Roy 'Jack' Hussey shot down a Macchi before he joined Sgt Bert Griffiths and between them they shot down another Me109, which crashed in the Syracuse/Catania area. There was reduced aerial activity in the afternoon with only small groups of Axis fighters making an appearance. It seemed that the Axis forces knew that air superiority had been gained by the Allies. Overwhelmed and exhausted, the surviving German and Italian pilots were withdrawn to the mainland leaving behind many unserviceable aircraft.

During the night more British paratroops were dropped over the plain at Catania to secure the key bridge over the River Gornalunga at Primosole, but as had happened before, the operation proved to be costly, with several C47s, Albacores and Halifax towing aircraft lost. The remaining paratroops did however succeed in capturing the bridge and removed the demolition charges.

14 JULY 1943

Logbook: 1. Patrol 'Acid' Red Line Augusta. 2. Patrol Catania. F/O Keith 1.5 destroyed and P/O Hussey 0.5 destroyed.

ORB: Sgt Morris reported missing on the 12th and then picked up by the Navy rejoined the Squadron today. The Hal Far Wing's Spitfires including 72 flew 3 further sweeps, with 3 Me109s claimed as destroyed, one by P/O Keith.

By morning the British Eighth Army had encountered enemy rearguard at Monterosso while the German counter attack on the seaplane base at Augusta was beaten back. US troops captured further airfields at Biscari, Mazzarino and Caniccatta, so the ground fighting was now going the Allies' way. First patrol of the day from 72 Squadron was at about 07.45 hours when 11 Spits saw several Me109s in the Augusta area and attacked them from above. Three were promptly shot down and claimed by F/O George Keith, F/O Ken Smith and George Keith and 'Jack' Hussey claimed a further one shared. US B17s Mitchells and Marauders from the NWAAF and Liberators from the US 9th Air Force continued to pound Messina.

15 JULY 1943

Logbook: Patrol to Catania. Fired at by considerable light and heavy flak.

ORB: Squadron as an operational unit left Hal Far for Sicily ready to conduct further operations from Comiso. One uneventful patrol flown over Catania from Hal Far and then in the afternoon the following pilots flew their Spits to Comiso. Sqn Ldr Daniel, F/Lt Jupp, F/Lt Johnston, P/O Hughes, P/O Shaw, P/O King, P/O Smith, P/O Hussey, P/O Barnfather, Sgt Clarkson, Sgt Connolly, Sgt Scott and Sgt Griffiths.

After the capture of the important bridge at Primosole, the British Eighth Army began to fan out over the plain at Catania. Despite numerous patrols, it proved to be relatively quiet in the air. More squadrons moved across from Malta to Sicily and 72 Squadron at Comiso were joined by 111, 43 and 93 Squadrons. The general state of the airfield and buildings paid tribute to the accuracy of the Allied bombing effort. Hangars and buildings had been completely wrecked and the airfield was littered with damaged Axis aircraft. It was also memorable because of the thick clouds of red dust thrown into the air as the Spits took off, the flies and mosquitos that were everywhere, which infested cuts and scratches and were most unpleasant. Comiso was also only about 30 miles from Gerbini, and the Axis-held airfields close to it were not captured until 21 July, so this made life interesting for a while!

US fighter bombers continued their attacks on retreating German motor transport and positions around central Sicily and US Mitchells continued to bomb Palermo and the railway yards at Termini to hinder further troop movements.

16 JULY 1943

ORB: Bulk of the Squadron had a great day at Hal Far and bathed. P/Os Keith and Cameron flew further Spits to Comiso where operationally the Squadron swept the Catania area.

The British Eighth Army continued its advance across the plain at Catania towards the River Gornalunga and the landing grounds at Gerbini while the Canadians took the Caltagirone further east. In the morning nine Spits from 72 Squadron led by F/Lt Arthur Jupp patrolled north of Augusta and across the Catania plain at around 10,000 feet and engaged about 15 Me109s three miles west of Augusta. Sgt Bert Griffiths was seen to shoot down one Me109 but his aircraft appeared to be hit by fragments from the downed Me109 and it fell out of control and crashed. One parachute was seen to open but it was unclear whether the parachute was German or that of Bert Griffiths. Later, Bert's body was recovered from the wreckage of his Spitfire.

In the evening warships off Syracuse, including HMS *Rodney* and HMS *Nelson* bombarded Catania.

17 JULY 1943

Logbook: 1. In Dakota Luqa Malta to Pachino. 2. Pachino to Comiso.

British Eighth Army continued push and advance across the Gornalunga, Canadians captured Ramella and its airfield and the Americans took Pietraperzia. More Spitfire squadrons made the move from Malta to Sicily.

> At the end of the week, in company with other pilots and ground crew, we were taken by Dakota first to Pachino and then to Comiso, a regular air force base with a 2,000-yard runway. Imagine our surprise when we found not only a number of unserviceable aircraft lying about but also cases of wine and Asti that presumably the Germans had been unable to load onto their last departing transport planes. The supplies were very welcome to us!

18 JULY 1943

ORB: Early morning patrol over the Catania plain and came across 4 Me110s with an escort of Me109s bombing Catania harbour.

One Me110 was claimed shot down and shared by Sgt Cliff Piper (RNZAF) and Roy 'Jack' Hussey after their first bursts had hit the rear gunner and stopped him shooting. The plane was seen to crash north of Mount Etna.

19 JULY 1943

Logbook: 1. Patrol Acid Beach x 2 10,000ft.

ORB: Patrol by Squadron failed to find any enemy in morning patrol in the Catania area but a large convoy was seen and attacked. Two lorries were destroyed by F/Lt Arthur Jupp and F/O John King, then the Kittyhawk fighter bombers were called up and destroyed half a dozen more.

On the ground the British Eighth Army had run into stiff opposition against the crack German Hermann Goring division, which had been reinforced by the 15th Panzer Grenadier Division. The Canadians had also run into stiffer opposition as the Germans fought hard to keep the road running eastwards open to help with troop movements.

20 JULY 1943

Logbook: Catania, Gerbini Patrol 10,000ft.

ORB: Rest of sqaudron personnel arrived from Malta. Convoy from marshalling yards, completed the tortuous route through Pachino, Ispica, Modica, Regusa and then to Comiso. Camp site at Comiso attractive with plenty of shade.

21 JULY 1943

ORB: Camp site converted into home. Pilots who had flown the Spitfires in on the 15th and had sleeping quarters in the Wing were moved into the camp site. Aerodrome was a mess, but offered ample evidence of the thoroughness of the air attacks before our occupation. Two further patrols over Catania.

22 JULY 1943

Logbook: Escort Baltimore bombers to Adrano 10,000ft. Good bombing by some of the babies.

ORB: Squadron dug in and a lone raider dropped bombs and shot up the areodrome. Squadron provided escort to Baltimores bombing Adrano.

23 JULY 1943

ORB: Comparitively quiet. Squadron provided cover for Kittyhawks bombing Catania and Baltimores over Misterbianco.

24 JULY 1943

Logbook: Sweep to Mount Etna 10,000ft.

ORB: First mail arrived, with a considerable number of airmail letters and bags and bags of parcels and newspapers. News that in the operation in Sicily itself, Palermo had fallen and the Allied forces held the whole island with the exception of a line north of Palermo–Catania.

25 JULY 1943

Logbook: Escort Kittybombers.

ORB: Air raid alarm. Lone bomber dropped several bombs in the aerodrome area but no more than a nuisance value. Squadron provided escort again to Baltimores over Adrano, Bronte and Gerbini.

26 JULY 1943

Logbook: 1. Ferry to Lentini East. 2. Ferry to Comiso 3. Shipping patrol Messina Straights. F/O Cameron missing in very accurate intense flak. Hit in tail plane. Plenty of melons unloading and curing wrinkles! Cameron later confirmed PoW.

ORB: News that Mussolini had resigned reached the Squadron. Squadron function changed to shipping reconnaissance and 4 sorties were flown, each with several aircraft. F/O Cameron was posted missing from the first of the day, last seen a few miles north of Messina.

27 JULY 1943

ORB: Reconnaissance from the previous day on shipping had meant the bombers of the American 57 Group were able to successfully attack them N/W of Reggio.

Squadron operations included bomber escort again to attack the shipping off the coast of Sicily.

28 JULY 1943

Logbook: Kittybomber Escort Milazzo area. Saw 2 Me109s going in the opposite diection.

ORB: Squadron 4 missions escorting Kittyhawk bombers twice to Milazzo, once to Randazzo and one ASR trip to an upturned sighting of a dinghy.

29 JULY 1943

Logbook: Kittybomber escort.

ORB: Less operations but news that another move for the Squadron planned, indicated by the order that the 'A' party consisting of approx 60 personnel were to be prepared to move out at short notice. Nobody particularly happy about this move as it is doubtful whether flying or general facilities would be as good as those at Comiso. Kittyhawk bombers were twice escorted today and the Spitfire pilots saw the railway station at Chettino destroyed by a direct hit from the bombers.

30 JULY 1943

Logbook: Kittybomber escort.

ORB: Move to Pachino commenced. 'A' Party moved off shortly after mid-day and later that evening the Squadron aircraft flew to Pachino, 6 landing after an armed recce during which nothing was seen. Other operations included escorts to Kittyhawks whose targets were Milazzo, Risposto, and Ciardini. Sqn Ldr Daniel flew the captured Me109 regarded as a trophy.

Pachino was about 30 miles south west of Comiso, on the southernmost tip of Sicily. It would not be the first time the Squadron had operated from a dust strip, as it was similar to those in Tunisia, but this one was only about 800 yards long and had been ploughed up and then prepared by the Royal Engineers, assisted by members of No. 3201 RAF servicing commando unit who had come ashore immediately behind the assault troops. There was some concern over the length of time the Squadron would take to take off and form up, because if they waited for the thick clouds of dust to clear after each pair took off, and the strip was only wide enough for pairs to take off, valuable fuel would be wasted in forming up. The only solution was to set the gyro and take off blind into the dust! Flies and mosquitoes continued to be the scourge of the Squadron.

31 JULY 1943

Logbook: Escort Mitchells. Randazzo Good bombing by 2nd twelve. Moved to Pachino South Sicily.

ORB: Move to Pachino completed, apart from small party remaining at Comiso on unserviceable aircraft. 72 Squadron made three bomber escort trips, two with Kittyhawks to Giardini and Randazzo and the third escorting B25 Mitchell bombers to Randazzo. Remarkably accurate bombing by the Mitchells.

> But our stay at Comiso was all too short. We were soon moved back to Pachino at the southeastern tip of Sicily. Hot and dusty, set amongst the olives and vines it was not a very good base. Flies in the daytime, mosquitoes at night, plus a very boring diet, the corned beef slices almost melted off your plate!

1 AUGUST 1943

Logbook: Escort Mitchells to Randazzo 14,000ft. Flew with 93 Squadron, Bombs jettisoned because of cloud over the target.

ORB: A little more achieved towards completing the move from Comiso to Pachino. Especially happy day for 'Sexton' Gear to whom Gp Captain Gilroy O.C. 324 Wing bought news about the award of his DFC. The CO Danny Daniels also had bar to his DFC, Roy Hussey the DFM and Sgts Connolly, Morris and Scottie all continued to put up the Squadron score. Tom Hughes second stripe

had also come through and he became a F/Lt. Squadron provided bomber escort to Adrano and Randazzo. Weather on second trip closed in and bombs had to be dropped away from target.

Some of the pilots and ground crew evidently did not appreciate the move: 'Comiso too good for us' because it had a two-thousand-foot runway, a camp and was in pleasant surroundings. In true RAF fashion, the move was made to a strip where taxying threw up dust and taking off was blind! Comiso lay in a flat valley at the foot of a ridge of hills. Fruit was available everywhere, bunches of grapes, lemons or peaches. Over the ridge was a town called Ragusa which was untouched by the war and beautiful and 'Sicilian'. It was built around the junction of two gorges and consisted of a new town and an old town. The new town had straight streets criss-crossing, a cathedral and a square where the male population met in the evenings. There appeared to be shops which were well stocked, though none had windows.

2 AUGUST 1943

Logbook: 1. Escort Kittybombers Etna area 12,000ft. Lost Kittybombers in haze and cloud. Strafed trucks on road.

ORB: Two further sweeps as a bomber escort to Adrano, but a third rendezvous was not kept by the bombers so Spitfires from 72 Squadron carried out an armed recce instead, which proved to be uneventful. Echelon moved into Pachino south from Comiso and several aircraft, which had been left at Comiso undergoing repairs were flown over. With the sea being in close proximity to the campsite, daily bathing parades were organised.

3 AUGUST 1943

ORB: Fairly quiet day, Squadron provided escort to bombers again over Adrano and an armed recce west of Etna. Few enemy aircraft were being encountered, the main problem continued to be friendly fire either from other Allied aircraft or from Allied troops or ships.

4 AUGUST 1943

Logbook: Escort Baltimores Giarre 11,000ft. F/O Keith hit by flak, baled out off Catania. Picked up by Air Sea Rescue but died same night.

That day the Squadron lost one of its outstanding pilots, P/O George Keith. While he was attacking ground targets in the Catania area, his aircraft was hit by flak and he had to bale out over the sea. The Air Sea Rescue Walrus soon picked him up but his left leg had been smashed when he baled out and hit his leg on the tail plane. An operation was carried out at No. 25 Military Field Hospital but he died the same day. He was buried at Cassabile the following morning. His loss had occurred during the second of the day's three missions, which were primarily bomber escorts to Adrano. George was killed before news of his DFC and bar had come through.

5 AUGUST 1943

The fall of Catania to the Allied forces was good news. 72 Squadron again provided cover to bombers over Adrano. Catania had shown signs of being difficult to take until the Herman Goering Division that had been defending it pulled out, so when British forces entered on the morning of the 5th there was little opposition. It was clear that the Germans were making preparations for their withdrawal to the mainland, across the Straits of Messina and they started to pull out immediately. For their part the Allies needed to be in a position to press home their advantage by using the full weight of their naval and air superiority. Air Vice Marshal Harry Broadhurst 'Broady' AOC Western Desert Air Force was also clear when he wrote to the AOC Tactical Air Force, Air Marshal Coningham that 'a combined naval and air plan was required but that the flak on both sides of the Straits of Messina would need the use of US Fortresses to prevent the evacuation'. The Germans could probably muster about 100 fighter and fighter-bombers to cover the evacuation plus about 100 long-range bombers. The plan was to use the Wellingtons of the Strategic Air Force to bomb Messina at night while B17s would do the same in daylight as well as bomb the landing ground in Crotone and Scalea.

6 AUGUST 1943

Logbook: Escort Bostons Bronte. Good bombing, but good flak. Saw bomber hit but crew baled out OK.

CO Sqn Ldr 'Danny' Daniel and F/Lt Arthur Jupp returned from a motor trip with a good yarn to tell and various trophies. It was an unofficial tour to see the army at work. They visited Catania where, under mortar fire for an hour south of Catania, they watched enemy positions around Adrano bombed and shelled. The Squadron again provided escort to bombers over Adrano and Bronte.

7 AUGUST 1943

Logbook: Escort 12 Mitchells Randazzo 16,000ft. Near misses.

Allied bombing attacks increased on Randazzo, there were numerous trips during the day, with Spits providing the escort. Troina fell to the Americans. There were further landings at Sant'Agata by the Americans to try and outflank the Germans.

9 AUGUST 1943

ORB: Squadron stood down at midday.

An Me109 had been made serviceable from one of several Me109s left lying around Comiso in various states of repair and had been bought across to Pachino when the Squadron had moved. The one chosen had just had a prop change so with Tom Hughes help, a German dictionary and various experiments, it flew! 'Sexton' Gear took the Me109 up and got mixed up in a barrage of anti-aircraft fire over Pachino because he had not told the gunners that the Me109 would be flying, nor did he have a Spitfire 'escort'. Most of the Squadron lay on the ground anticipating that Sex and the Me109 would be shot out of the sky, but Tom Hughes ran out to a parked Spit, climbed in, started it up and took off into the flak and machine gun fire. By circling the Me109 and weaving gently, waggling his wings he was able to persuade the gunners the Me109 was friendly so 'Sex' was able to land, very shaken but otherwise unhurt, though he bent the Me109 when landing on one wheel.

Tom Hughes:

After flying this machine I spent a lot of time writing flying notes having explored the cockpit layout. I found that one wheel did not always lock down satisfactorily in flight. However, if the manual release was pulled, the undercarriage dropped down and locked under gravity. F/O Gear was a very experience pilot, also one-time instructor from Training Command.

He was anxious to fly our Squadron's Me109, and I spent some time showing him my notes. I also told him the trouble I had had with the reluctant starboard wheel lock. He decided to take a trip in the machine one hot Sicilian afternoon. Somehow the warning message did not get through to the Army gunners who infested the local vineyards with light machine guns to ward off low flying attacks on our landing strip.

F/O Gear flew straight out to sea and a 'trigger happy' Navy boat took a shot at him. They recognised the characteristic profile of an enemy fighter, but were not too bothered with the RAF markings crudely painted over the German crosses and swastika. He turned back to the shore and the Army now let loose with everything they had got at him. The bullets whistled across the landing strip from all sides. I was not very far away from my own Spitfire and jumped into it after a fine hundred-yard sprint. It started first time on the internal batteries and I took off as smartly as possible straight down the runway at full boost. Although it was said that I had neither a parachute, nor my straps fastened, that was certainly not correct. I quickly found F/O Gear in the Me109 being skilfully flown among the treetops amid a barrage of anti-aircraft fire from our troops.

I was terrified by the tracer but managed to get fairly close behind the 'friendly' enemy waggling my wings violently and hoping the Army would be kind enough not to hit me in the Spitfire or my friend in the Messerschmitt. By then all

F/O Gear wanted to do was to get his mount back to our landing strip as quickly as could be. Unfortunately he forgot my careful briefing about the starboard undercarriage. It simply did not lock down and although I was still behind him I was helpless for there was no chance of a radio message as we never got round to studying the German radio frequencies, or their equipment in any case.

He did a fair landing on one wheel with the other leg still tucked up. I am not sure if the shooting had stopped by then. The Me109 swerved as it slowed down and ran off the runway into the vines but Gear stepped out rather smartly with a smile on his face. He survived the war and his photograph was shown in the press when he became the Chairman of the Handlebar Club for he still had the most enormous moustache, the sort you can see from behind! I am glad of that.

10 AUGUST 1943

Logbook: Escort 12 Baltimores Randazzo.

ORB: Three further escort trips to bombers over Randazzo again. Sgts Leach and Gridley posted to the Squadron.

11 AUGUST 1943

ORB: Three further escort trips to bombers over Randazzo. Had news of a large raid by the Germans on Lentini where some 26 Spitfires and Kittyhawks were hit and unserviceable and 27 were killed, mostly from 244 Wing.

12 AUGUST 1943

Logbook: 1. Escort Baltimores Falcone 12,000 ft. 2. Escort Bostons Mascali 13,000 ft.

ORB: Three trips, this time to Falcone and Olivari, Navarro and Mascali and a patrol covering shipping in the Catania area.

13 AUGUST 1943

ORB: Two bomber escorts to Piedmont and Falconi and a high cover patrol north east of Etna.

14 AUGUST 1943

Logbook: Escort 12 Bostons Messina area 12,000ft. Germans evacuating across Straits of Messina.

ORB: Patrol to the north east of Sicily and bomber escort to Messina.

15 AUGUST 1943

ORB: F/O Tom Hughes had to bale out of another captured Me109 he was flying which had developed a glycol leak. He landed in a vineyard not far from Pachino and returned unscathed and apparently all the happier for his experience.

Tom Hughes:

I joined the Caterpillar Club on 15 August 1943. The entry qualification is unusual; all members have to save their lives by parachute. There is no clubhouse but the badge of membership is a little golden Caterpillar with eyes of amethyst and I wear it on my tie.

72 Squadron were based at Pachino in southern Sicily and following F/O Gear wrecking our best Me109 we were left with a rather decrepit G4 model. This sounded very rough when I started it up but nonetheless we thought it would be interesting to compare its speed with the Spitfire in level flight. So one fine afternoon with some trepidation and sitting on my RAF parachute, which did not properly match the German fighter's seat, I taxied out.

F/Lt Jupp taxied his Spitfire IX out to accompany me. This time we had alerted all the army units in the vicinity following their unprovoked attack on Gear the previous week. As I got to the end of the runway I found that only one brake was working and I wondered how I should manage to do a successful landing. However, the 109 had a lockable tail-wheel and as soon as I was rolling straight I engaged the lock, which at least kept me straight for take-off. We climbed together to 6,000 feet and I flew westwards at cruising speed. As I opened the throttle to maximum and increased the revs the engine sounded horrible. I thought it would be sensible to return and land at once and turned back eastwards to Pachino; Jupp was slightly behind. Suddenly there was a fearful escape of steam from under the instrument panel, some sort of leak in the coolant system had developed and I found it not only hot, but choking to breathe. I immediately jettisoned the hood and was pleasantly surprised with the excellent arrangement of it, which allowed quite easy escape. I realised however that there was so much steam around my legs that it would be better to abandon ship.

At this point I should say that the RAF stopped their parachute training early in 1939 and apart from precise briefing to aircrew on how to escape from each particular aircraft no actual parachute drops were made during training. I think the incidence of broken ankles simply made such training uneconomic.

I had come to a point of decision and I may say my last thought was to preserve a captured aircraft. It had already been examined a score of times by Air Ministry experts and this made my decision a little easier. I undid my straps and started to climb out. I had a sudden change of mind, were my parachute straps tight? I tried to climb back in and somehow knocked the control column. In a trice I was catapulted straight up and clear of the cockpit and somersaulted over and over. I pulled the D-ring without bothering to count to three, which was part of the training advice. As the parachute opened I was startled by the shock from dropping freely. I was now supported underneath the canopy and saw galaxies of stars before my eyes, but what a joy it is to be safely lowered to the ground on a silken thread. It is why Mr Irving decided on the Caterpillar as the badge of his Club.

Two Sicilians appeared by magic. How could they tell whether I was German, American or British, at least they knew I was not Italian. They took me to a little shack nearby and I was introduced to a tiny, ancient, shrivelled woman who must have been their grandmother. They gave me a glass of wonderful red wine and soon I was as cheerful as they were. With my parachute rolled up I got on their donkey cart and headed for the main road back to Pachino. A Jeep driven by Greggs Farish with Pearson on board rounded the corner and I was transhipped and returned to base, but only after we had all been back and had another drink of their famous wine.

That night the three of us, with our largest wooden keg, returned to the vineyard to try and buy as much of the red wine as we could. They took us to the outhouse of the nearby mansion, which seemed quite deserted and from four great tuns siphoned several glasses. We eventually filled our cask with one of them but all agreed that it was not the same brew as I had had that afternoon. I paid the packer in the parachute tent 10 shillings, which I was told, was the traditional price for a repacking job. I also noted that the Secretary of the Caterpillar Club seldom got complaints from dissatisfied customers!

16 AUGUST 1943

ORB: No operational flying, the end of the Sicilian campaign is evidently near.

Although 72 was not required, other Allied squadrons continued the relentless assault on the retreating Axis forces across the Straits of Messina. Despite this, the vast majority were able to evacuate safely to the mainland. Of the 122,000 Axis troops taken prisoner, about 119,000 were Italian. There would be recriminations on the Allied side when the success of the German evacuation was realised. The Germans for their part could not believe their luck and could not comprehend why they had been allowed to get away. General Montgomery was livid:

> There has been heavy traffic all day across the Straits of Messina and the enemy is without doubt getting his stuff away. I have tried to find out what the combined navy-air plan is to stop him but I have been unable to find out and I fear the truth is there is no plan. The trouble is there is no high-up grip on this campaign, Eisenhower the Supreme Commander is in Algiers, Cunningham the naval C in C is in Malta, Tedder the Air C in C is in Tunis and Alexander, in command of Land Forces is in Syracuse, so it beats me how you think you can run a campaign with the commanders of the three main services about 600 miles from each other. The enemy should never be allowed to get all his equipment out of Sicily and we should round up the bulk of his fighting troops.

Following the withdrawal an inspection of the airfields in Sicily revealed over 600 aircraft abandoned and in various states of repair.

> One extraordinary thing about the campaign in Sicily was that the Germans and Italians were left to get back across the Straits of Messina without any concerted effort being made to prevent their escape to the toe of Italy. So different to what had happened in Tunisia.

17 AUGUST 1943

Logbook: 1. To Lentini West. 2. Escort Monitor Task Force. 3. Escort Monitor Task Force returning. 4. From Lentini to Pachino. Messina falls, organised resistance in Sicily at an end.

ORB: Allied troops in Messina. 72 Squadron sent 4 aircraft to Lentini where they flew 5 patrols escorting naval vessels and Kittyhawk bombers to Palmi.

18 AUGUST 1943

ORB: All organised resistance in Sicily now over – no operational flying.

20 AUGUST 1943

ORB: Twelve aircraft went to Lentini and provided escort to bombers across southern Italy.

'Spanner' was the nickname for Greggs Farish, an engineer officer for the Squadron who had been with them since November 1942 in North Africa. An Italian-made Caproni Saiman 200 had also been made serviceable enough to fly just as the Me109 had been. The Caproni was a dual control bi-plane made of wood and fabric with a 248-hp six-cylinder air-cooled Alfa Romeo 115 engine, which was pretty new. It had a maximum speed of 135 mph and a range of about 295 miles. The ground crews called it the 'Maggie' but the pilots called it the 'Pisser'. It was a joy to fly and became the Squadron 'hack', faster than a Tiger Moth and safer than a Maggie. They had to modify the tail wheel forks to take a Spitfire tyre because no spares were available! It was 'pranged' one day when Roy Hussey and Scottie took it across to Lentini to try and find Griff's grave (he had been lost when debris from a Me109 hit his Spitfire on 16 July). During the trip they got shot at by 'ack ack' and were beaten up by two Me109s. When they returned, Scottie, who had not flown it before and was evidently in the front cockpit, asked Roy to land it because the crosswind was a bit awkward. Roy therefore landed it, touched down fast across the runway but they found themselves heading towards a bomb crater and a pile of rubble, so Roy hit the brakes and they both ended up in the front cockpit, the plane with a broken undercarriage. It took about a month to mend it.

The plane was a Caproni Saiman. After some weeks we were able to make her airworthy. She was a two- seat bi plane and faster than a Tiger Moth. We found the Pisser very useful as a communications aircraft, shifting mail, messages and passengers too. Of equal benefit we could offer familiarisation trips to any of the ground crew that wanted to get airborne.

21–25 AUGUST 1943

Logbook: Practise, good fun, bags of steepers ho!

ORB: No operational flying, though P/O A.H. Gear left for hospital, tour-expired.

26 AUGUST 1943

Logbook: 1. To Agnone 2. Sweep south eastern tip Italy. 3. Patrol Catania 4. Back to base.

ORB: Fifteen aircraft moved to Agnone for the day and from that landing ground carried out a bomber escort to Bianco in southern Italy. Two further patrols over Augusta and Catania. News of the DFC to the late P/O Keith was received. F/Sgt Hermiston left the Squadron tour-expired.

29 AUGUST 1943

Logbook: Ferry to Pane Beanco.

ORB: Approx half the Squadron moved to Pane Beanco but the pitching of a camp in the new location was hampered by thunderstorms. Remainder of Wing HQ and Squadron left Pachino and proceeded to Pane Bianco and Squadron aircraft followed. Just after their arrival a thunderstorm broke and the ground quickly became a quagmire that made the erection of tents impossible.

No further operational flying in the month but there were 'big events in the air'. A conference at Wing Headquarters discussed the move north in preparation for further operations.

30 AUGUST 1943

ORB: Landing area still bogged down after the deluge and the airfield remained unserviceable, not fit for landing. Instructions received to proceed to Milazzo area tomorrow pending embarkation.

CHAPTER NINE

ITALY INVADED, SEPTEMBER–DECEMBER 1943 – 72 SQUADRON

It had been agreed by the Allied Chief of Staff as early as 20 July that Italy was to be invaded as soon as Sicily had been captured. Amphibious operations however were to stretch the limits of the fighter cover based in Sicily and the key to the invasion would again be air superiority. The early capture of airfields was therefore considered to be a priority. The plan was that the Allies were to put three divisions ashore around Salerno, a small port on the west of Italy about 50 miles south of Naples under the code name Operation *Avalanche* and further divisions would be landed at Taranto, again a port, right on the 'heel' of the foot of Italy, under the code name *Slapstick*. Once established ashore, fighter squadrons would fly into Monte Corvino airfield near Salerno to provide air cover. The landings at Salerno would be under the command of Mark Clark and his US 5th Army and the landings at Taranto and Messina would be under the command of General Montgomery and his British Eighth Army and the plan was for the two armies to link up following the Eighth army drive north from their landings at Messina and Tarranto. It was also hoped that Rome could be seized by a coup de main, dropping a US airborne division to reinforce the Italian troops when they suddenly switched sides.

From 18 August to 2 September, the Allied air forces mounted a concerted attack on lines of communication in southern Italy, dropping over 6,500 tons of bombs.

1 SEPTEMBER 1943

Logbook: Caproni 'Saiman' 1. To Lentini West. 2. To Pane Beanco. 3. Various 'Erks' Joy Rides Local. 4. To Cassala. 'Spanner' Farish injured starting this later in day.

ORB: Initial movement for Squadron in Operation *Avalanche* for which 324 wing squadrons including 72 Squadron **were to operate under the American 12th Army Air Support Command. F/Lt Pearson moved off with the wing advance party. Having just settled at Pane Beanco the Squadron was once more on the move and headed for Casala that is less likely than Pane Beanco to be unserviceable in the event of further rain. The CO and 'Spanner' [Greggs Farish] the Chief Engineer Officer flew across in the 'pisser' to make preliminary arrangements. Unfortunately when they were about to return F/O Farish was seriously injured when trying to start the engine by swinging the propeller.**

Danny Daniel and Spanner had gone across to Cassala near Gerbini to have a look around as preparation for the Squadron to move in. They had chosen the dispersal when Danny had apparently climbed into the front cockpit of the 'pisser' and Spanner was preparing to swing the propeller to start the engine which was the only way of doing it, Danny apparently waited for him to climb aboard with the engine then running but he did not appear so he put the brakes on to stop the 'pisser' rolling forward, jumped out to find Spanner underneath, unconscious and covered in blood. He apparently managed to shove Spanner in the rear cockpit and flew him back to base, still unconscious, where he was rushed to No. 21 Field Hospital nearby with severe wounds to his head and hand. He remained critical for several days but regained consciousness and made a full recovery.

2 SEPTEMBER 1943

ORB: Squadron moved to Cassala from Pane Beanco. Warrant Officer Price arrived on attachment as replacement for F/O Parish.

3 SEPTEMBER 1943

ORB: Italy invaded in the south by the Eighth Army at 04.30 hours today. There was still no rest for the Squadron. Warning notice that the 'A' party comprising roughly half the ground crew strength and a few pilots are to be ready to travel tomorrow with half the Squadron motor transport and ground equipment to Falcone on the north coast of Sicily. Packing soon in full swing. Squadron patrolled 3 times today over Allied shipping north east of Augusta. No observations made. Sgt Pilots Johnstone, Pullen and Street reported for duties.

At 0430 on 3 September, under the cover of a massive artillery barrage and the firepower of fifteen Royal Navy warships, XIII Corps of Eighth Army began the crossing from Sicily to Italy in 300 landing craft under Operation *Baytown*. 5th Division landed to the north, while 1st Canadian Division led the attack on the southern flank. The Italian coastal units surrendered almost immediately, leaving a single German regiment to defend 17 miles of coastline. That evening, British commando forces were landed in the rear of the Germans, at Bagnara, securing the success of the immediate landings. However, the difficult terrain in Italy – the dominant factor in the fighting for the next two years – coupled with skilful German demolition operations, slowed the advance. The roads in Bagnara itself had been so badly damaged that only troops on foot could enter the town. The 76th Panzer Corps covered the German withdrawal north as Eighth Army slowly advanced through Calabria. In reality the crossings had gone by the book because the Germans never had any intention of fighting for the strategically useless 'heel and toe' of Italy, they merely wanted to delay matters as much as practically possible to allow the Axis ground forces to withdraw in good order to re-establish themselves to contest the landings at Salerno. Most enemy airfields in the 'toe' of Italy were abandoned.

4 SEPTEMBER 1943

ORB: F/Lt Hughes left Squadron to become a flight commander in No. 43 Squadron. 'A' Party left for Falcone in the early afternoon. Sqn escorted Kittyhawk bombers to the 'toe of Italy' and landing beaches. Operated between 5/10,000 feet patrolling Messina Straits. Flak was reported but no enemy aircraft encountered. Later patrol at 12.45 again over Messina Straits contacted 5 Me109s and these were chased north east to Capistrano but had to give up the chase – short of fuel.

5 SEPTEMBER 1943

ORB: 'A' Party already at Falcone, 'B' Party at readiness for same move. Squadron was to be based here to provide high cover for the landings at Salerno. The latter party were unlucky as their ration wagon went astray and they were more than a little hungry by the time it followed them into Falcone. Two patrols over the landing beaches and Allied shipping east of Augusta with a Ju88 reported but not seen.

The problem with any sorties was that they could only be made with the aid of 90-gallon drop tanks and this was to test the Spitfire's capabilities flying across 180 miles of sea.

6 SEPTEMBER 1943

Logbook: From Cassala to Falcone. Hit tree at end of runway, aircraft Category III.

ORB: All squadrons released. Everything bustle at Cassala. 'B' Party started for Falcone and the aircraft flew to the new location shortly after the motor transport departed. The route taken by the M/T was interesting with magnificent scenery, though tortuous and hilly. Travelling as the 'A' Party had done before, via Catania, Misterbianco, Palermo, Adrano, Bronte and Randazzo, they saw something of the havoc and destruction wrought by the Allied bombing during the fighting. The party camped at 4000 feet up a hillside overlooking Vittoria and although chilly, everyone was in good humour, despite the rain, which meant that numerous temporary shelters were rigged. When the Squadron aircraft arrived at Falcone, F/O Scrase crashed on landing but only received minor injuries.

> 'Sunshine' was the Gift of War name to a brand new Spit IX MA520 which on September 6th I was asked to fly on a 35-minute ferry trip from Cassala to Falcone. She was still fitted with her 90-gallon long-range tank. One black mark as coming into land I hit some trees at the threshold of the runway as I did not allow sufficient height over the airfield boundary. On landing the undercarriage collapsed and the propeller blades were broken off. Yes, I did feel I had let the plane and the donor down, as the aircraft was a Gift of War. For me no damage except a bruised forehead and a bloody nose and a little hurt pride! I was back flying the next day.

7 SEPTEMBER 1943

Logbook: Falcone Sicily.

ORB: 'B' Party continued journey to Falcone which they reached at about 18.00 hours, through Floresta, Naso and Cape D'Orlando. All pilots attended a briefing by Grp Captain Ronnie Lees, its former CO where they were briefed on the proposed landings at Salerno and Operation *Avalanche*.

8 SEPTEMBER 1943

ORB: The struggling vehicles on the Cassala-Falcone journey due to mechanical troubles finally arrived. The Squadron learnt that their role in Operation *Avalanche* was to support and then make landings on the Italian mainland south of Naples. More preparations for the sea party move.

> Now we were to prepare for the Invasion of Italy. We used Falcone on the north coast of Sicily as our base from which to fly for the Invasion. 'Peaches Beaches' was the name given to the strip of coast south of Salerno that we were to patrol. This was about 180 miles away and about as far as we could go using slipper tanks and still carry out an effective patrol. About one third of the way to our patrol point was the Aeolian Island of Strómboli, a live volcano. Our heading point showed puffs of smoke and occasional bursts of red flame day and night and served as a marker. From there all you had to do was head north.

9 SEPTEMBER 1943

Logbook: Patrol Peaches Beaches 16,000ft. Italy surrendered last night. Operation *Avalanche* the landing of the Allied 5th Army between Salerno and Agrigento commenced today. No joy for us.

Although General Castellano had signed the Italian surrender in Sicily on 3 September, it was not declared until 8 September, as the convoys carrying the Allies neared their target at Salerno. The plans to seize Rome had to be abandoned, after a covert Allied reconnaissance visit decided that there was no possibility of successfully reinforcing the Italian garrison sufficiently. The German 2nd Parachute and 3rd Panzer Grenadier Divisions quickly overran the Italian troops in the capital. However, at Taranto six Allied cruisers safely put ashore the 1st British Airborne Division to help the Italians secure the important naval base.

Meanwhile at Salerno, in the early hours of 9 September, Operation *Avalanche* saw the British 46th and 56th Divisions of X Corps land on the northern flank, with the US 36th and 45th Divisions coming ashore to the south. Three German armoured divisions – the Hermann Goering, the 16th Panzer and the 15th Panzer Grenadier – were in the area and launched a series of counter attacks. By the end of the day, Italy had unconditionally surrendered, the culmination of arrangements made, according to broadcasts, on 3 September. The Squadron's first operation under Operation *Avalanche* was patrolling the beaches south east of Naples and although fitted with 90-gallon drop tanks, they could only maintain standing patrols over the beaches of about 25 minutes. The 90-gallon drop tanks extended the range of the Spitfire's flying time by about an hour or so and although they increased drag, did not affect the handling of the aircraft to any great extent. To start with, they were jettisoned once empty, but after several trips, when it was realised there was little enemy air opposition, they were retained. In this way the aircraft could be airborne for up to 2 hours 40 minutes.

10 SEPTEMBER 1943

ORB: Beaches patrolled were 'Peaches Beaches' in the Salerno area, with the Mark VCs at 16,000 feet and the IXs at 20,000 feet. Landing craft and M/T reported but no enemy aircraft in the air.

Logbook: Patrol 'Peaches Beaches' 18,000ft. The army doing better today. Found SM 79 and escorted it home!

ORB: 'A' Party moved to marshalling yards at Milazzo for waterproofing the vehicles prior to embarkation to Italy where they are to support the 5th Army in the Salerno area. F/Lt Johnston badly shaken when his aircraft overturned on take off. Two uneventful patrols over 'Peaches Beaches' again near Salerno. P/O Kennedy from 111 Squadron destroyed a Fw190 in the morning over Peaches beach.

Gp Capt Gilroy had also flown with 111 Squadron during the day. He liked to keep his hand in and flew with one of the squadrons whenever he could. He also had a reputation for being able to spot enemy aircraft before anyone else had spotted them. Peaches beach by this time appeared to be a complete shambles. Men and equipment, tanks and landing craft, smoke and flashes of guns and shell bursts made flying hazardous. Allied ships continued to fire on targets inland. The rest of the Wing were at Monte Corvino and were told that the American 31st Fighter Group were to occupy the aerodrome so they had to move to Tusciano landing ground. Very little sleep was had by anyone on the aerodrome and camp site as they were located in front of three artillery batteries. The noise of the shelling together with the anti aircraft fire made it impossible.

11 SEPTEMBER 1943

Logbook: Patrol 'Peaches Beaches' 16,000ft. Salerno captured.

ORB: During the first two patrols of 'Peaches Beaches' F/Sgt Leech landed at Paestum in Italy due to engine trouble but returned to Falcone later in

the day. Sqn Ldr Mackie from 243 Squadron destroyed a Dornier 217 over the beaches in the morning. P/O Newman reported as Engineer Officer in place of F/O Farish, posted from the unit, non effective to RHQDIAF in view of his injuries. News was also received that P/O Shaw, formerly of Squadron, now tour expired, awarded the DFC.

12 SEPTEMBER 1943

Logbook: Patrol 'Peaches Beaches' 16,000ft. Saw 7 Me109s. They dived away and Mark IX 's chased Con 1 destroyed, 1 damaged. Smithy 1 damaged and Bruce 1 destroyed 1 damaged.

ORB: While 'A' Party was being embarked at Milazzo the LSTs sailed at about 19.00 hours, the pilots operating from Falcone continued to push up the Squadron score. During the first of the days two patrols over Salerno, 7 Me109s were encountered and two were destroyed by P/O Ingalls and Sgt Connolly and two were damaged by F/O Smith and Sgt Connolly. F/O Smith's aircraft was hit by flak and P/O Ingalls, short of fuel had to crash land on his return to Milazzo West.

The initial successes on the ground for the Allied ground forces were reversed when General Kesselring's Panzers counter attacked with some force and re-captured Battipaglia from the British, just three days after the initial beach assault.

13 SEPTEMBER 1943

Logbook: To Tusciano, Italy.

ORB: Aircraft of 72 Squadron and 243 Squadron arrived Tusciano so Sqn was able to begin operations from the Italian mainland. F/Sgt Clarkson overshot on landing and damaged his aircraft but was unhurt. First job was to patrol Dakotas to Stromboli and then patrol 'Peaches Beaches' again, both without incident. 'A' Party disembarked whilst the navy were shelling enemy land positions. Some enemy air activity reported and a few bombs were dropped in the vicinity of the camp during darkness. One enemy aircraft bought down north of the camp. With guns all around pounding away there is not much sleep to be had.

The recent death of Sqn Ldr Macdonald had served to highlight the dangers of aircraft operations and recognition in close proximity to the battle area. In moving to Tusciano, they would be the first RAF unit to operate in front of their own artillery, not that the pilots were told before they arrived! The British 25-pounders were situated in olive groves on the seaward side of the landing ground and appeared to fire continuously over the landing strip, even when Spits were in the circuit, so it was a little disconcerting to say the least. Barney Barnfather recalled later that the landing at Tusciano was probably the most nerve-wracking experience he had faced since his landing on Malta some 18 months before after taking off from the USS *Wasp*. Coming into land they had to turn over the enemy positions at a greatly reduced speed with wheels and flaps down and the concussion of the guns firing caused the Spits to rock and buck with the very real danger that they would lose flying speed and of course, loss of control at such a low altitude made a fatal crash inevitable. They were told later that the gunners did not, at least in theory, fire when aircraft passed in front of them, the Wingco Cocky Dundas was told 'in any event whoever heard of a 25 pounder shooting down a Spitfire'!

What few tents the Squadron had were pitched that night on the southern end of the runway and the personnel and pilots lost no time in digging in their 'slit' trenches. Sleep was impossible because of the noise of the 25 pounders, so most of them stayed awake and watched the vivid flashes of the guns, followed by the screams of the shells. The tents shuddered under the gunfire. There was a small enemy raid when the aerodrome was dive bombed and a small fire was started at the end of the drome. On the ground the Germans re-took Altavilla and Perano from the Americans. Plans for other squadrons to move to landing strips on the beach-head had to be delayed because there was a real danger that it would be lost. The Luftwaffe were largely kept from interfering with troops and supplies because of air superiority but it was undoubtedly accurate and destructive naval firepower that helped turn the Germans back.

> Then on the 13th it was time to fly over to our newly constructed landing strip at Tusciano close to the river of the same name. British artillery units were in the field next door to us. Our first full day at the base and German infantry came down to within two miles of the airfield and it was only much later that we came to know that General Mark Clark had considered whether to withdraw the 6th Corps from the beach head!

14 SEPTEMBER 1943

Logbook: 1. patrol 'Peaches Beaches' 19,000ft. Enemy infiltrated to within 2 miles of airfield. 2. air test – Kalamity Kate IV OK.

ORB: 'B' Party moved from Falcone to the marshalling yards near Milazzo, the beginning of a long and later tedious wait there until the shipping was available on 21 September. At Tusciano, the remainder of the Squadron saw evidence of the increased Allied air attacks on enemy positions and the bombers passing overhead was almost endless. During the night again disturbed by gunfire. Gp Captain Gilroy flew with Squadron on the first of the days two missions, comprising bomber escort to Avellino and a further patrol of the beach area. Aircraft of 43 Squadron arrived Tusciano. Wing Cdr Dundas flew. Sgt Connolly reported the enemy gun positions and the army was informed. Pilots were instructed to sleep with pistols at hand in case of enemy paratroops or intruders as the potential was there for enemy attacks at will.

Sleep remained impossible because of the noise of the barrage, ack ack fire and shells. The mosquitoes out in force, the large, fierce variety that proved resistant to all repellents and these arduous living and operating conditions sapped their strength. Within a few weeks many would be suffering from malaria. Examining the aircraft each morning also became a chore to assess any damage caused during the night. Shell fire damage was an obvious risk but several aircraft were damaged by great white oxen that roamed the field at night and scratched their hides on the wings, which damaged the all-important pitot head extensions, the externally mounted tubes that measured air speed. The field guards had a thankless task trying to keep the huge beasts away from the aircraft, occasionally firing their own guns at them to keep them away, but it was quickly realised that any bullets just bounced off their tough hides! They were not to know it but 14 September appeared to be the turning point in the battle. About 700 sorties were flown that day by Allied fighters and fighter-bombers, largely against German transport near Eboli.

15 SEPTEMBER 1943

Logbook: 1. Cover Battleships shelling Naples. Returned early. CO got 1 destroyed in later show.

ORB: Bombers again lively over Salerno, encountered intense flak. Enemy aircraft encountered during the second of two 'Peaches' beach patrols. Sqn Ldr Daniel destroyed a Me109 and later in the Naples area. F/O Smith probably destroyed a Fw190 and F/Lt Johnston damaged another Fw190.

16 SEPTEMBER 1943

Logbook: Patrol 'Peaches Beaches' 16,000ft. Saw 3 109s going home at 400+ mph. Disappeared in haze. Smith and Pearson brought the Squadron score to 201. Sgt Piper missing, force landed behind enemy lines.

ORB: Three patrols of 'Peaches Beaches' with more Squadron successes and the start of a great adventure for F/Sgt Piper who after shooting down a Me109 during the second patrol, crash landed because of engine trouble near Lacino, within the enemy lines and was reported missing. On the same patrol F/O Barnfather damaged a Me109 and during the last operation of the day F/Lt Pearson and F/O Leach destroyed a Fw190. The enemy aircraft destroyed by F/Sgt Piper was the 200th destroyed by the Squadron.

Some of Montgomery's Eighth Army moving up from Calabria in the south joined with the Yanks at Salerno beach and it appeared the crisis and threat of being stuck on the beach head or even turned back into the sea was averted. The beach head had been secured. HMS *Warspite* was attacked by a squadron of German aircraft, armed with early guided bombs. She was hit three times, one of them striking near her funnel, ripping through her decks and causing immense damage, making a large hole in the bottom of her hull and crippling her. Casualties were minor; 9 killed and 14 wounded.

Reinforcements by sea and the effects of shelling by heavy guns of the fleet helped to restore the situation but this was at some cost. The Germans used Dornier 217Ks to bomb, hit and seriously damage a number of our warships including HMS *Warspite*.

17 SEPTEMBER 1943

Logbook: Patrol 'Peaches Beaches' 20,000ft.

ORB: Artillery fire in the Tusciano locality abated, the guns evidently having moved forward in the wake of the enemy retreat. Between the two Squadron patrols over the beaches, Sqn Ldr Daniel and F/Lt Jupp were to have shared in the protection of P38 Lightning on a ground strafing expedition, but the P38s did not keep the rendezvous. The two therefore did their own ground strafing and damaged enemy aircraft on the ground. Enemy aircraft reported over the beaches and despite an intense barrage one ship in the bay was bombed.

18 SEPTEMBER 1943

Logbook: Patrol 'Peaches Beaches' 16,000ft.

ORB: Comparatively quiet day with only one operational mission, another patrol over 'Peaches Beaches' in the Salerno area. News of the Eighth Army advance towards the 5th Army was encouraging. The landing of more British and American troops on the beach head ensured the Germans began their withdrawal towards Salerno.

19 SEPTEMBER 1943

Logbook: Patrol 'Peaches Beaches' 25,000ft. Took a look at Naples!

ORB: Two beach patrols and over Naples. Two unknown pilots baled out in camp vicinity.

20 SEPTEMBER 1943

Logbook: Patrol 'Peaches Beaches' 20,000 ft. With P/O Hussey, saw him get 2 Do 217s, stooged around with U/S engine. Saw 7 bail out but one parachute caught tail. Suspected radio bombers.

ORB: Twice today, Fw190s made low level bombing and machine gun attacks on the aerodrome and camp site. Casualties in other units but none to 72 Squadron. Squadron escorted bombers to Avellino and subsequently patrolled the beaches. On the patrol P/O Hussey destroyed 2 Do 217s. 6 Me109s were engaged by 243 Squadron but they had to break off thinking 72 Squadron was also enemy aircraft. The same me 109s were attacked and F/Lt Pearson got 1 damaged and P/O Ingalls got 1 probable.

An interesting story from one of the other squadrons in that on patrol at 23,000 feet they saw a group of Fw190s at very low altitude that just appeared to be 'stooging around' so the Squadron came down in a steep curving dive and just as they came up the back of the still unsuspecting Fw190s, about 400 yards away and ready to fire, the front armoured windscreens clouded over completely and they could see nothing. It was evidently the result of leaving a very cold altitude at 23,000 feet quickly for much warmer air in a very short time. This strange and disquieting occurrence would happen several times in Italy.

> Flying with Roy Hussey on a catch-the-bombers two-man patrol, we engaged two Dornier 217s. We were at 20,000 feet and to my chagrin I had trouble with my supercharger cutting in and out. I descended 1000 feet or so to put the matter right. Roy continued with his attack and engaged first one and then the second Dornier, destroying both. As I came up to join the melee I flew past the second aircraft from which one after another, the seven-crew members were baling out. Sadly, the last one to emerge got his parachute entangled with the tail plane and he went down with the plane.

21 SEPTEMBER 1943

Logbook: Patrol 'Peaches Beaches' 21,000ft. 'Pip' came home 40 miles through the lines!

ORB: 'B' Party having languished in the marshalling area for a week were embarked at Milazzo and sailed for the Italian beaches at 19.00 hours. Two beach patrols were flown. Sgt Piper returned to the Squadron with a grand story to tell, the truth was at least as thrilling as the fiction! At first befriended by an Italian soldier in the hills with other Allied troops who were seeking to escape from enemy lines. The Germans persistently patrolled the scene of Pip's crash and searched houses and buildings. When Pip eventually reached Capagnia, there were evidently doubts to whether it was still occupied by Allied troops or Axis troops. While Pip was being bought back by road by the Yanks to the Tusciano area, some Piper aircraft were noticed in a field and the offer of one of the pilots to fly Pip back was readily accepted, so that on arrival at his home landing strip Sgt 'Pip' Piper was bought back by a Piper!

22 SEPTEMBER 1943

Logbook: Patrol 'Peaches Beaches' 23,000ft.

ORB: A 'hit and run' bomber dropped bombs near the runway at Tusciano. Two freelance patrols between Salerno and Capua and on the beaches. 'B' Party disembarked on the beach a short distance from Tusciano while the bay was under heavy shellfire so they were not able to reach camp until darkness.

23 SEPTEMBER 1943

Logbook: Patrol Avellino area 16,000ft. Army attack towards Naples. We cover.

ORB: Ground personnel working normally. Three patrols of 'Peaches Beaches', Battipaglia and Salerno. Aircraft of 93 and 111 Squadrons arrived Monte Corvino.

Montgomery and his Eighth army linked up with Clark's 5th Army and started to push the Germans back.

24 SEPTEMBER 1943

Logbook: Patrol Salerno 13,000ft. Wingco Dundas and F/Sgt Larlee destroyed a Reconnaissance 88. We climbed to 30,000ft in attempted interception.

ORB: Our aircraft covered the reconnaissance Spitfires over Naples and later in the day patrolled the Salerno area led by Wing Cdr Dundas (Wingco Flying) who shared with F/Sgt Larlee, a Canadian, the destruction of a Ju88. Also escorted transport near the Volturno river. Heavy flak over Capri though Tusciano area now quiet.

25 SEPTEMBER 1943

Logbook: Patrol Salerno 14,000ft. Saw 36 Mitchells do splendid bombing tunnels and viaduct north of Nocera.

ORB: Enemy motor transport and railway transport seen during a sweep north of Naples and reported to the ALO with a view to bombing them. Squadron afterwards patrolled Salerno again.

26 SEPTEMBER 1943

Logbook: Tac R Avellino, Benevento and Capua. A little transport and lively flak!

ORB: After morning patrol north of Naples, the position of enemy flak batteries was also reported to the ALO. Later the Squadron patrolled over Salerno again.

27 SEPTEMBER 1943

ORB: No activity. Airfield unserviceable following heavy rain in the early morning.

First sign of the weather, that it, along with the Germans, would be difficult during the coming winter. 243 Squadron had to divert to Paestum because Tusciano was unserviceable but there two collided on the runway on take off and a third lost power and crashed into a tree.

28 SEPTEMBER 1943

Logbook: Patrol Salerno Nocera 10,000 ft.

ORB: Squadron first offensive sweep between Benevento and Gaeta was curtailed because of cloud. The second patrol of the Salerno area reported that our own motor transport appeared to be under fire from our own guns. Torrential rain and a thunderstorm in the night wrought havoc in the tented accommodation.

29 SEPTEMBER 1943

ORB: Aerodrome unserviceable due to rain. Fortunately a fine day that helped with the drying out.

30 SEPTEMBER 1943

ORB: Aerodrome still unserviceable. During the afternoon flak batteries fired at enemy aircraft high above the camp but no bombs were dropped.

September 1943 was a busy month, 28 hours operational flying. On the ground it was hard going. Mosquitoes and high temperatures, poor tented accommodation and basic rations. We thought this would have been livened up when one of the cooks slaughtered a cow from a nearby field. The Squadron Coles crane was used from which to hang the beast but no one was prepared to wait and let it hang properly so it proved a tough old beast to eat!

1 OCTOBER 1943

ORB: 6 aircraft Peaches beach patrol. Good news for the CO Sqn Ldr Daniel who was awarded bar to his DFC. Also news that DFCs had been awarded to acting Sqn Ldr Evan Mackie and F/Lt Bamey Bamberger of 243 Squadron, so celebrated in the mess that evening with Gp Capt Gilroy as guest of honour. More general good news in that Naples had fallen to the Allied forces.

2 OCTOBER 1943

Logbook: Patrol Naples 12,000 ft.

ORB: 10 aircraft Peaches patrol. More torrential rain shortly before noon made the aerodrome unserviceable for the rest of the day. US Tomahawks had prepared the ground for a further Eighth Army landing at Termoli on the Adriatic by bombing and strafing troops and transport on the the roads north and west of the town.

Posted to 74 Squadron

The island of Leros was part of the Dodecanese islands in the south-eastern Aegean that had been occupied by German and Italian forces. With the surrender of Italy on 8 September 1943 however, the Greek islands, which were strategically vital to Churchill, became reachable for the first time since the loss of Crete.

The Italian garrisons on most of the Dodecanese either wanted to change sides and fight with the Allies or just return to their homes. The Allies attempted to take advantage of the situation, but the Germans were ready. As the Italian surrender became apparent, German forces, based largely in mainland Greece, were rushed to many of the major islands to gain control.

By mid-September, however, the British 234th Infantry Brigade had secured the islands of Kos, Kalymnos, Samos, Leros, Symi, and Astypalaia, supported by ships of the British and Greek navy and two RAF Spitfire squadrons on Kos including No. 74 Squadron.

In September Sqn Ldr James Chilton Francis Hayter, a New Zealand farmer known as 'Spud', had led nine aircraft of 74 Squadron to Antimachia on Kos with disastrous results. On 3 October, the Germans effected amphibious and airborne landings and reached the outskirts of the island's capital later that day. The airfield was then overrun and Hayter and four others took to the hills. The British meanwhile withdrew under cover of night, and surrendered the next day. The fall of Kos was a major blow to the Allies, since it deprived them of vital air cover for the islands.

3–7 OCTOBER 1943

Logbook: Posted from 72 (Basutoland) Squadron to A.H.Q. – A.D.E.M. Douglas Dakota, Monte Corvino-Cassible-Catania-Luqa-Marble Arch-Cairo, West-Nicosia, Cyprus.

> No one had explained properly but a request from HQ for a flight commander for 74 squadron, then in Cyprus, led to my being posted away. Ferry flights by Dakota via Malta, Libya, and Cairo before I was on my way to Nicosia in Cyprus. There I did two reconnaissance flights. Next I met Sqn Ldr Hayter, the boss and five of his pilots who had just returned from Kos. The invasion of the Dodecanese Islands had gone badly wrong and four of his pilots had been captured and remained there as PoWs.

> This was no place for a chap like me so within a week I was back in Cairo at HQ ADEM and from there it was Dakota flights back to good old 72 Squadron. I was just in time to make a further trip from our new base at Capodochino in Naples.

Guy de Pass, one of the pilots of 74 Squadron, put in a report which read:

> On the morning of 3 October I awoke at about 04.30 hours and heard the sound of aircraft above me but didn't take much notice. The aircraft continued to fly around and I heard in the distance the sound of a motor launch. By this time I was very apprehensive. Shots from the direction of the landing beaches strip were heard. We arose and moved off in the direction of the road. The firing became more persistent. Flares were being fired and mortar fire could be discerned. It appeared to all of us that the island was being invaded and that enemy troops were in the vicinity. We began to run towards the main road as we were unable to put up any sort of defence and considered that the best policy was to join up with the main party of British troops. It was still fairly dark with plenty of cloud. I saw F/Os Bates and Norman, F/Sgt Maxwell, Sgt Harris and a South African and joined up with them. When we reached the main road we saw a jeep driven by a South African. We piled in and went straight to Kos. The people in the hotel at Kos, a Major and some RAF Regiment chaps did not believe that the invasion had started. I took the jeep and warned British HQ, the Bofors gun battery and all and sundry. I then handed the jeep over to an RAF Regiment officer who wanted to go to Kos aerodrome to collect some of his men. We pilots of 74 Squadron did not know that a party of our ground crews had landed by air on the previous night on Kos aerodrome, and by 11.00 hours we had boarded an Italian boat in Kos harbour and set sail for Leros. On the way out we ran into some German boats so we turned for Kefalcha on the Turkish coast eventually reaching Castelrosso and Paphos by high speed launch.

The CO ('Spud' Hayter), and four others all went into the hills south of the salt flats and lived on sheep that they killed with their bare hands, eventually reaching Cyprus in a fishing boat.

Sqn Ldr Hayter escaped with two pilots, a squadron leader from Ops and an MT driver. They wandered the hills and with the help of a shepherd made a raft – Spud had farmed in New Zealand and he killed a sheep which they cooked as they started to build it. Eventually they escaped to the Turkish coast with the Special Boat Service's help on 7 October 1943.

(No. 74 (Trinidad) Squadron – Nicosia Cyprus)

9 OCTOBER 1943

Logbook: No. 74 (Trinidad) Squadron Nicosia. Spitfire Vb Sector Reconnaissance. It had been a fiasco of an operation, and fewer than 50 airmen, untrained in land warfare, had beaten off the attack of more than double that number of German commando troops. No. 74 Squadron had shown that they could fight on the land as well as in the air. It was not without sacrifice however, as 20 Squadron personnel were dead and missing.

ORB: All 74 Squadron personnel evacuated from Bone Nauthett 14.00 hours 10 October, 1943. Wish to record appreciation magnificent piece of work by all ranks under the most trying and strange conditions.

This was the final entry of the Squadron's Official Record Book. Air Vice-Marshal Saul, the Air Officer Commanding, when forwarding this message, added his own to the Commanding Officer of No. 74 Squadron, Sqn Ldr J.C. ('Spud') Hayter, DFC.

> I would like to add my own appreciation of the magnificent spirit shown by No. 74 Squadron as a whole throughout the operations on Kos Island. Their unity, loyalty and devotion to duty under exceptionally difficult and trying conditions is a fine example of courage and determination to the Air Force as a whole, and reflects considerable credit on your personal leadership in bringing your unit to such a fine state of esprit de corps.

12 OCTOBER 1943

Logbook: Nicosia to Peristerona. S/L Hayter and 5 pilots of the 9 that went returned from Kos after hiding in the hills for 5 days.

Peristerona Cyprus

13 OCTOBER 1943

Logbook: Posted from 74 (Trinidad) Squadron to AHQ – A.D.E.M. Wellington Nicosia, Aqir Palestine, Maryut, Alexandria. Dakota Cairo West, Benina (Lord Gort as a VIP passenger) Luqa, Catania, Bari, Foggia, Naples.

Back to 72 (Basutoland) Squadron Capodichino Naples

23 OCTOBER 1943

Logbook: Patrol area north-east of Volturno River.

Naples aerodrome was a large grass airport and was much better than the landing strips in what had now become the rainy season. Capodichino became shortened to 'Cappo'. With the villas and offices empty everyone began to scour around to see if anything of any value could be scrounged. It seemed that every Squadron had the same idea. Looting was forbidden but most squadrons 'acquired' transport, a few cars and motorcycles ran very well on high octane aircraft fuel until the practice was stopped!

Naples itself was crowded with people begging for food and cigarettes and made movement around the city difficult. The city had suffered badly from the bombing, street fighting between Germans and Italians had added to the damage and the docks had been totally destroyed, with sunken ships alongside almost every pier and dockside. It would take some considerable time for the docks to be made serviceable again. The most serious damage was carried out by the Germans. As they withdrew from the city and with almost total disreguard for humanity, they had cut the sewer mains allowing them to run into the water mains and contaminate them. The city was quite literally without water apart from a few scattered wells around which women and children queued for hours to get a few pints of the precious liquid. Despite the crowds and wandering vendors selling fruit, ices and wines the city appeared more dead than liberated. The smell of the broken sewers was overpowering and filth lined the streets. The shops on the other hand appeared well stocked with perfumes, silks and art objects. The city was also infested with booby traps and time bombs. Prostitutes, some diseased, were only too glad to ply their trade amongst the very willing Allied soldiers. Dirt was everywhere, people were lice ridden and typhus because of the broken sewers was a real threat. Much of it was contained by the introduction of a new insecticide called DDT.

Capodichino was a big improvement on the landing strips and tents they had been used to. Naples also had its attractions, despite the description given, though they rarely went into town. The place was steeped in history. Within sight of the aerodrome was the volcano Mount Vesuvius, about eight miles away with Pompeii at its base. About 50 miles north was Mont Cassino, a great abbey built by Saint Benedict and north of Mont Cassino a further 70 or so miles was Rome iteself. After the Salerno beach head had been established and the Allied ground forces had driven north to capture Naples and the surrounding area, it became clear that Kesselring would provide stern resistance across what became known as the Gustav line which hinged on Mont Cassino. It would later prove almost impossible to take. First, however, the 5th Army had to establish bridge-heads across the Volturno river, about 20 miles north of Naples and it was the job of the RAF to support the army's push to secure this bridgehead. When not escorting bombers they patrolled the air over the river to ensure the army was not harassed. By this time the Volturno river was a formidable obstacle, the rain had swelled it so that it was between 150–300-feet wide and anything up to 6 feet deep in mid-stream. The current was swift and the water icy cold and in such circumstances and against battle-hardened troops, it took a good 10 days of ferocious fighting to cross the river and the Volturno line. During the night Wellington bombers had hit rail bridges to prevent German reinforcements reaching the battle area, supplemented in daylight by the Kittyhawks, Bostons and Maurauders hitting anything that moved. The Spits continued to provide escort duties as well as standing patrols and Allied air strength and superiority cleared all resistance. It was only when clouds and the rain clamped down that effective flying stopped. The foul weather was a double hit, it made the advance by the Army even harder over an already difficult terrain and it often rendered the Allied air superiority irrelevant.

That air superiority also allowed them to introduce a new system of close air support for the Army. To provide quicker and closer support than had been previously possible, mobile observation posts with the forward troops and Brigade HQ were linked by direct radio contact with aircraft in the air. Both the controller and pilots were issued with photographic maps of the area on which there were reference grids to help both to identify targets. From the patrols maintained overhead by the fighter-bombers, in formation in line astern that became known as 'cab rank', they were directed to target areas by radio and by using the grid maps. Known as 'Rover David' the system was widely and successfully used, but only because Allied air superiority allowed it.

News was filtering through of delayed action bombs going off in Naples and the surrounding areas laid by the retreating Germans. Several hundred mines had been laid under principal buildings. One had gone off near the Central post office, senselessly killing many innocent Italian civilians and the prospect of other large municipal buildings being mined meant they were evacuated temporarily. Engineers trained in bomb disposal could not cope with the number of alarms and suspicious wires running everywhere. The situation not helped that evening by the first German air raid back on Naples itself with further damage caused to the port area.

The British Eighth Army managed to force its way across the Trigno despite the appalling weather. Torrential rain, icy mountain storms, almost impassable mud and the lack of billets, which had been destroyed by the retreating Germans, all combined to lower the morale of the Allied units.

The 5th Army, having managed to get across the Volturno river, had continued their push north towards the Garigliano river from where the valley of the Liri led past Monte Cassino towards Rome. It was this valley that was dominated by almost impregnable mountain peaks including Cassino itself that had to be bombed before the army could consider any sort of assault. The patrols changed to bomber escorts of Fortresses, Baltmores and Bostons, sometimes three squadrons at a time or alternatively up to nine squadrons of Mustangs or Kittyhawk fighter-bombers against the German mountain positions. Strafing transport north of the line became their role as well, though there was not much to see in daylight. Flying in mountain valleys was exhilarating and dangerous. On more than one occasion inexperienced pilots were lost because they got too close to the hills or the ground. The trick was to concentrate on the strafing rather than the perspective of the hills and mountains but mistakes were made by less experienced pilots. It also became clear that chasing Me109s was alright in the Spitfire Vs, which were a match in performance terms, but it was no good trying to catch a Fw190 in a Spit V because the Fw190 could outrun it. The introduction of the Spit IXs gave them the performance to compete with the Fw190s.

Before the end of the campaign almost 60 per cent of Squadron personnel would be affected by malaria or jaundice. There were severe cases of worms, they all had fleas and many suffered considerable discomfort. The field hospitals were kept busy. By the end of October the US 5th Army and English Eighth Army held a line running from the Garigliano river in the west, across the Abruzzi mountains, along the course of the river Sangro into the Adriatic. The Desert Air Force wings moved forward to the captured airfields around Foggia and then onto all-weather strips prepared for them by airfield construction units close to the front line. Enemy aircraft were seen less frequently. For the all-weather strips an ingenious 'runway' was laid down with pierced steel plates or PSP which were sections that were hinged and fitted together to form a continuous landing surface for aircraft that provided a safe landing surface no matter how wet and muddy the rest of the airfield became. It became a godsend in the wet and muddy Italian winter, and without it many airfields would have been rendered unserviceable.

Squadrons from the US 15th Strategic Air Force also moved into the airfields around Foggia and this extended the range of operations to targets deep in Southern Europe and the Balkans. The industrial areas of Silesia, Czechoslovakia and the oil-fields in Romania now came within range of these bombers. Fighters could, with long-range tanks, also provide escort.

On a morning drive from the mess to the aerodrome, which was actually located on the edge of the plain above the city near the foot of Mount Vesuvius, the Squadron personnel had to drive through literally thousands and thousands of Italians all walking out of the city. It looked like one continual stream of people choking the road and making movement nigh on impossible. It appeared to be the same all over town, and the reason for it was that the electricity was due to be switched back on that day and there had been rumours that there were booby traps and mines set to go off when that was done, pretty much as had happened at Salerno. The rumour had taken such a hold on the Italians that they decided to evacuate.

The German defence beyond the Volturno were generally referred to by the Allies as the Winter Line and actually consisted of three different lines, each progressively tougher than the first. They had all been prepared by Kesselring. The first one was called the Barbara line and this was a series of strong points designed to hold up the 5th Army advance while defences behind it were strengthened and completed. The line stretched across part of the Italian peninsula from Monte Cassino, seven miles north of the Volturno in the west to the Matese mountains in the spine of Italy, to the villages of Teano and Presenzano. Approximately ten miles behind the Barbara line was a much stronger line called the Bernhard line, which ran from the mouth of the Garigliano river to the Matese mountains, again to the west, where the mountains around Monte La Defensa and Monte Camino formed another natural barrier. Finally there was the most intensely fortified position known as the Gustav line, which ran along the Garigliano river where the Gustav and Bernhard lines were one and the same. Inland however, the Gustav line snaked some twelve miles to the rear to ther natural mountain fortress of Monte Cassino. The German defence of these lines was made all the more easier because there were so few well defined corridors through which a motorised Army could advance. There were only two main roads from Naples to Rome and it was along these and on precipitous mountain tracks that the 5th Army was obliged to attack. One of the main roads was Highway 6, which passed Monte Cassino and then filtered into the Liri valley, from where the Allies could deploy their tanks and advance quickly across the remaining 80 or so miles to Rome. First though, the Barbara line would have to be taken and then the Mignano gap would have to be negotiated. Cassino would also have to be taken before a crossing could be made across the Rapido river, a natural barrier that ran across the entrance to the Liri valley. Knowing full well which route the Allies would have to take, the Germans were able to concentrate their defences using the natural barriers of mountains and rivers that blocked their route.

Most personnel went round the shops in Naples. All personnel were by now in billets and requisitioned cars were the order of the day. Their new surroundings were the lap of luxury compared to the tented accommodation that they had been used to on the landing strips. The aerodrome had been Naples City Airport and although there had been several days of consecutive rain, it had not, as yet, been unserviceable. It had a large expanse of grass and surrounding it was the concrete perimeter track. Beyond this track were, on three sides, hangars, office blocks and garages and on the far east side a wood. Houses on all sides surrounded the airfield and of the fifteen or so hangars either the Allied bombing or the Germans had destroyed all but one when they had pulled out. Overlooking it was Mount Vesuvius, always smoking, changing colour and at night it appeared to glow red at the summit. The rest of the Wing and Squadron were scattered about all over Naples so that the Squadron was actually more widely dispersed than before. The officers mess was situated in two quite pleasant houses and the Wing sick quarters were about a half a mile up the road towards the airfield. Pompeii, Sorrento and the Island of Capri were all within easy reach. At times the airfield seemed crowded with Spitfires everywhere, DC3s from the Yanks transport, Austers from the Air Observation corps and more Spits from the Army Co-Op unit.

> In Naples we were billeted in splendid houses adjoining the main railway station that had probably been reserved for us by wealthy Fascists. The contrast between our life in the fields in Tunisia or Sicily was beyond belief. Now restaurants and bars offered a very real social life where you met all sorts of people. Our quarters were cleaned by local people, very probably so employed by the previous residents. The price of goods and services increased day by day as the locals realized we knew very little about the cost of life in Naples!
>
> As a squadron and group of pilots our favourite dinner spot was the Giardini degli Aranci or Orange Garden high up on the hillside and with lovely views across the Bay of Naples. Cars were commandeered to get us to this or that restaurant and another favourite haunt was the Opera House, the San Carlo. A return visit many years later reminded me of a leap I had made as a young pilot, slightly the worse for

wear, in an effort to catch the chandelier. By some great good fortune I landed on a table some ten feet below and did myself no physical injury!

The Eighth Army launched their push against Tuffilo along an 8-mile front. The village had been bombed and strafed by the Kittyihawks but it had been a difficult target to hit from the air and the attack faltered against the German defence.

5 NOVEMBER 1943

Logbook: 1. Capodochino – Foggia 2. Foggia – Capodochino.

ORB: 12 aircraft provided escort to two squadrons of Boston's that proved uneventful. However later in the day enemy bombers attacked the Naples dock area for more than an hour. One bomb fell about 300 yards from the Squadron billet.

The last German rearguard had left Tuffilo so the Italians apparently raised the white flag to signify that the village was no longer in German hands so that our troops could enter. The Germans had withdrawn, not because of our assault, but because the Trigno line as a line of defence was no longer sustainable as Allied troops elsewhere had broken out and had threatened the German flanks. The US 5th Army had also, by now, reached the Garigliano outside Mignano ready to push through the valley.

6 NOVEMBER 1943

Logbook: 1. Capodochino – Bari 2. Bari – Capodochino.

ORB: 12 aircraft on free-lance sweep over Rome One Spitfire shot up by Me109. Aircraft was Cat E destroyed. P/O McIntosh slightly injured.

Other squadrons on the Wing were more successful. 43 Fighting Cocks and 111 Squadron encountered 30+ Me109s and Fw190s on their morning patrols. Victories: 43 Squadron F/Lt Turlington 1 Me109 destroyed, F/O Reid 1 Me109 destroyed, W/O Johnson 1 Fw190 probable, F/O Craig 1 Me109 damaged. 111 Squadron F/Sgt Plumridge 1 Me109 destroyed and F/Sgt Gray 1 Me109 probable.

The Americans tried to capture the Mignano gap, the forward position on the German defensive position known as the Reinhard line, a stretch of ground about 6 miles long over which the Via Casilina ran through the mountains before reaching the open valley of the Rapido. Despite tough German resistance some progress was made but by taking advantage of the difficult mountainous terrain, the Germans were able to set up a dogged defence on the Garigliano, the strategically important river line between central and southern Italy.

Some of the airmen went again into Naples. If they were prepared to pay on the black market some decent meals could be had, but it did not sit comfortably with many because most of the city's population was starving. Shops of luxury goods had been well stocked when they had first entered the city but were now running out of supplies because of the influx of the military. Nurses and local beauties were regularly entertained! The 78th Division of the Eighth Army reached the River Sangro in the east but any attempt to cross it could not be carried out as it remained flooded from the heavy rains.

The Wing said goodbye to 243 Squadron who completed a move to 322 Wing in the east of Italy. 324 Wing was reduced to four squadrons, 72, 93, 111 and 43.

11 NOVEMBER 1943

Logbook: Patrol minesweepers off Volturno 16,000ft.

ORB: 8 aircraft naval patrol over the mouth of the Volturno River again. 10 aircraft bomb line patrol. 43 Squadron again encountered 9 enemy aircraft with F/Lt Turlington claiming 1 Ju 88 destroyed. 6 aircraft bomb line patrol. As it was Armistice Day the Squadron had poppies on sale in the mess and contributed £1.5s 0d to the Earl Haig fund and the Officers Mess £1.7s 0 d.

12 NOVEMBER 1943

Logbook: 1. Patrol bomb line Cassino – Formia 17,000ft. 2. Top cover minesweeper patrol 18,000ft.

ORB: 8 aircraft bomb line patrol. 43 Squadron again came across 20+ enemy aircraft including Me109s and Fw190s on their patrol. Victories: W/O Hedderwick 1 Me109 destroyed, F/Sgt Booth 1 Me109 destroyed, F/Sgt Leighton 1 Me109 destroyed and F/Sgt Smith 1 Me109 probable. 12 aircraft bomb line patrol 11.10–12.20. 12 aircraft minesweeper patrol 13.50–15.15. F/Lt Arthur Jupp OC 'A' Flight was tour expired and left the Squadron on posting to take over 324 Wing Training Flight. F/Lt Hussey DFM, a former Sgt Pilot in the Squadron, succeeded him in charge of 'A' Flight.

13 NOVEMBER 1943

Logbook: 1. Free Lance delousing sweep. 2. Patrol bomb line 18,000ft to 21,000ft. Ended up as a private sweep with the Group Captain!

ORB: 8 aircraft minesweeper patrol. 9 aircraft sweep. Fifteen Fw190s encountered. F/Sgt Morris 1 Fw190 destroyed and 1 damaged.

Gp Capt Sheep Gilroy was about to leave at the end of his tour. He wanted one last flight north over the Appenines. As his No. 2 we did a flight in clear blue skies at 21,000 feet looking down over the snow-capped mountains to see the sea far away below us. The memory of that flight is still clear to me today.

14 NOVEMBER 1943

Logbook: Patrol bomb line 14,000ft. 5 Me109s destroyed today. CO got 1, Larlee 2, Mcleod 1 and Morris 1.

ORB: 10 aircraft naval patrol. 2 aircraft calibration escort. 4 aircraft bomb line patrol and came across 5 Me109s. Victories F/O McLeod 1 Me109 destroyed, Sqn Ldr Daniel 1 Me109 destroyed, F/Sgt Larlee 2 Me109s destroyed without firing a shot.

Larlee had pursued the aircraft in a dive at terrific speed but had pulled out at about 10,000 feet. The two enemy aircraft failed to pull out of their dive and crashed within several yards of each other. The speed of the dive had also damaged F/Sgt Larlee's aircraft so much so that he crashed on landing when his undercarriage failed to lower but he was unhurt. The Me109s were reported to have had long range tanks fitted.

The Army was advancing beyond Naples towards Capua. Much of our time was spent in giving escort cover to destroyers shelling coast towns such as Minturno. We did have one major engagement with Me109s on a freelance 'de lousing' sweep. The lice, as they were known, were shot down, 5 of them.

15–17 NOVEMBER 1943

ORB: 72 Squadron stood down – no flying. F/Lt Tom Hughes posted back to take over 'B' Flight.

18 NOVEMBER 1943

Logbook: Patrol bomb line.

ORB: 6 aircraft minesweeper patrol over the mouth of the Volturno river. 6 aircraft minesweeper patrol. 4 aircraft bomb line patrol.

19 NOVEMBER 1943

Logbook: Patrol minesweepers.

ORB: 8 aircraft bomb line patrol 09.30–11.00 . F/Lt Johnstone was tour expired and left the Squadron for No. 2 BPD to await disposal instructions.

The problem of solving the issue of getting to Rome by some other means than through the mountains now faced the Allied Chiefs of Staff. There was a school of thought, including General Eisenhower that believed an amphibious landing around the German lines to threaten their rear would cause them to abandon their positions south of Rome. For this landing to have any effect however, at least one or two divisions would have to be landed and this would require a large number of transport landing craft or LSTs, which were now in short supply as most were scheduled to be withdrawn to England in preparation for the proposed landings in Northern Europe the following year. Any landing would have to be close enough to the battlefront so that the landing forces could link up with the troops advancing overland, otherwise the landing forces could be pinned down on the beach-head and maybe pushed back into the sea.

The plan was for Montgomery's Eighth Army to attack along the east coast, break through the defences of the Sangro river and drive north-west to the Winter Line at Pescara and threaten Rome from the east. As the rivers were flooded, roads were poor and the German defences strong, this was a tall order. In the meantime Clark's 5th Army was to break through the Mignano gap, advance and cross the Rapido river and capture Monte Cassino before driving up the Liri Valley to Frosinone about 50 miles south-east of Rome. When they reached Frosinone, 2 divisions of the 5th Army would be landed at Anzio, about 35 miles south of Rome, and the two elements would link up and push towards Rome. It was anticipated that the Germans, fearful that their supply and escape routes could be cut, would retreat beyond Rome.

20 NOVEMBER 1943

ORB: 6 aircraft naval patrol. 6 aircraft minesweeper patrol.

The fresh push by the US 5th Army towards the Rapido river began but progress was extremely slow. A simultaneous attack by the British Eighth Army had to be postponed because the River Sangro was still overflowing.

21 NOVEMBER 1943

ORB: 72 Squadron stood down – no flying due to poor weather.

Field Marshal Kesselring was appointed commander of Army Group and took over defence of Italy. Field Marshal Rommel was posted to France to prepare for the expected invasion there.

22 NOVEMBER 1943

Logbook: 1. Patrol Gaeta–Cassino area 15,000ft.

ORB: 8 aircraft bomb line patrol, 8 aircraft bomb line patrol and 10 aircraft sweep to Rome.

23 NOVEMBER 1943

ORB: 72 Squadron stood down – no flying again due to weather.

24 NOVEMBER 1943

Logbook: 1. Top cover bomb line patrol 18,000ft. 2. Escort destroyers shelling coast 13,000 ft. 3. Fleet destroyers shelling near Minturno.

ORB: 8 aircraft bomb line patrol, 8 aircraft bomb line patrol, 5 aircraft bomb line patrol, 4 aircraft minesweeper patrol.

25 NOVEMBER 1943

One patrol by 43 Squadron in the morning.

26 NOVEMBER 1943

Logbook: 1. Patrol minesweepers, Recalled the minesweepers were not sweeping! 2. Patrol bomb line 16,000ft.

ORB: 4 aircraft minesweeper patrol.

43 Squadron on their morning bomb line patrol reported one Ju88 and this was attacked and shot down with all six pilots in the section claiming a share.

ORB: 5 aircraft – Sweep to Rome and 7 aircraft bomb line patrol.

111 Squadron came across 8 + Me109s, F/O Whitney claimed 1 probable.

27 NOVEMBER 1943

ORB: 6 aircraft patrol south of bomb line.

The British Eighth army began to attack across the River Sangro. This had been postponed from the week earlier due to the rain and the overflowing river. Very heavy fighting followed and the Germans were again pushed back so that a few bridgeheads over the Sangro were established. Mozzagrogna, the king pin of the German defensive line, was captured.

28 NOVEMBER 1943

Logbook: Patrol bomb line 16,000ft.

ORB: 6 aircraft sweep Rome area and 2 aircraft Naples patrol.

93 Squadron whilst ground strafing targets lost F/O Swain as missing when his aircraft hit a tree and he crashed in flames.

ORB: 2 aircraft Naples patrol, 8 aircraft bomb line patrol.

San Maria and Fossacesia fell to the Allies and the 78th Division continued to advance up the coastal road. Canadians were on hand to relieve them.

29 NOVEMBER 1943

Logbook: Patrol bomb line 13,000ft. 10/10 cloud over the area.

ORB: 8 aircraft bomb line patrol.

30 NOVEMBER 1943

Logbook: Patrol Naples 17,000ft. Lots of cloud.

ORB: 2 aircraft Naples patrol and several aircraft detailed for convoy patrol had to be recalled because of bad weather.

1 DECEMBER 1943

Logbook: Bomb line cover for bombers. 100+ mediums and fighter bombers blasting gun positions.

ORB: 12 aircraft gave cover to medium bombers over the South Apollinare district. No enemy flak reported.

The US 5th Army, after waiting for Monty's drive to pull German troops across to the Adriatic and to thin the defences at the Mignano Gap launched their main attack. The initial objectives were to take the rugged mountains at the left of the entrance to the gap: Monte Camino and Monte de la Defensa, hence the cover to the medium bombers.

2 DECEMBER 1943

Logbook: 1. Bomb line patrol 12,000 ft. 9/10 Cloud 2. Bomb line cover for bombers. Ended up as BK1.

ORB: eight aircraft bomb line patrol and a further twelve gave cover to Bostons which bombed Trocchio. Flak positions strafed and two guns were destroyed.

Bari was bombed by about a hundred German bombers. Bari was being used to unload vital supplies for the Allied push and to help save time, all the lights had been switched on around the harbour area so that work unloading the ships could carry on at night. The attacks lasted only about 20 minutes but no Allied fighters were scrambled and the Germans were able to bomb unopposed. Nineteen transport ships were destroyed and a further seven seriously damaged. There were about 1,000 casualties and the harbour was put out of action for several weeks.

3 DECEMBER 1943

Logbook: Bomb line Patrol. Flying 3 x fours – first time for months. Recalled 10/10 Cloud.

ORB: Bad weather meant bomb line patrol aircraft were recalled.

4–7 DECEMBER 1943

ORB: No operational flying due to weather and notice received that kit in transit had been destroyed after the attacks on Bari three nights before.

US 5th Army managed to take the strategic summit of Monte Camino.

7 DECEMBER 1943

Logbook: 1. Capodochino – Bari. 2. Bari – Capodochino.

ORB: 10 aircraft bomber escort to Civithivechia where the Mitchells bombed with excellent results.

8 DECEMBER 1943

Logbook: Patrol bomb line 11,000ft.

ORB: Major A.C. Bosman DFC, a South African was posted superannuary to the Squadron with a view to his taking over from Sqn Ldr Daniel DFC and Bar who is tour-expired. W/O Turgion a French Canadian also posted in for flying duties. 8 aircraft bomb line patrol. 12 aircraft over Frosinone escorted Mustangs, which bombed the town.

German defence now centred around the Gustav Line, the heights on either side of the River Liri and behind the Rapido and Garigliano. US artillery was within range of Monte Cassino. Radio bought news of the declarations following the conference between Roosevelt, Churchill and Stalin at Tehran.

9 DECEMBER 1943

Logbook: 1. Escort A36s Furbara airfield, 18 Invaders well north of Rome. Quite good. 2. Patrol bomb line 13,000ft. Too much cloud. F/Lt Jack Pearson and Sgt Tom Larlee missing after strafing Rome area in earlier show.

ORB: F/Lt Pearson and W/O Larlee both posted missing after an armed sweep over the Rome area in the afternoon. F/Lt Pearson was last seen going down to strafe enemy motor transport and Sgt Larlee called up on the radio transmitter when 12/15 miles south of Rome saying that he had engine trouble and would have to bale out, but he was not seen by the rest of the Squadron.

In fact, though reported missing he evaded capture and came back to the unit on 26 May 1944.

ORB: 6 aircraft escorted Mustangs bombing Civitavechia and a further 6 patrolled the bomb line.

10 DECEMBER 1943

ORB: 8 aircraft patrolled bomb line in bad weather and on their return W/O Turgion had to crash land his Spitfire VC near Gingliano. The Crash landing was exceptionally good as the pilot miraculously put his aircraft down in a small clearing in an apple orchard. The apple orchard sorters were obviously very shaken as they gave Sqn Ldr Daniel a large quantity of their best apples when he went to collect his pilot!

11 DECEMBER 1943

Logbook: Escort A36s Ostia 7,000ft.

ORB: 2 aircraft on a bomb line patrol at first light. 6 aircraft later escorted Invaders to Ostia but due to poor visibility no bombs were dropped.

12 DECEMBER 1943

Logbook: Escort A36s Civitavecchia 12,000ft. No Bombing – cloud over target.

ORB: Weather again poor but 6 aircraft flew as bomber escort north of Rome, uneventful.

13 DECEMBER 1943

Logbook: Bomb line patrol 12,000ft. 4 Me109s reported Cassino, chased north but no engagement.

ORB: 6 aircraft sweep over Rome. 8 aircraft bomb line patrol, both uneventful.

14 DECEMBER 1943

Logbook: Escort Mitchells Ceccano 10,000ft.

ORB: Escort to Mitchells dropping leaflets over Ceccano.

15 DECEMBER 1943

Logbook: 1. Close Escort to 36 A 20s to Frosinone 20,000ft. 2. Patrol bomb line 12,000ft. 10+ Me109s and Fw190s attacked bombers. Went down – One x Me109G Destroyed. Street, Coles and Scott 109s damaged. Shaky doggers with another Me109 on return. We were all very short of fuel.

ORB: Escort Bostons on two bomb line patrols.

Rodney's combat report for the day records:

> Spitfire VC
> I was leading section blue escorting the bombers after they had bombed Frosinone and had turned to port towards Privermo. I noticed the third box of six A20s, which had just passed over the thin cloud at 9,000 feet, were being followed by three aircraft when I recognised them as two Me109s and one Fw190. I detailed two aircraft of the section to remain with the bombers and I and Blue 2, 5 and 6 dived down on the enemy aircraft. The enemy aircraft had come up from below cloud and were at 9,000 feet, the same height as the bombers. In my dive from 12,000 to 9,000 feet I noticed one of the enemy aircraft attacking the rear starboard A20 and black smoke came from the port engine of the A20. The enemy aircraft broke away down to starboard – I was rapidly closing range from 400 yards. The enemy aircraft then went under the cloud and I followed. We then came out of cloud still diving and I was only about 200 yards away and at 5 degrees. I fired a short burst of cannon and machine gun fire and observed strikes on the port side of the fuselage. I closed in to about 100 yards dead astern and fired another short burst and observed more strikes along the fuselage. The

enemy aircraft turned over into a steep dive from 2000 feet and crashed into the side of a hill amidst a lot of black smoke and debris. This combat took place at 11.15 hours.

Claim: One Me109G destroyed.
December we had a busier spell. For the first time in months we flew 12 aircraft in a three fours formation. On December 15th and while escorting A20 bombers to Frosinone we met formations of Me109s and Fw190s. They attacked the bombers. I got one Me109G destroyed and others claimed a number of enemy aircraft damaged. Then it was a shaky dogfight with another Me109, the sweat pouring off me as we turned and fought before we both flew off home. The fight left us very short of fuel and I landed with about one gallon left!

16 DECEMBER 1943

Logbook: Escort 36 A 20s St Elia 14,000ft.

ORB: 10 aircraft bomb line patrol and escorted Bostons in the afternoon.

17 DECEMBER 1943

Logbook: Escort 24 B25s Orte 11,000ft. Returned early, visibility was 1,500 yards.

ORB: Escort Mustangs to Civittivechia and patrol over Pontecorno. Sweep over Orte but aircraft again recalled due to bad weather.

18 DECEMBER 1943

Logbook: Escort 24 A 36s Civitavecchia 12,000ft . Tom missing, later confirmed as a PoW.

ORB: Sadly marked by the loss of F/Lt Hughes posted missing who turned back from an escort mission when he was near Capua. Called up on radio transmitter 'that he was going back to see the controller' but was not seen again.

Tom Hughes recalled the incident years later in correspondence:

> We were flying together over the Bay of Naples on 17 December when I suspected that I had engine trouble with my Spitfire IX. As I was leading the flight and we were waiting for some American bombers, who were late, I handed over to 'Barney' and dived back towards Naples airport. The Merlin engine immediately picked up as I got down to 2000 feet and I thought I would have a look at the great battle

> that was raging at Monte Cassino. I flew very low and very fast around the ruined monastery and engaged a flak gun in a duel! I was hit. My engine stopped, my trousers were alight and I crashed into a hillside! I woke up on the operating table of a German field hospital.

> On the 18th we lost Tom Hughes. He was hit by ground fire and crash-landed. Made a PoW. He required considerable hospital treatment. Later he was to be one of the last PoW exchanges made through the Red Cross in Switzerland.

Tom Hughes luck had finally run out when he was shot down just north of the Monastery at Monte Cassino. His Spitfire was brought down by machine gun fire when he was making a strafing attack. It caught fire and he was too low to bale out. His trousers were burned off his legs below the knees and he hit his head during the crash landing and remembers little of the crash. The Germans treated his burns, and he was then moved, stretcher bound from Italy to Germany. He was 'exchanged' in a 1 for 3 schemes with German prisoners, having been assessed by doctors as requiring repatriation. He then spent four days crossing Germany by train, worried sick that the RAF would find the train and either bomb them or shoot them up. From Switzerland he was taken to Marseilles, where he boarded the liner Arundel Castle and sailed past Gibraltar to Liverpool where his father was anxiously waiting to meet him on the quayside.

ORB: Later 11 aircraft patrolled the bomb line without incident.

19 DECEMBER 1943

Logbook: Scramble 20+ Bandits Gaeta. Hussey, Mcleod, Coles and Connolly Me109s and Fw190s destroyed in later shows.

ORB: Squadron provided bomber escort to Arce. Seven went up, all Spitfire Vs. One extra by mistake and then there appeared to be a mad panic to find more pilots because there was further sweep due to take off later that morning. F/O McLeod destroyed a Fw190, F/Sgt Coles a Me109G and F/Sgt Connolly another Me109G aswell. On later afternoon bomb line patrol, F/Lt Hussey DFM destroyed a further Fw190 and Sgt Pullen damaged a Me109. Unfortunately, F/Sgt Bouchier was hit by flak when chasing a Me109 and it was believed that his aircraft crashed south of Ceccano, well behind enemy lines. Major A.C. Bosman assumed command of the Squadron today.

20 DECEMBER 1943

ORB: Squadron patrolled bomb line twice but weather again was poor so the second patrol was recalled. F/Sgt Wood was posted from 324 Wing Training Flight for flying duties.

21 DECEMBER 1943

Logbook: 1. Sweep to Viterbo 15,000ft. Airfield straffed. 2. Patrol bomb line 14,000ft. Weather closed in badly.

ORB: Squadron an armed sweep. Bomb line patrol plus one bomber escort over Ortona. Canadian 1st Division began assault on Ortona, a small port on the Adriatic Coast. Lots of fighter- bombers, twelve Baltimores and twelve Bostons were up with the mountains visible all day, the first day with decent visibility for a while.

22 DECEMBER 1943

No operational flying.

23 DECEMBER 1943

Bad weather meant recall from only patrol.

24 DECEMBER 1943

No operational flying. The Squadron was released at 12.00. Sqn Ldr Daniel DFC and Bar left the Squadron with their best wishes for the future.

25 DECEMBER 1943

Logbook: Patrol bomb line 15,000ft. Weller hit by flak, baled out our side OK.

ORB: One bomb line patrol on Xmas day. F/Sgt Weller was hit by flak over enemy lines and had to bale out but a kindly wind blew him just within our lines, where he was sheltered by Italians and later bought back to the base by Americans just in time for Xmas dinner. Xmas dinner was a tremendous success. The Officers and NCOs waited upon the airmen, who had food such that one could not wish to better at home in the most prosperous days. A concert was held in the airman's dining hall after dinner and was a fitting end to the day.

> There was one bomb line patrol on which F/Sgt Weller was hit by flak while over enemy lines but a kind wind blew him just within our own lines. He was sheltered by Italians and later brought to base by Americans in good time for Christmas dinner. All's well that ends well. the dinner was a tremendous success.

Roy Hussey sent home to his mother a signed copy of the Squadron Menu for the day signed by all the pilots together with some ribald comments. Dinner was a positive feast and consisted of:

Vegetable Soup
Turkey with Seasoning
Pork with Apple Sauce
Creamed Potatoes
Baked Potatoes
Cauliflower and white sauce
Followed by:
Christmas Pudding
Mince Pies
Jellies and Custard
Washed down with:
Bianco and Rousse wine

On the reverse were the words to the Squadron song.

Who as a squadron came,
Out overseas to fame
Flying to dusk from early sunrise
Chasing the Hun from Africa's skies
Who, feared throughout the land
Who were that gallant band?
Known as Basutoland
Who – Why Seventy Two

Who, with their hopes of home
Moved on a Malta drome
Keeping their kills way up ahead
Chasing the Luftwaffe out of the Med
Who on a record day
Got the old Hun to play
Put fourteen of them away
Who – Why Seventy Two

Who on their new campaign
Are sweeping the skies again
Out every day defending the ports
Or up at the front as bomber escorts
Who'll make old Goering pack
Who when thoughts going back
Can say we have done our whack
Who – Why Seventy Two

26 DECEMBER 1943

No operational flying due to bad weather which got worse and worse. Cold, windy and lots of rain.

27 DECEMBER 1943

Logbook: Bomb line patrol 14,000ft.

ORB: Two bomb line patrols.

Ortona captured by the Canadians after fierce fighting but the Eighth Army was forced to a halt. It snowed and rained almost ceaselessly and the roads had turned into a quagmire making transportation impossible. Whilst Monty had managed to cross the River Sangro, his plan to push onto Chieta and then to Rome was hampered by a determined and dug-in enemy, weather that bogged down tanks and transport which made supply impossible and grounded the RAF or at least made them ineffective in their bombing and ground support roles. For the Army, with trucks bogged down and supplies difficult, morale was at an all-time low. Clothes became encrusted with mud and tent areas surrounded by water. Men rarely washed because it was so cold and most of what food they were able to get was canned and dreary. Small iron stoves used for heat had a tendency to blow up!

28 DECEMBER 1943

Logbook: Sweep delousing Ciampino airfields 19,000ft. 48 Mitchells bombed others on Guidonia.

ORB: Air Vice Marshal Broadhurst DSO, DFC and AFC gave an interesting talk to the pilots at dispersal this afternoon. Squadron patrolled bomb line in the morning and in the afternoon deloused the Rome area for the Mitchells to bomb.

29 DECEMBER 1943

No operational flying due to bad weather.

30 DECEMBER 1943

Logbook: 1. Patrol bomb line. F/Lt Hussey Fw190 damaged, they had bombed in Garigliano River area. 2. Testing cannon flights x 2.

ORB: Squadron patrolled the bomb line three times and on the second 8 Fw190s were seen near the Gulf of Gaeta. F/Lt Hussey managed to damage one.

31 DECEMBER 1943

Logbook: Sweep delousing Frosinone Area 19,000 ft. 9/10 cloud.

Summary of all flying for the year:
Total Hours for the Year 259.45, operational 210.40, non-operational 55.45 and as a passenger 48.10. Spitfire 9–137.20 operational hours, Spitfire 5–73.20 operational hours.

ORB: Covered Frosinone in very poor weather. New Year's Eve – a happy time had by all.

Montgomery did not have the strength to force his way through to Pescara and onto Rome through the winter, so he recommended to General Alexander that the Eighth Army offensive should be halted, amidst almost incessant rain and snow. Meanwhile, news filtered through that Monty had left Italy to assume command of troops in England for the preparation of the invasion of France.

The US 5th Army assault on the Bernhardt line towards Cassino now included plans of a landing of at least one division by amphibious craft at Anzio, about 25 miles south of Rome but this meant the retention of vital landing craft that had been earmarked for the preparation of the landings in Normandy and southern France. These landing craft were in short supply but the planned landing of troops near Anzio was considered vital because it would cut the German lines of communication and threaten the rear of the crack German 14th Division.

A young Rodney Scrase, 1938.

Cadet R. Scrase, 1942.

Rodney in the cockpit of a Stearman, Clewiston, 1942.

Harvard, Clewiston, 1942.

Passing out ceremony at Clewiston, March 1942.

Cadets No. 3 Course Clewiston, March 1942.

Leaving Clewiston with wings 1942.

Rodney aged 21 with wings, June 1942.

Rodney at No. 10 Course 58 OTU Grangemouth, October 1942.

Wing Commander Roland Bob Stanford Tuck, Rodney's station commander at Biggin Hill, December 1942.

Gibraltar from the air, January 1943.

The Ox – F/O Bobby Oxspring who would become Rodney's first squadron leader at 72 Squadron in Tunisia, 1943.

No. 72 Squadron pilots, Tunisia 1943.

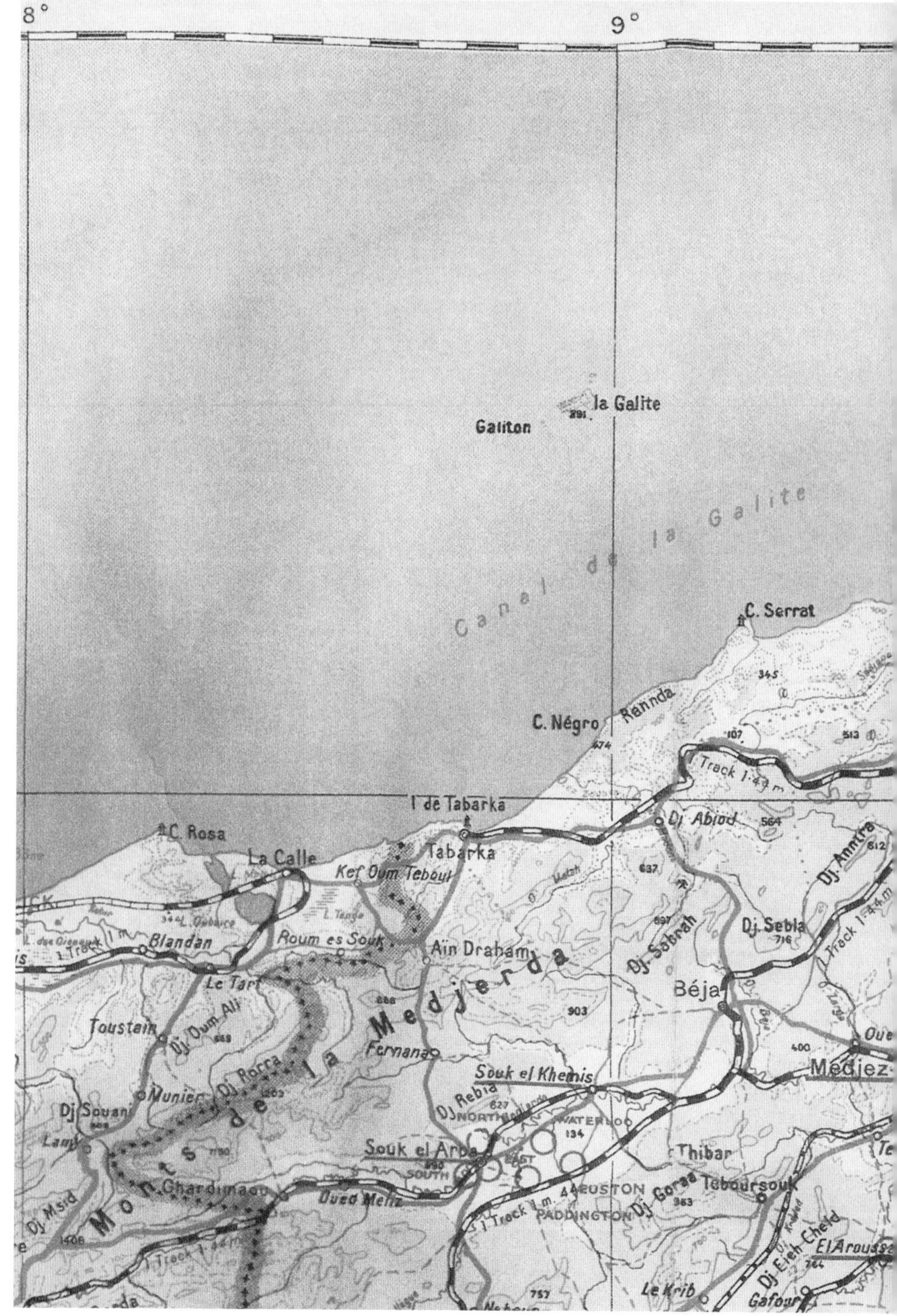

Tunisia, the site of the final push into North Africa, May 1943.

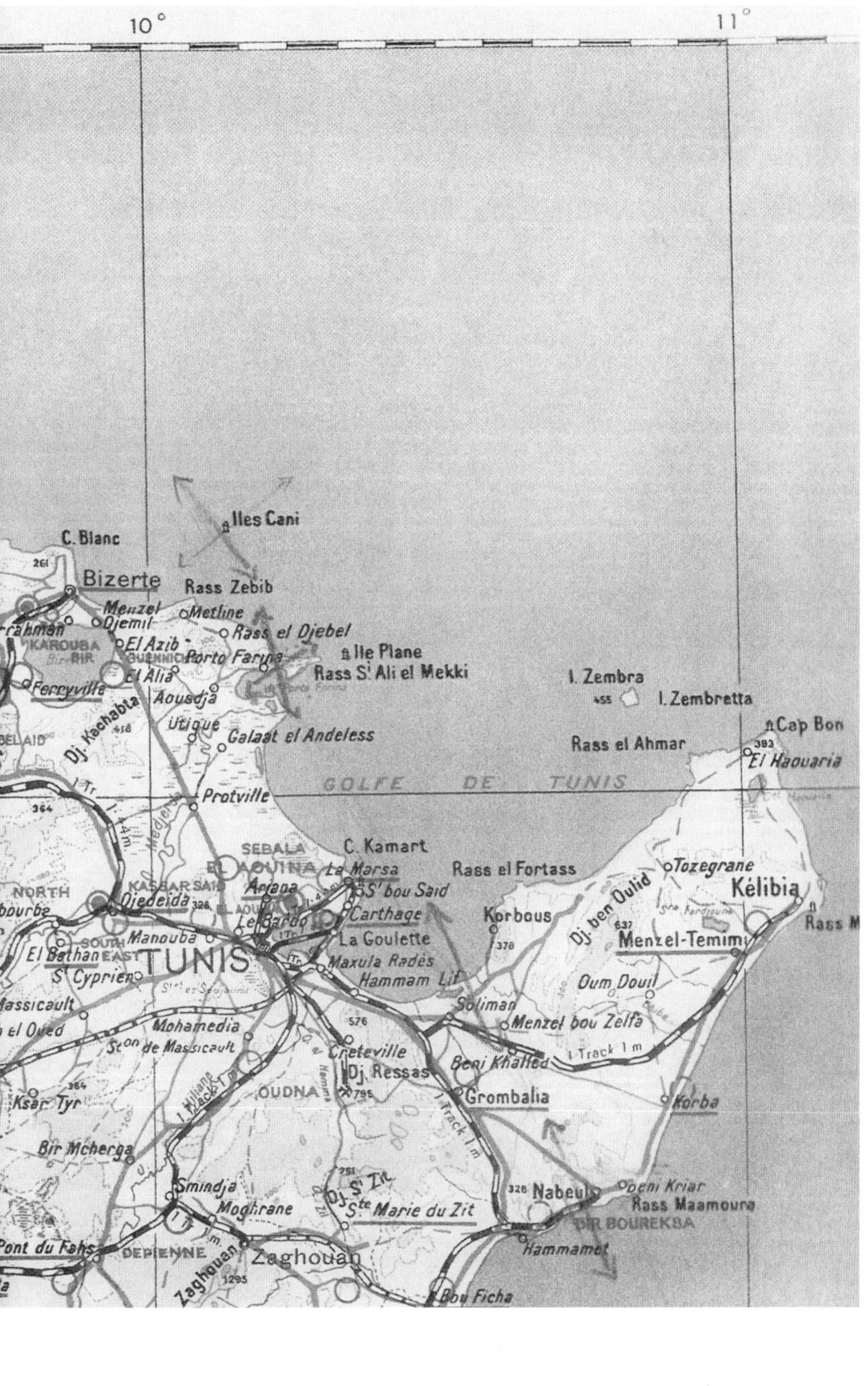

10°
11°
Iles Cani
C. Blanc
Bizerte
Rass Zebib
Menzel Djemil
Metline
Rass el Djebel
El Azib
Porto Farina
Ile Plane
Rass S. Ali el Mekki
El Alia
Ferryville
Aousdja
I. Zembra
I. Zembretta
Cap Bon
Dj. Kachabta
Utique
Galaat el Andeless
Rass el Ahmar
El Haouaria
GOLFE DE TUNIS
Protville
C. Kamart
SEBALA
EL AOUINA
La Marsa
Rass el Fortass
Tozegrane
Kélibia
Ariana
S. bou Said
Djedeida
Carthage
Korbous
Dj. ben Oulid
Le Bardo
La Goulette
Menzel-Temimi
Manouba
TUNIS
Maxula Radès
El Bathan
S. Cyprien
Hammam Lif
Oum Douil
Massicault
Soliman
Menzel bou Zelfa
Mohamedia
Creteville
Track 1 m
Beni Khalled
Dj. Ressas
Ksar Tyr
OUDNA
Grombalia
Korba
Bir Mcherga
Smindja
Nabeul
Beni Kriar
Moghrane
Ste Marie du Zit
Rass Maamoura
BIR BOUREKBA
Pont du Fahs
DEPIENNE
Zaghouan
Hammamet
Bou Ficha

Conditions on a Sicilian airfield, July 1943.

Spitfire landing in Sicily, July 1943.

Captured Me109s at Comiso Airfield, August 1943.

Roy Hussey in the cockpit of the 'Pisser' in Italy, September 1943.

Roy Hussey in Italy, September 1943.

Spitfire IIa – 72 Squadron.

Tom Hughes in the cockpit of a captured Me109, September 1943.

The damage to the Port of Naples, September 1943.

Opposite: The damage to Naples airfield, September 1943.

72 Squadron Spitfire in Naples, September 1943.

Fergus King and Keith Clarkson, 72 Squadron pilots, October 1943.

Appalling conditions in Italy, October 1943.

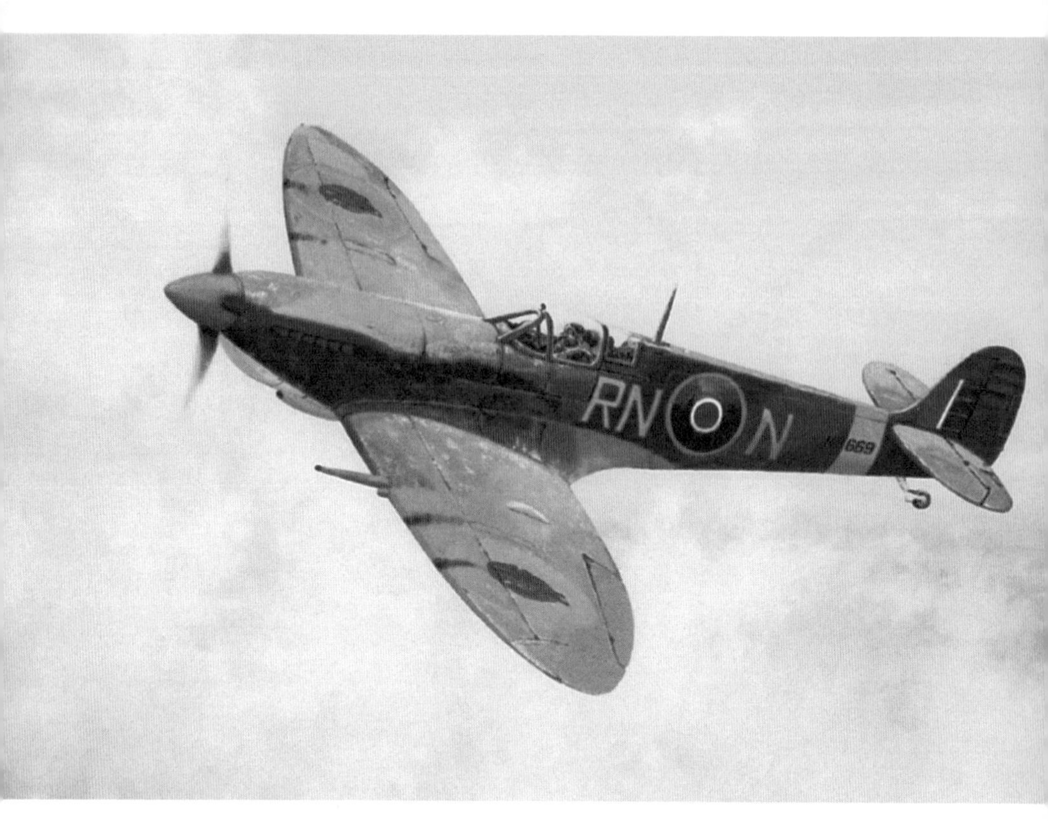

Rodney's own Spitfire RN – N with 72 Squadron, by Barry Weekley.

Spitfires in Italy, 1943.

72 Squadron Spitfires at Nettuno, a small landing ground near Anzio, January 1944.

The ruins of Monte Cassino, February 1944.

Ken 'Red' Weller No. 1 Squadron, 1945.

Squadron Leader David Cox – 'Coxy' No. 1 Squadron, 1945.

Gravestone of F/Lt E.B. Mortimer Rose DFC and Bar in Tunisia, 2005.

Medjez el Bab War Cemetery in Tunisia, 2005.

Remains of La Merdja Railway Station used as the officers' mess in Tunisia, 2005.

Site of Souk El Khemis Airfield in Tunisia, 2005.

Rodney with medals, 2005.

Reunion with 72 Squadron pilots and ground crew, 2005.

On the tail of an Me109 and not for the first time, YAM Elvington, 2006.

On Spitfires again in North Weald, 2007.

Rodney's first meeting with the author, 2008.

Rodney and Sue Scrase at the White Hart in Brasted 2010 – the public house frequented by pilots from RAF Biggin Hill just up the road.

CHAPTER TEN

THE LANDINGS AT ANZIO, ITALY, JANUARY–MARCH 1944

The Anzio landings soon developed into a major operation planned as a giant pincer movement. The invasion itself would be preceded by a strong feint attack against Pescara on the Adriatic coast while at the same time the US 5th Army would launch a series of attacks along the Rapido and Garigliano rivers in an attempt to pierce the Gustav line and break into the Liri Valley. This would be followed about ten days later by the amphibious landings at Anzio with the aim to force two fronts against the Germans and threaten their supply lines and route of retreat. The beaches chosen for the landings seemed ideal. The harbour at Anzio, although not large, was suitable for putting further troops ashore and was reasonably well protected by a mole.

About an hour's drive from Rome the towns of Anzio and Nettuno lie on the western Italian coastline with long, fine white sand beaches, famous for bathing pre-war. About ten miles north lay the Moletta river and man-made Mussolini Canal and about 20 miles inland lay the vineyard-covered Alban Hills, which rose to about 3,000 feet from the plains. The two main routes into Rome were the historic Appian Way, otherwise known as Highway 7 and the Via Cailina or Highway 6 that bisected the Alban Hills, the strategic approaches into Rome.

1 JANUARY 1944

ORB: No operational flying and in view of the bad weather Squadron stayed in billets. New Year celebrated in a quiet and sober fashion.

The mountains were covered in a thick blanket of snow with most road communications cut. A gale blew and after the snow, there was driving rain and further freezing conditions. Lloyd Snell recalled:

> New Years Day 1944 and we were in tents north west of Naples, less than a mile from the Mediterranean. We were close enough to Naples to see ack ack when they were bombed and see the smoke from Vesuvius when it erupted a little later. We could also hear the artillery at Cassino. We had a marquee for a dining tent and we had eight-man tents rather than our pup tents. We had a kerosene stove in our tent workshop, the wireless personnel were in three different tents so we could take turns using the

stove in our sleeping tents, each tent getting it every third night. The other nights we would use a charcoal burner that was actually a two-gallon tin punched full of holes with a long wire handle. The charcoal we made during the day. Some large trees had been bulldozed down so we would start a fire with the drier wood and any that had been charred through we would rake out and extinguish. The charcoal warmed us twice, once when we made it and then at night. There must have been a party somewhere. We had turned in when we heard a couple singing a little the worse for wear and so we pretended to be asleep so that they would leave us alone. No such luck, they piled into the tent and were joined by a couple of others also singing. They seemed to stay for ages but it wasn't until the guy next to me suddenly jumped up, put a magazine in his sten gun and shouted 'I'll get rid of these buggers' and pulled the bolt back that they left for a more appreciative audience!

2 JANUARY 1944

Logbook: Shoot testing modified magazine x 3.

ORB: Twelve aircraft patrolled the bomb line without any incident apart from the intense flak.

3 JANUARY 1944

Logbook: 1. Patrol bomb line 15,000ft. 2. Escort Mitchells – Nickelling Atina 14,000ft.

ORB: There were two shows of 12 aircraft patrolling the bomb line without incident. Major A.C. Bosman DFC posted to the Squadron from No. 7 SAAF Wing as Wingco flying. F/Lt John MV Carpenter DFC and Bar assumed command with Major A.C. Bosman.

Danny Daniels' replacement had been Major A. Bosman but he was with us for only a short time before he took command of a SAAF Wing. In January came 'Chips' Carpenter, a Battle of Britain veteran who had spent time as a flight commander during the siege years of Malta.

'Chips' Carpenter had been one of the few survivors of the ill fated Norwegian campaign when outdated Gladiators had been sent to try and fend off the Luftwaffe. He had also flown during the Battle of Britain but had been shot down and badly wounded. Having recovered he had then been posted to Malta and flown there from *Ark Royal* back in 1941 and joined 126 Squadron. After six months of intensive operations he had been awarded the DFC for 'consistently showing great courage and fighting spirit'. After a period instructing fighter pilots in South Africa he had returned to operations with the Desert Air Force with Spits on 145 and 92 Squadrons before his promotion to squadron leader. Rodney recalled he had a wicked sense of humour, and a light hearted approach to most things. He was extremely popular. It was noticeable that something was afoot in respect of the plans for the landings at Anzio. The Squadron operations largely consisted of escort missions to bombers that pounded the communications, military installations and airfields north and south of Rome. These operations were typical of the build up to a land offensive and were designed to soften up the targeted area for the prospective battleground. In between there were still fighter sweeps to try and lure the Luftwaffe into the air and standing patrols over the Army's forward positions.

4 JANUARY 1944

ORB: Twelve aircraft were employed de-lousing the Frosinone area. F/Lt Graham J. Cox DFC was posted to the Squadron from No. 111 Squadron for flying duties.

5 JANUARY 1944

ORB: No operational flying.

US 5th Army made another push on the approaches to the Gustav line. On days off the pilots continued to explore.

> It was in our minds to climb Mount Vesuvius, so Roy Hussey and I with a local guide climbed the volcano above the slopes of Pompeii. The views from the top were breathtaking right across the bay of Naples. At a height of 4,203 feet it was not a great height but we needed a guide to be able to get there and back safely, this at a time when the volcano was not quiescent. The trick for the guide was to get us to give him a coin that he then pressed into the next flow of molten lava to land nearby. Hard to believe but I still have my souvenir, a 1942 Italian coin with its black lava surround.

Rodney was not to know but less than 2 months later, in March 1944 Vesuvius was to erupt, a major eruption in fact, and provide a spectacular backdrop to their operations in Italy.

6 JANUARY 1944

Logbook: Sweep Frosinone south of Rome 18,000ft.

ORB: Two patrols of twelve aircraft over the bomb line. F/Lt JH Gray was posted to the Squadron for flying duties.

7 JANUARY 1944

Logbook: 1. Patrol bomb line 16,000ft. Squadron re-equipping with 9s!!! 2. Patrol bomb line 16,000ft.

ORB: Weather reconnaissance by two Mark 9s during the morning and there were two bomb line patrols of eleven aircraft each.

> In January we became an all Spitfire Mark IX Squadron again. My plane MH 669 RN-N was my pride and joy and most of the sorties we made were at 4 or 6 aircraft strength. For a number of these I was leader.

8 JANUARY 1944

Logbook: Patrol bomb line 13,000ft.

ORB: One bomber escort of six aircraft with a further 12 from 43 Squadron and one bomb line patrol of eight aircraft.

9 JANUARY 1944

ORB: No operations. F/Sgt Piper and F/Sgt Clarkson were this day posted OTE [Operational Tour Expired] to No. 2 Base Personnel Depot. F/O J. Howarth RCAF was posted to the Squadron.

Again torrential rain did its worst playing havoc with operations and morale and the gloom was deepened by the departure of Squadron stalwarts such as Piper and Clarkson.

10 JANUARY 1944

ORB: No operational flying.

The Squadron, with No. 43 Squadron, was to move into tents at Lago airfield. With the rain and the weather bitterly cold and the enemy about 12 miles away this was not an exciting prospect. The Italian definition of Lago was Lake – it was to be an apt description.

11 JANUARY 1944

Logbook: 1. Bomb line patrol 16,000ft. My new kite – Wizzo!

ORB: Weather reconnaissance by two aircraft during the morning and there were two bomb line patrols of twelve aircraft each.

12 JANUARY 1944

Logbook: Sweep – delousing bomb area. One Boston took a direct hit by flak – Flamer!

ORB: There were twelve aircraft that engaged in delousing ARCE area. Leave for aircrew was introduced to the Squadron today. One medium bomber was seen to break into two pieces after being hit by flak.

In atrocious conditions of blinding snow and freezing slashing rain, units of the French Expeditionary Corps broke through to the Gustav line and reached Sant Elia and occupied Monte Santa Groce. US troops had also taken Monte Trocchia by storming it so the Allied forces were now along the entire length of the Gustav line. Artillery began to shell the monastery at Cassino and forward troops reached the River Rapido.

13 JANUARY 1944

Logbook: Patrol bomb line 14,000ft.

ORB: 12 aircraft patrolled the bomb line and 11 aircraft gave area cover over the south of Rome. News received today of the following awards. A DFC to F/Lt Roy Hussey DFM and DFMs to F/Sgt Keith Clarkson and F/O K. Smith.

14 JANUARY 1944

Logbook: 1. Bomb line patrol 10,000ft. 2. Bomb line patrol 12,000ft.

ORB: Two bomb line patrols of 2 aircraft and one bomb line patrol of 10 aircraft were operations for the day.

News received of the pending movement of the Squadron from Naples Capodochino aerodrome to Lago airfield.

15 JANUARY 1944

Logbook: Weather Reconnaissance 24,000ft north of Pane.

ORB: Weather recce by two IXs in the morning. One bomb line patrol of 10 aircraft and an area cover over the south of Rome by 8 aircraft with 90 gallon tanks. 'A' Party moved from Naples to Lago.

'Capo' as they regularly called Capodochino had become their home but they were on the move to allow the build up of further Allied aircraft in the preperations for Anzio. They were to be replaced by the American 79th Fighter Group with their P40 Warhawks, but 'Capo' was also crowded with the Bostons of a medium bomber group, another P40 outfit, three squadrons of B25s, an air transport section and an Air Sea Rescue unit. The US II Corps took Monte Trocchio in the centre of the Gustav line and were pushing up to the River Rapido.

16 JANUARY 1944 – LAGO AIRFIELD NEAR CASTEL VOLTURNO

Logbook: 1. Ferry Capodochino to base. 2. Bomb line patrol 14,000ft.

ORB: A bomb line patrol of two aircraft and two-bomb line patrols of six aircraft were carried out today. 'B' Party moved to Lago today. F/O Smith was posted OTE to No. 2 base Personnel Depot.

Lago airfield was a little wooded island strip along the north bank of the Volturno River by the sea. With water and mud everywhere, the conditions could only be described as miserable for all. One joker repainted the famous cock of the 'fighting cocks' on 43 Squadron motto with a duck outside their flight office! The limited range of the Spitfires had prompted the move of the Squadron. It was necessary to construct a landing strip closer to the front line. Lago was a little village of no more than 100 people originally but was now a few bombed out apartments and stores. The inhabitants had fled when the Germans had pushed through. PSP had been laid for about 1,200 feet as a runway in a wooded area no more than a hundred yards from the sea. The runway was the shortest they had ever used and took some getting used to and it gave no margin for error on a fast approach. Several times the much heavier P 47s from a nearby US squadron attempted to use it but changed their minds when the pilots realized how short it really was.

The only place for the campsite was alongside a stream that flooded with the slightest rainfall turning the floor of their tents into lakes. The nights in sunny Italy were still bitterly cold adding to their misery. It was hard to forget those dark pre dawn hours waiting for first light. The silence would be accentuated by the chirping of crickets and the occasional distant rumble of cannon fire and then suddenly be shattered by the explosion of backfire as the ground crews ran up the Merlin engines avoiding the need for any batman calls to wake them up.

> We said goodbye to Naples and went off to Lago an airfield by the sea and just north of Castel Volturno. All though this was a canvas camp again and conditions were atrocious at least we had the pleasure of sea bathing. In the small village 20 miles from Capua there was an atmosphere more closely resembling the Medjerda Valley.

The only way of keeping clean was to wash in the stream. After they would grab their battledresses and clothes again and hurry towards the briefing through trees that were still wet from the overnight rain or the early morning dew. It was invariably an exciting start to the day.

17 JANUARY 1944

Logbook: Sweep Area Cover Viterbo 18,000ft. Liberators, Mitchells and Marauders bombing airfields in Rome area.

ORB: Six aircraft with six aircraft from 43 Squadron and six from 111 Squadron gave area cover over the north of Rome with 90 gallon tanks attached. Two patrols of two aircraft at high altitude were operated over the Gaeta and four aircraft patrolled over Naples harbour.

The British X Corps attacked across the rain swollen Garigliano to capture the town of Minturno on the extreme left flank of the Gustav line.

18 JANUARY 1944

Logbook: Patrol Gaeta Bay 22,000ft.

ORB: Seven aircraft patrolled the Terni area. Two IXs and four IXs of 43 Squadron patrolled Gaeta at high altitude. Eight IXs patrolled the bomb line and Two IXs patrolled the Gaeta area at high altitude later in the afternoon.

19 JANUARY 1944

Logbook: 1. Patrol Gaeta Bay 22,000ft. 2. Sweep Guidonia –Viterbo area 19,000ft. Viterbo airfield once more – Mitchells! 3. Escort 36 Bostons Colleferra 14,000ft. Excellent Bombing as the blast furnace was blown apart.

ORB: One bomb line patrol of seven aircraft and one patrol over Gaeta consisting of two aircraft and nine aircraft were employed de lousing the north of Rome. Eight aircraft escorted Bostons to Colleferra.

20 JANUARY 1944

Logbook: 1. Escort Mitchells Viterbo.

ORB: Four IXs and six from 93 Squadron and six from 111 Squadron escorted Bostons to Mount Seauri. Two IXs patrolled Gaeta at 25,000 feet and eight IXs escorted Mitchells to Viterbo. Four South African pilots were posted to the Squadron and these were ex 324 Wing Training F/Lt J Franks, Lt P.J. Van Schalkwyk, Lt J.M. Jackson and Lt S.V. Richardson.

21 JANUARY 1944

Logbook: Patrol bomb line 16,000ft.

ORB: There was one bomb line patrol of eight aircraft and three convoy patrols. Two of four and one of three aircraft and two high altitude patrols.

A disastrous dress rehearsal for the landings, that wasted men and materials but there was no time for further practice. That night the invasion convoys sailed out from Naples harbour on route for the landing beaches at Anzio.

22 JANUARY 1944

Logbook: Escort Marauders 21,000ft. Operation *Shingle* VI Corps land at Anzio – Nettuno, little opposition.

ORB: Despite the rain and mud the squadrons had to cover the Anzio landings. The Squadron was detailed to escort Marauders to Pondi with four aircraft and Velletu with nine aircraft.

The Anzio landings began under cover of darkness, with the 6th US Corps consisting of the 3rd US and 1st British Divisions. The plan also included standing patrols over the beach head from dawn until dusk. The operation was codenamed Operation *Shingle*. Intelligence reckoned that there could be at least 300 German fighters within striking distance of the beach head so standing patrols of Spitfires and Warhawks were kept over the beaches and approaches. Spits from 244 Wing and American 31st Fighter Group patrolled between 12,000 and 25,000 feet while the Warhawks or P 40s cruised at lower altitudes but it wasn't until the afternoon that the Luftwaffe reacted to the presence of the Allied invasion force. The spectacle of the Invasion Forces was awesome, hundreds of ships with barrage balloons above them, countless landing craft plying back and forth, everywhere troops, vehicles, bulldozers, artillery, and tanks rolled down the ramps and onto the sand. Men covered with equipment were scrambling ashore and faced shellfire on the beaches when they landed. It appeared chaotic.

Over the beach head, Gp Capt Duncan Smith (Smithy) leading the Squadron spotted about 6 Me109s at about the same height flying in a long line astern formation. Before he could get the Squadron into a good attacking position, the Me109s avoided combat by rolling on their backs and diving inland. Other squadrons had better luck. 43 Squadron in the morning flew a 12-ship escort to B25s returning from their target. They came across about 20 Me109s and one was destroyed by P/O T.E. Johnson. Commander of 324 Wing. Wing Cdr M.J. Loudon also claimed a Me109 damaged and F/O R.W. James damaged another Me109. Hovever the action was not without loss as they lost F/O P.J. Richards during the engagement. The US 79th Warhawks were even more successful, accounting for six Fw190s over the beaches when the Luftwaffe had ventured out. The Spitfire pilots generally at higher altitude came across little action and a common view was that they were being made to fly too high for effective interception and would never have any joy especially as it seemed that the Luftwaffe usually ran in from the sea at about 12,000 feet, delivered their dive bombing attacks and escaped inland at low level.

The landings appeared to have caught the enemy completely by surprise. Almost inconceivably the invasion ships had sailed into the Anzio area undetected. It appeared that the German radar had failed at a critical moment. The bombing of Perugia on the 19th had taken out the German long range recce aircraft on the ground while Allied air superiority over German aerodromes on D Day rendered the rest of the Luftwaffe ineffective. By nightfall on the first day VI Corps had about 3,000 vehicles and most of the assault force ashore. It had gone almost too well. Whilst every effort had been made to keep the actual landing point secret, the plans allowed for some resistance and to dig in allowing the beach head to be consolidated in anticipation of a German counter attack from the hills. Caught off guard by the lack of resistance, the plan was not revised and they dug in anyway, though, in hindsight, if they had pushed on the route to Rome was actually wide open.

> Just a few days later came the Army landings at Anzio and Nettuno. We had some activity but these were limited in scale and encounters with the enemy were almost always by chance.

23 JANUARY 1944

Logbook: 1. Patrol 'Shingles Beaches' 16,000ft. 2. Patrol 'Shingles' convoy 2,000ft. 10/10 cloud. Visibility very poor.

ORB: Squadron patrols over Anzio beaches. There were four patrols over the beaches, two of ten aircraft and two of eight aircraft.

A typical mission, pilots were now dressed in helmet and goggles, oxygen mask, gloves, shirt, sweater, trousers and jacket (for protection against fire as well as the cold) and they were advised to wear boots that would enable them to be able to walk in the event they baled out. A Mae West with a dye marker was worn over the jackets and they sat on a parachute pack that contained a dinghy, paddle, water bottle, emergency rations for three days, and a first aid kit with morphine and either a flare pistol or smoke grenade as a marker.

24 JANUARY 1944

Logbook: Patrol 'Shingles' convoy 16,000ft. F/Lt Hussey and F/O King shared a Fw190.

ORB: Eight aircraft patrolled the 'Shingles Beaches' and later, ten aircraft patrolled the beaches when four Fw190s were seen to dive bomb the convoy without effect. F/Lt Hussey and F/O King between them destroyed one of them.

25 JANUARY 1944

Logbook: Escort Bostons 16,000ft.

ORB: One bomber escort of twelve aircraft today.

The US 34th Division succeeded in getting across the River Rapido with strong artillery support but had to retreat back after strong German counter attacks because the Yanks had no tanks supporting them. The Scots and Irish Battalians of the 24th Guards Brigade were beaten back as they attacked Campolene on the road to Rome and their HQ staff were captured. A landing ground had been made in the beach head at Nettuno for emergency landings and the use of casualty evacuation and communications aircraft.

26 JANUARY 1944

ORB: No operational flying.

Attacks continued on the ground in the Cassino sector but with limited success. The Tunisian 2nd Battalian captured Colle Abate and closed in on Terelle but were running short of ammunition and had had their supply lines cut by a counter attack from the German Panzer Grenadiers. Fierce hand to hand fighting.

27 JANUARY 1944

Logbook: 1. Patrol 'Shingles Beaches' high cover 21,000ft. Self one Fw190 destroyed 10 miles SW of Rome 2. Patrol 'Shingles Beaches' aircraft U/S. F/O Ingalls, F/O McLeod and F/S Leach 109s and 190 destroyed. F/S Halliday missing.

ORB: There were four patrols over the beaches, two of ten aircraft and one of seven aircraft and the last of eight aircraft. On the third patrol, enemy aircraft were intercepted at the beaches area. Led again by Gp Capt Smith, the mixed formation consisted of Me109s and FW190s with the 109s stepped above.

Rodney's combat report for the day records:

> Spitfire IX. Operation *Shingle*. High Cover.
> I was Pink 1 leading section as high cover over 'Shingles Beaches' at 21,000 feet. Control had plotted several bandits and at 0830 hours I observed several aircraft flying over the ships from south to north at approximately 8,000 feet. They appeared suspicious and the next second bomb bursts were observed on the sea amongst the ships. Flak came up from the ships and shore batteries. I identified the aircraft as enemy aircraft by their hostile actions and dived down north to about 10,000 feet when I again observed enemy aircraft and Warhawks flying parallel to the coast road about 10 miles inland. I picked out 5 or 6 FW190s on the deck as yet unengaged. I dived on one of them and closed to within 300 yards astern where I fired a short burst of cannon and machine gun fire. I did not observe any results so closed in a

> further 200 yards and fired a second burst from about 150 yards and then a third burst from which I observed strikes around the cockpit. The enemy aircraft was crossing a small gully and did not climb the other side, breaking up on crashing. Claim: One FW190 destroyed. Approved wing commander Flying.
>
> On the 27th flying as Black 1 I found and destroyed an FW190. This was 10 miles SW of Rome. Following the early days after the beach landings we did get some enemy reaction but it was very much in and out flights by enemy aircraft bombing or attacking our ships off the beach head.

Gp Capt Smith turned behind an Me109 and opened fire and saw strikes on the wing root and started streaming smoke. He followed him down but was then engaged by another Me109 at about 10,000 feet and had to break off and the rest of the Squadron was completely spilt up and it was everyone for them selves. On landing it became apparent that F/O McLeod had destroyed one Me109, F/O Ingalls and F/O Scrase had destroyed one Fw190 each and F/Sgt Leach had destroyed a further Me109 and W/O Turgeon damaged a further Fw190.

On the ground the build up of the beach head continued. VI Corps had swelled to the equivalent of 4 divisions or 70,000 men. The plan was after an extensive naval, artillery and air force preparation, the British 1st Division would push down the Albano road towards Highway 7 and the US 3rd Division would advance on Cisterna, cut Highway 7 and then circle the southern edge of the Alban Hills towards Valmontone. However the attacks on Cisterna and Campoleone were driven back by German reinforcements and the bridge- head was coming under fire from German railway mounted guns and also homed in on the captured Harbour of Nettuno which the Allies used.

28 JANUARY 1944

Logbook: Escort 36 Bostons to Cisterna 14,000ft. Wizard bombing crept up main street.

ORB: There was one bomber escort of eight aircraft sweep over the north of Rome led by the group captain with nine aircraft and a beaches patrol with six aircraft.

Between Anzio and Nettuno an area of ground about 15 miles wide had been gained.

29 JANUARY 1944

Logbook: 'Shingles Beaches' high cover 21,000ft.

ORB: Two beaches patrols with ten aircraft each were operations today.

US engineers on the ground had constructed tank roads on the approaches to Cassino so that stronger armoured forces could advance. The Luftwaffe attacked Anzio itself and sank the British anti-aircraft crusier Spartan and damaged the freighter Samuel Huntingdon which exploded the following morning after fire reached its cargo of ammunition and fuel.

30 JANUARY 1944

Logbook: 'Shingles Beaches' 10/10 cloud recalled.

ORB: Two aircraft provided high cover for the beaches.

Push from the beach head began. The US 3rd Division was cut to pieces and had very few survivors after trying to get to Cisterna. The British 1st Division and US 1st Armoured Divisions had also attacked towards Albano but came to a halt in boggy marshy ground near Campoleone. With the armour stalled and bogged down the British flank was exposed so the advance was halted and they went on the defensive again. There was still no link between the US VI Corps which had landed at Anzio and the US 5th Army fighting outside Cassino but a pause was needed before a full scale assault could begin and they dug in, in preparation for the expected German counter attack.

31 JANUARY 1944

Logbook: Escort Bostons Artina.

ORB: One bomber escort with twelve aircraft.

LAGO AIRFIELD FEBRUARY 1944

1 FEBRUARY 1944

Logbook: Patrol convoy 'Shingles' area 10,000ft.

ORB: Weather recce was carried out by two aircraft over the Anzio sector. 12 aircraft patrolled the Anzio beaches at high and medium altitudes and later in the day 4 aircraft patrolled a convoy approaching Anzio.

Weather was very bad. General House had originally intended to base a large number of fighters close to the beach-head perimeter immediately after the landings. A shortage of shipping, the confinement of the beach head itself and the proximity of the fighters available to him from Naples – about 15 minutes flying time, curtailed his initial plans. A Squadron of the 31st Fighter Group Spitfires began providing spot cover from a strip at Nettuno near the beach-head but the strip almost immediately became a target for the German artillery as it was within easy range. The runway was very short but planes were regularly lost due to the shelling and landing or take off accidents. It would become familiar to 72 Squadron later in the month.

On the ground the invasion force had been increased to about 70,000 troops but the Anzio–Nettuno beach head had been sealed off by about 5 German divisions, though they were of course without air superiority. In thick fog at daybreak the 34th Division started an attack from Cairo north of Cassino towards Monte Calverio with further pushes towards Monte Castellone and Colle Sant Angelo.

2 FEBRUARY 1944

Logbook: Patrol 'Shingles Beaches' 15,000ft.

ORB: Patrol carried out by 8 aircraft over the beaches. 2 Fw190s were observed but no contact was made. A patrol of 11 aircraft gave medium and high cover over the beaches and a further patrol of 8 aircraft were over the beaches again when 2 Me109s broke cloud at 3,500 feet about 5 miles off shore of Anzio. They were too far away for our aircraft to make contact.

Four members of Ralph Readers 'gang show' put on a show in the airmens mess. In thick fog the ground troops pushed onto within 2 miles of Highway 6 and the Via Casilina and the Americans were on the outskirts of Cassino itself though were coming up against stiff German resistance in the form of crack German paratroops.

3 FEBRUARY 1944

ORB: Ten aircraft fitted with 90 gallon tanks were detailed from 43 SQuadron to R/V with 36 Maurauders over Civitivechia. The Maurauders did not R/V, probably because of the cloudy weather conditions. One Maurauder seen to ditch at F.2545. Our aircraft gave mayday on Channel D and one of our aircraft landed at Nettuno to give further details. Gp Capt Duncan Smith DSO and DFC, Officer commanding 324 Wing visited the Squadron to make an appeal for contributions on behalf of the Battle of Britain Memorial to be erected at Westminster Abbey.

The Germans also started their expected counter attack at Nettuno. German railway mounted guns, nicknamed the Anzio Express by troops opened fire on the harbour at Anzio and the transport ships and the landing beaches became targets for the German artillery.

4 FEBRUARY 1944

ORB: No operational flying.

Though on the ground the newly formed NZ II Corps under Lt General Freyberg with the British 78th Division attached to it was to take advantage of the expected US breakthrough by capturing Cassino and the Monastery, pushing on up the Liri Valley and cutting Highway 6 to stem the German retreat. There was heavy fighting around Cassino itself.

5 FEBRUARY 1944

Logbook: Patrol 'Shingles Beaches' 15,000ft.

ORB: Two patrols were carried out of 8 aircraft each over the Anzio beaches and Sgt Pullen force landed at Nettuno with temporary engine trouble. Pilot and aircraft returned to base OK.

43 Squadron were also over the Anzio beach head that day. Returning from their first mission of the day they apparently shot up a suspected ammunition dump north of Gaeta but encountered heavy flak and F/Sgt H.A. Booth was hit. He managed to limp to the coast where he baled out near the Dutch gunboat Flores but by the time the crew were able to pull him form the water, he had died. An Aussie W/O C.S. Luke was also hit by the heavy flak and killed instantly.

6 FEBRUARY 1944

Logbook: Escort and withdrawal cover Marauders bombing Orte 14,000ft.

ORB: Twelve aircraft flew to a point 20 miles S/E of Civitivechio to escort Maurauders flying west after bombing Orte. R/V was successfully made and our aircraft returned to base after escorting the bombers 30 miles west of Rome without incident.

German ground troops were still holding out on the high ground around Via Casilina and Monte Calvario but once these were taken, the US troops would be able to control Cassino.

7 FEBRUARY 1944

Logbook: Escort Mitchells Viterbo 15,000ft. Bombing short 20+ Me109s and Fw190s attacked us as we left target. F/O Ingalls and Sgt Pullen – 1 x 190 destroyed. Some of the Fw190s had DB engines.

ORB: Patrol of 8 aircraft carried out over the beaches. Some bogies reported but no interceptions made though it became clear that the lower flying Warhawks of the Yank 79th Fighter Group had better luck.

The Fw190s were set upon, and one, in an attempt to gain altitude, jettisoned his bombs which unfortunately fell on the 95th Evacuation Hospital killing about 30 patients and seriously wounding another 64. Further successes followed for the 79th. By the end of the day 17 enemy fighters had been destroyed with a further twelve probable, while the anti-aircraft gunners claimed a further seven. The German raids were still causing considerable damage and destruction so plans were made to launch countermeasures including retaliatory air strikes by B24s on the German airfields and this included attacks against Viterbo, Tarquinia and Orvieto. A patrol of 6 aircraft with 6 from 43 Squadron and 6 from 111 Squadron escorted Mitchells to Viterbo. 20+ enemy aircraft encountered, some were Fw190s with long noses were seen north of Rome. One solitary Fw190 was seen and destroyed by F/O Ingalls and Sgt Pullen but no bombs were observed to be dropped by the Mitchells. Despite this the attacks must have been effective because enemy air activity was considerably reduced over the next few days. German counter attacks reclaimed Monte Calvario and this strategic hill was to change side again and then remain in German hands until May 1944.

8 FEBRUARY 1944

Logbook: 1. Patrol 'Shingles Beaches' 12,000ft 2. Patrol 'Shingles Beaches' 2,000ft but 10/10 cloud.

ORB: Better weather so today 3 patrols over the beaches were carried out by 8 aircraft and one bomber escort by 2 aircraft with 6 from 111 Squadron. R/V with Maurauders at Hadispoli. Bombers escorted 50 miles out to sea without incident. Missions appeared to be split between area patrols, covering the fighter bombers straffing German transport, bombers attacking bridges and communication links and C47s carrying VIPs.

9 FEBRUARY 1944

Logbook: Escort Bostons 15,000ft – No bombs dropped!

ORB: 12 aircraft escorted 36 Bostons to F.8137, and this was the only detail for the day. No bombs were seen to drop. News received today that Sgt J.B. King who had been reported missing on the 12/7/43 and later re-classified as a PoW was now safe in neutral territory.

10 FEBRUARY 1944

ORB: Two beaches patrols were carried out and were flown without intercepting enemy aircraft. Two US Liberators who had been flying in company with our aircraft for some 5 minutes or more then unnobligingly fired on the Squadron, fortunately without scoring any hits.

The weather had started to deteriorate again and they had to dodge snow and rain squalls between Lake Albano and the coast. Further German counter attacks on the ground around the beach head because Kesselring's aim was to seal the beach head and prevent the Allies breaking out.

11 FEBRUARY 1944

ORB: No operational flying.

The Americans tried to capture Monte Calvario and Cassino by frontal assaults. In appalling conditions, a severe blizzard blew up preventing artillery from correctly shelling intended targets and had grounded any potential air support. American troops were decimated by German Paratroops dug in on the slopes and by the evening the US 11 Corps gave up the fight for Cassino, not only had they suffered huge losses but what remaining troops there were, were absolutely exhausted. They were to be replaced by Freybergs New Zealand 11 Corps and the 4th Indian Divisions including the famous Gurkhas. It was to be Freyberg who asked for the monastery at Cassino to be bombed and destroyed convinced that it was being used to help German artillery accurately shell Allied troops and this would then assist the second attempts to capture the strategically important site.

12 FEBRUARY 1944

Logbook: Patrol 'Shingles Beaches' 8,000ft.

ORB: Two beach patrols, one of 9 aircraft and one of 7 aircraft. A smoke screen was reported over the railway station F.8738 and a big explosion seen at Fondi.

13 FEBRUARY 1944

Logbook: Patrol 'Shingles Beaches' 8,000ft.

ORB: During the first beach patrol of the day 10 Fw190s were contacted and as a result of the Combat W/OMorris destroyed one and damaged two more. He had attacked five in all. A further Fw190 was damaged by F/O McLeod. Three further patrols were carried out, two of 8 aircraft and one of 9 aircraft but both were uneventful.

14 FEBRUARY 1944

Logbook: 1. Patrol 'Shingles Beaches' 14,000ft. Met 8 x Fw190s and 8 Me109s escort 10 miles north of Anzio. F/Sgt Coles and F/Sgt Leach 109s damaged. Self one x Me109G destroyed 30 miles up the coast from Anzio.

ORB: There were 4 beach patrols today, two each of eight aircraft and two of nine aircraft. The first three were uneventful but the last patrol provided combat with 6 Fw190s and their top cover of Me109s. F/O Scrase destroyed one Me109 and F/Sgt Leach and Sgt Coles each damaged one Me109 apiece.

Rodney's combat report for the day:

> Operation *Shingle*. Bomb line patrol from Lago airfield, 12 miles north-west of Anzio. I was leading aircraft. We were flying at 12-13,000 ft when we observed 6 Fw190s bomb the road junction at B628. There was a top cover of 8 Me109s. As soon as they saw us they turned and dived for cover. The Me109s broke up into two groups. I chased the rear one consisting of 3 aircraft. They headed for a small patch of cloud and then engaged in a turning match. Two broke off north but the third turned in towards cloud again. I fired from line astern at 300 yards giving 2 x two-second bursts. The enemy aircraft dipped in and out of cloud and on firing a third burst I observed part of the tail plane breaking off. He then went into a spiral down crashing near a farm where it burst into flames.
> Claim: One Me109 destroyed.
>
> On the 14th and while leading six aircraft we met a gaggle of 6 FW190s escorted by 8 Me109s about 10 miles north of Anzio. There followed an encounter and we claimed several enemy aircraft damaged. I got a good burst in on a Me109G and claimed it as destroyed.

Much later after the war and following the publication of a book in 2009 on the History of one of the Luftwaffe's elite fighting units, *JG4 – The Luftwaffe's 4th Fighter Wing* by Eric Mombeck. Rodney was asked to review the book.

> In any combat it is always interesting to identify the opposition, against which unit you were fighting, what was their type of aircraft and what tactics did they employ. Unless you lost a battle or unless you were taken prisoner this was something you would never to get to know at the time. On 14 March there is reference in the book to the unit losing a pilot of 2/JG4 Officer Hans Roscher who was shot down by a Spitfire over Nettuno beach near Anzio.

It may well be that this was Rodney's victim and nearly 68 years after the event Rodney was asked to write a review of the very book that gave him the information about his opponent that day.

15 FEBRUARY 1944

Logbook: 1. Patrol 'Shingles Beaches' 13,000ft 2. Escort area cover Marauders bombing Monastery Hill Cassino 15,000ft. Good bombing first batch.

ORB: Two beach patrols by 10 aircraft and 8 aircraft were duties for today. Shell bursts were seen over the railway station at F.8739 and flak was reported in the area.

> In 1944 the bombing of Monte Cassino on February 15th will always be a memory I hold with sadness. Flying at 15,000 feet as Red 1 in my own Spitfire Mark IX I was leader of the escort to the Marauders flying in two groups of six. We saw all too clearly what was happening and my comments that it was a wonderful show were widely reported in the press back home. Little did we realize it would be another 3 months before the Allies could finally break through on the road to Rome.

Rodney's remarks about the accuracy of the bombing and damage to the monastery were widely reported in the UK Press.

At Cassino 140 B17s from the US 15th Strategic Air Force based at Foggia began the destruction and bombing of the Monastery, and a second wave of 47 Mitchells and 40 Maurauders continued the battering. Some Indian troops caught close to the Monastery and unaware of the intended bombardment were killed, as were many civilians still in the Monastery itself. The bombing was not entirely accurate, some American casualties were hit when bombs were inadvertently dropped on the HQ of the US 5th Army at Presenzano which was 15 miles from Cassino! Most of the Monastery and the Basilica were reduced to piles of rubble, only the strong outer walls of the west wing and entrance steps managed to defy the bombs. Any survivors from the first wave were slaughtered by the second wave. In hindsight the bombing of the Monastery acted against the Allies because it was transformed into an impregnable fortress with bomb and artillery proof subterranean passages and cellars. The Germans would become masters of using the rubble and ruins in the defence of the monastery.

By now the Wing kept a squadron at Nettuno, the emergency landing ground on the Anzio beach head so that standing patrols could be kept up right until dusk and again at dawn the following morning. The Squadrons were rotated each day but the ground crew were left there for up to two weeks before being replaced. Conditions were pretty grim, pilots and ground crew had to sleep and eat in dug outs because the landing ground was regularly shelled by the German guns that were also dug into the hillsides overlooking the beach head. Lloyd Snell with 43 Squadron recalled:

> About the middle of Feb we moved up to Nettuno, part of the Anzio beach head by small landing craft at night. It was quieter then although a few shells would be lobbed over from some railway guns that spent their days in a tunnel. We were advised to dig down inside our tent but that would have been a mess if it had rained. At night when we were woken up by shellfire we always said that we would dig down the following day but we never did. The most exciting thing that happened was a visit by an American fighter that landed amongst our tents when everyone was there. We had just eaten. I was standing in front of one tent with my head ducked down, talking to the fellows inside. I straightened up at once and there was the fighter going at right angles, silently. His wingtip was nearly touching the tent

I was at. The pilot had his oil-covered face outside the cockpit and his windscreen was also covered in oil. As he touched down his guns fired, putting three holes just under the ridge pole of one tent. Not one injury!!!

16 FEBRUARY 1944

ORB: Four beach patrols again stirred up some enemy aircraft. The first of 8 aircraft observed some 20+ Fw190s approaching Anzio from the south-west diving from 13,000 feet to 4000 feet. As a result of the combat F/OIngalls destroyed a Fw190. The second patrol of the day of 6 aircraft was uneventful. The third patrol of 8 aircraft came across 15 Me109s over the Anzio sector and as a result one Me109 was damaged by Lt Richardson SA. On the fourth patrol of the day a further 15 Fw190s were seen over the beaches area. F/O McLeod damaged a Fw190 after a chase which took him 8 miles south-east of Rome.

After a heavy barrage the Germans counter attacked across both sides of the Aprilia – Anzio road against the Anzio–Nettuno beach head. Supported by artillery and tanks the Germans came up against stiff Allied resistance and against very boggy conditions off road. As result, they had to use the few roads available and this made them easy targets for the Allied fighter bombers and artillery so the German infantry divisions were left without support and made only slow progress.

ORB: Judy Shirley a radio star and 4 other members of the 'Gang Show' visited the Wing and two shows were arranged in the airmens mess, one for the Squadron and one for the other units in the Wing. The awards of 'Mention in Despatches' were made to F/Lt Hussey and F/Lt Prytherch (missing in Sicily) today.

17 FEBRUARY 1944

On the ground after some probing the previous night, the Germans renewed their assault along the shell cratered Albano–Anzio road and had penetrated about 4 miles into the Anzio–Nettuno beach head with air support provided by about 35 German fighter bombers. The Americans fell back under the onslaught and after another push supported by Fw190s fighter bombers again, the Germans succeeded in driving a wedge two miles wide and about 4 miles deep into the US positions. The Allies last ditch lines of defence were under threat and and the landings at Anzio were on the brink of disaster. It was all in the balance. Reserves were poured into the battle and a plea was made for all available aircraft for support. The Allied air forces responded with about 800 sorties alone that day. Nearly 1,000 tons of bombs were dropped on the German positions, most of it on the roads between Carroceta and Campoleone. Warhawks, Spitfires and Mustangs straffed the German guns, tanks, troops and battle lines as well and continued to harry them with RAF Baltimores, and Bostons came down low to bomb within 400 yards or so of the US positions in an attempt to stem the push. The overwhelming Allied air superiority provided such a weight of support to the hard pressed troops on the ground together with naval bombardment and artillery that the German push faltered. The Indian Corps at Cassino attempted to storm Monastery Hill and Monte Calvario but they were caught in heavy German cross fire and pushed back.

ORB: On the first patrol of the day over the beaches we saw Kittihawks bombing a viaduct at F.8843 but all the bombs dropped south of the target area. Very heavy and intense flak at Genzano. On the second patrol of the day 10 aircraft flew over the beaches with nothing to report. An incident on the runway at Lago by one aircraft from 43 Squadron made it necessary for 6 of our aircraft to land at Castel Volturno until such time as the runway at Lago was repaired. A further patrol over the beaches provided nothing of interest. 43 Squadon also came across 50+ enemy aircraft on their patrols with Sqn Ldr 'Polly' Parrott able to claim a Me109 damaged but in the same combat the Squadron lost F/Sgt Williams who had only been with them about a week.

P/O Barnfather left today on posting to No. 2 BFD as tour expired. He had been acting adjutant this month owing to the illness of F/Lt D.K. Rice.

An amazing story with 'Spanner ' Farish, the Chief Engineer Officer at the centre of it, then unfolded. 111 Squadron had been equipped with new Spit IXs powered by Rolls Royce Merlin 66 engines. The engines had been developed by Rolls to give a better performance between 13,000 feet and 20,000 feet but the first few operations carried out with them were a disaster because of continued engine failure. Some Spits were lucky to get down at Lago or Nettuno, some pilots bailed out and some crash-landed. 111 Squadron was grounded as a result. 'Spanner' was not popular.

A team was called out from Rolls Royce to investigate but it turned out to be nothing to do with the engines, it was the petrol that had been used, which apparently had been taken from drums and had some rust or something else in it. This meant that the plug points were smeared with crap and meant that at maximum power, the complete bank of cylinders had a tendency to cut out. 'Spanner' was mortified and decided that in an effort to get all the Spits back in the air again, including those grounded at Nettuno, he would have to sort the problems himself and get up to Nettuno. The problem was apparently, how was he going to get there. Nettuno was still being shelled and there were four Spits grounded there. 'Spanner' being an engineer officer had never flown before other than with a qualified pilot in a dual plane such as the 'Pisser' but he apparently took it upon himself, with a manual to fly another Spitfire up to Nettuno to see if he could get the rest back in the air again. 'Spanner' going solo in a Spitfire without his pilot's wings had immediate repercussions. Merlyn Rees, the Ops Officer immediately got onto 'Smithy' (Gp Capt Duncan Smith) who took off in another Spit to cover 'Spanner' or to persuade him back to Lago where he thought he would have to bale out rather than try and land the Spitfire. However around Nettuno he apparently already found 'Spanner ' had landed amidst the shelling of the airfield so he managed to land as well and let 'Spanner' carry out what he had set out to do, namely to get the other Spits back in the air. Remarkable story, but it did not end there. 'Spanner' was Court martialled apparently.

The weather on the 18th turned bad again grounding most Allied aircraft apart from a few sorties by A 36s and P 40s. The Germans tried to take advantage again by massing a large number of troops and tanks near Campoleone but they came under heavy artillery fire and after several hours of fierce fighting the last serious bid by the Germans to push through to the sea was halted and they were beaten back. The counter attack had cost the Germans about 5000 men but the beach head had been saved and the 'crisis at Anzio' was over.

Rodney was granted a seven-day period of leave.

> Seven days leave at a five-star hotel near Sorrento, the Cocumella at Sant' Agnello. It really was a splendid place, provided for RAF Officers. We were feted and treated as very special people. It was only 2km from Sorrento town centre with its wonderful club for visitors and its long time links with the British people I had a really super time. Made even more pleasant during the visit was the friendship I enjoyed with a PMRAF Nursing Sister whose Uncle had been appointed British Government Port Manager for Naples. He gave us the use of his chauffeur driven limousine and in that vehicle we spent some days traveling along the Amalfi Coast to see such sights as Positano, Amalfi and Ravello. I suppose as young men, I boastfully told her of our role in the Salerno landings and the occasion when in the Squadron 15 cwt we had driven from Tusciano for a day out, traveling beyond Salerno to Vietri sul Mare. The Germans were still controlling the road north to Cava dei Tirreni. You needed road traffic control going along the coast road as every minute or so an 88 shell would land. When you had the signal to go you went like hell and the number of burnt out vehicles showed this was no idle threat. Well we made it safely and she listened politely and I thought of the number of more serious medical cases with which she would have had to deal.

Some years later in 2003 Rodney returned to the Hotel Cocumella at Sant' Agnello as a guest. This time they showed him their record books and he was asked to write about his stay and sign the VIP Guest book.

A further push against the Anzio beach head at the end of February was put back, and both sides, exhausted, began to settle down and wait for dry weather. Although there were constant patrols and skirmishes there were no major ground operations on the Italian peninsula, with the exception of Clark's 5th Army assault on Cassino in March, for the next two months. The Germans worked to strengthen the Gustav Line while at Anzio the Allies continued to pour materials and supplies ashore. Cassino would not be taken until May later in the year.

25 FEBRUARY 1944

Logbook: Patrol 'Shingles Beaches' 9,000-12,000ft. First trip after 7 days rest at Sorrento and the last for No. 72 Squadron.

3 MARCH 1944

Logbook: Posted OTE [Operationally Tour Expired].

Rodney had flown 200 operational flights with 72 Squadron and clocked nearly 275 hours operational flying with a further 50 hours non operational flying. He was without doubt exhausted and sad to leave his colleagues. His combat record was four enemy aircraft destroyed, one probable and two damaged.

> It was a very happy period of my life and to this day I remain proud to have served with No. 72 'Basutoland' Squadron.

Whilst this was the end of Rodney's time with 72 Squadron the Italian campaign continued. Fighting at Anzio lasted for months. In May 1944 the war of attrition, affected by the Germans' growing problem of supply and manpower needs everywhere, allowed the Allies to break out of the Anzio beach head and Polish soldiers, taking heavy casualties, conquered Monte Cassino.

The Germans retreated and the Americans drove northeast from Anzio. The Allies had an opportunity to cut off and destroy the German forces retreating north, but under General Mark Clark they decided to head for Rome. Entering Rome on 4 June 1944, they had no way of knowing that the Allied landing in Normandy in France two days later would knock the liberation of the ancient capital from the public eye.

Instead of a quick campaign, the Italian Campaign had taken 275 days and cost nearly 125,000 Allied dead. And they were not close to the end of the fighting. The Germans' defensive positions behind the Gothic Line stood firm until the Allies opened a new offensive under very different circumstances than the attack on the Gustav Line. Again the Italian mountains helped the Germans. The British Eighth Army, the American 10th Mountain Division, and many other units, fought a hard battle through Ravenna and up the Po Valley through April 1945. On 27 April roving bands of Italian guerrillas captured Mussolini and executed him the next day. German forces surrendered on April 29 with 72 Squadron now flying in the north of Italy from Ravenna before heading into Austria as an occupying force.

In April 1944 Rodney was awarded the Distinguished Flying Cross and his award recommendation read as follows:

> F/O Scrase joined the Squadron in January 1943 and took part in the North African, Sicilian and Italian campaigns. His aggressiveness, outstanding leadership and keenness to engage the enemy has resulted in many successful combats for the squadron. He has himself destroyed four enemy aircraft, probably destroyed one and damaged two others. F/O Scrase took part in the Salerno Invasion and his enthusiasm and devotion to duty were an example to the whole squadron. I strongly recommend this award.
>
> Dated 12 Feb '44 Signed by Sqn Ld J.M. Carpenter CO 72 Squadron

CHAPTER ELEVEN

ISMAILIA AND BALLAH, EGYPT, MARCH–OCTOBER 1944

Logbook: No. 3 Base Personnel Depot (BPD) Portici Naples 8/3/44 –16/3/44.

The RAF had depots located around the world during the war; they not only catered for the arrival and departure of personnel and their kit, they provided meals and accommodation, and they also acted as accommodation 'holding' units until postings came through to personnel's next units.

The Italian winter of 1944–45 was one of the coldest in memory and the comforts presented to them at the transit camp were few. The camp was situated at Portici at the foot of Vesuvius, which had had its very spectacular eruption the year before and although still smouldering, failed to provide them with any warmth. They were billeted in a bare stone villa with boarded-up windows and tiers of Hessian bunks, in which they tried to sleep and keep out the cold with an absolute minimum of blankets. Sadly there were still some people worse off than themselves. The local Italians hung around the camp fences, tattered, cold, hungry and defeated. They waited patiently for a hand-out of the scraps or uneaten portions of the appalling food that was presented to them. Desperate times of course, and for most of them a salutary experience.

Logbook: No. 3 Base Area Transit Camp Naples 17/3/44–28/3/44.

Whilst most of Naples was still devastated and filthy it was still possible to sit in restaurants overlooking the bay, watch the fishing boats that had now been allowed out, with Vesuvius smoking in the background. Clams, fried octopus, boiled fish and the local delicacy, roast veal with fried potatoes with loads of olive oil and a delicate white wine could be found. One could dance at local nightclubs that the nurses also frequented. By the same token driving through some parts of Naples remained difficult because of the starving population, dirt and disease. Traffic was sometimes appalling, and the streets were crammed with lorries, jeeps, taxis, ambulances, carts and crowds of people.

Logbook: No. 67 E.V. Transit Camp Taranto 29/3/44–4/4/44.

On leaving Italy to go to Egypt, Rodney found himself at the transit camp at Taranto with very few duties to carry out and plenty of time to have a look around the town and search for presents to send home. Either that or he just lazed about! He wanted particularly to have a closer look at the sleek Italian destroyers that were moored up in the harbour.

Logbook: SS *Fort Capot River* 4/4/44–17/4/44 (Taranto – Augusta – Port Said).

The majority of Empire ships built during the war were freighters of a fairly austere and purely functional design. However, on the outbreak of war many cargo-liners with higher speeds had been requisitioned by the Admiralty for rapid conversion to merchant cruisers, hospital and depot ships etc. There soon became apparent a growing need for a fast, cargo-liner type of vessel with facilities for carrying heavy and awkwardly shaped war equipment. The SS *Fort Capot River* was built in 1943. The Fort ships were Canadian-built of various types. In 1941 agreement had been reached between Canada and the US for the US to purchase some 90 Canadian ships and transfer them to Britain under the Lend-Lease agreement. They were known as Empire ships. The SS *Fort Capot River* was 7,130 tons and 424 feet in length and had a beam of about 57 feet.

Logbook: 22 PTC Almaza Cairo 18/4/44–22/4/44.

No. 22 Personnel Transit Centre was at Almaza just outside Cairo. All transit camps were horrible places for those passing through. By now Rodney had had experience of many and noted that the permanent staff invariably lived in good quarters and had good food whilst those going to or coming from the war got very shabby treatment. The reason for this was that they, as personnel in transit, were not to be there long, whereas the permanent staff were and they needed to have their morale kept up.

The camp itself consisted of row upon row of square tents with one window each and was capable of housing eight men to a tent. Catering for so many personnel was a challenge without poisoning them! Milk had to be boiled even when fresh and was often delivered dirty and watered down. Meat came from Sudan and Abyssinia and while the armed forces had hired decent slaughterhouse and storage facilities, the rest of the abattoirs used by the local population and restaurants that catered for personnel when not in the camps were in appalling condition. As for the local sausages, they were not be trusted! Beyond basic board and lodging other facilities on the camp included little more than a couple of football pitches and a bar that was furnished with one or two chairs and a battered refrigerator chest that contained the local beer. Anyone who needed more would have to take the tram into Cairo. It may not have been all that long a stay there but it certainly seemed to Rodney to be too long and the more perceptive noted that there was no daily roll call, so without further ado Rodney went to Cairo.

Logbook: 203 Group HQ 22/4/44–6/5/44.

With the war moving away from Egypt it had been possible to merge No. 203 (Training) Group into Air HQ Eastern Mediterranean, that meant Air HQ Eastern

Mediterranean took over responsibility for training aircrews at the operational training units in Egypt, Palestine and Cyprus.

In Cairo Rodney was free to search out such amusement that suited him. There were shops where one could buy all kinds of novelties and of course souvenirs of Egypt. There were canteens and bars, and, the most novel thing of all, outdoor cinemas showing both old and new films, some of which he had seen at home and others that had only recently been issued. It was a new experience sitting under the star-filled Egyptian night sky watching American musicals and comedies.

Rodney was eager to see Cairo, having read so much about it, and was quite impressed with what he saw. There was no blackout, because by now the war had moved a long way westwards into Europe. He was surprised to find out too, how many forces canteens there were in Cairo. Money came via Thomas Cook – not far from the famous Shepheard's Hotel which, after the Pyramids, was the most famous landmark in Cairo.

The founding of Shepheard's Hotel in 1841 and its association with the earliest expeditions organised by Thomas Cook in the 1870s provided a base camp for all travellers to the Middle East. It had a famous terrace, set with wicker chairs and tables and commanded a lofty and shaded view of Ibrahim Pasha Street and a Moorish Hall. It was cool and dimly lit by a dome of coloured glass that hung above it and leather chairs around octagonal tables gave a feeling of intimacy and discretion. The ballroom featured pillars modelled on the temple at Karnak – some found it oppressive, some likened it to the British Museum. Others like Rodney found it a haven to have a quiet drink in the Long Bar, where women were not allowed and where you could relax and be quiet. (The hotel was wrecked on 26 January 1952 during riots as a precursor to the Suez crisis.)

No trip to Cairo would have been complete without a visit to the Pyramids, althought he had heard that many apparently came back disappointed by what they saw. There was a long straight main road with trams running close by and the first view in the distance reminded him of a slagheap outside a coal mine. However on closer inspection the more awe inspiring and the more spectacular they became and he forgot about the modern-day noises of trams and cars and he realised that there really was nothing quite like them.

One evening he had supper at the Empire Services Club. The Empire Club had been an Officers Club in the pre-First World War days when Britain had been closely involved in administering Egyptian affairs, and it had retained its Victorian and Edwardian appearance and atmosphere of a 'gentleman's' club. Cairo offered a wide variety of entertainment and cultural facilities and you could always find something in the city and its surroundings of interest. The service clubs were first-class, not only for the food they offered, but for all kinds of amenities – music, games, cinemas, baths, laundries, barber shops, writing rooms and libraries.

Cairo had its dangers, however, and it was not wise to frequent some of the sleazier bars and cabarets down the darker alleys of the city for all manner of reasons. Alan Moorehead describes Cairo during the war in his *African Trilogy* (1944):

> The Turf Club swarmed with officers newly arrived from England, and a dozen open-air cinemas were showing every night in the hot, brightly lit city … We had French wines, grapes, melons, steaks, cigarettes, beer, whisky, and abundance of all things that belonged to rich, idle peace. Officers were taking modern flats in Gezira's big buildings looking out over the golf course and the Nile. Polo continued with the same extraordinary frenzy in the roasting afternoon heat. No one worked from one till five-thirty or six, and even then work trickled through the comfortable offices borne along in a tide of gossip and Turkish coffee and pungent cigarettes … Madame Badia's girls writhed in the belly dance at her cabaret near the Pont des Anglais.

Clot Bey's brothels filled to overflowing with British Tommies. Shepheard's and the Continental were jammed with staff officers with suede boots, fly whisks and swagger sticks. As during the previous war, the night-shirted street Egyptian began to invent a thousand new ways of getting a few piasters out of the pockets of the red-faced soldiers. But as it was before, so it was again – the street Arab got the pickings, and the European and Levantine speculators and black marketeers and the rich Egyptians and the British also made their fortunes.

Cairo blossomed. British soldiers seeing sun and desert and clean air for the first time in their lives looked hungrily at the beautiful European girls who showed their pretty legs in the streets and on the trams and in the cafes. Many of these soldiers had come from appalling conditions in the black and grimy back streets of British cities not yet recovered from the Depression. Many of them had never seen before what they now enjoyed every day in Cairo, and Cairo's Europeans were generous with friendship and help. But it was not long before the relationship between the British soldiers and officers and the European girls in Cairo became an intricate and complicated entanglement which very few escaped, and many good British marriages foundered in those soft Cairo evenings when love rushed through the city on the wings of an exotic escape.

71 OTU ISMAILIA MAY 1944

After a few days off in Cairo Rodney boarded a train for Ismailia, approximately 60 miles to the north east of Cairo and approximately 10 miles north of the Great Bitter Lake. Close to the Nile the Delta was unexpectedly green and flourishing. On the train journey he saw in the fields asses carrying huge loads on their backs. There were oxen turning the old water wheels that irrigated the soil. Most of the view however consisted of bare sand except for pear-shaped cacti lining the rail side. The train was packed with locals, many clinging to the outside of the coaches, a common practice out there.

The villages were brown and drab, dirty muddled houses made of mud bricks dried in the sun. After about two hours Rodney came to Ismailia. Apart from the old European quarter south of the railway track that had elegant colonial-like streets with some beautiful old villas, he remembers very little of Ismailia itself except for tall, tumbledown tenements and mud-walled slums. It was a pretty uninspiring place.

Ismailia itself was and is close to the Great Bitter Lake about half way along the Suez Canal and about two miles north of the halfway point between Port Said in the north and Suez in the south. It also has Lake Timsah close by. The canal had been opened in 1869, a man-made sea level waterway about 119 miles long allowing water transportation between Europe and Asia without navigating around Africa. It contains no locks and seawater flows freely through the canal into the Great Bitter Lake, close to Ismailia, with the Mediterranean to the north and the Red Sea to the south.

Formed at Ismailia, originally under the control of No. 202 Group on 1 June 1941, the OTU's main task was to train pilots to fly and acclimatise fighter and army co-operation pilots to desert conditions.

He arrived at Ismailia station in the early afternoon and hired a taxi to take him on the final leg of his journey to the airfield. He was given a warm reception and it was at the OTU that Rodney trained pilots on Harvard Mark IIs, some old and battle-weary Hurricane Mark IIs and equally old but wonderful Spitfire Mark Vs.

> In March 1944 I was posted OTE [Operationally Tour Expired] from No. 72 Squadron and sent to Egypt to join No. 71 OTU – Ismailia as a flying instructor. As with all postings there is a certain amount of lost time while you settle in and are given the necessary briefing.

7 MAY 1944

ORB: No. 60 Course was brought up to full strength by the arrival of a warrant officer of the Royal Egyptian Air Force. Other movements affecting the Training Wing personnel concerned the arrival of Sqn Ldr S.W. Daniel who arrived to take over the duties of Chief Instructor and F/Lt R.D. Scrase for flying instructor duties.

The desert station consisted chiefly of tents, with a few wooden huts for the messes. There was a small village and a mosque quite close by, together with a railway station. In Rodney's tent there was a homemade electric light and the station had its own open-air cinema. All the water was brought in by train and the water-jugs were invariably old petrol tins so if they had not been cleaned properly the water tasted of fuel. He remembers the sounds of the morning when the braying of the donkeys and the grunting of the camels woke him together, of course, with the wailing from the mosques.

> Ismailia was in those days the headquarters of the Suez Canal Company. The RAF station had been in existence for some years and was a location run in very

traditional style. My memory is of tall Sudanese bearers, wearing white jellabas and topped with a red fez. They were responsible for looking after our quarters. For a briefing of instructors, information appeared on long sheets affixed to a notice board by the entrance to the Mess. These were often subject to rude amendments!

11 MAY 1944

Logbook: Hurricane 11B. Naval co-operation low attacks against HMS *Aurora* and HMS *Kimberley*.

HMS *Aurora* was a 6-inch cruiser, with a crew of 600 navymen and marines. She was attacked in the Mediterranean by Italian planes, and one of her gun turrets and the officers' quarters had taken the brunt of the attack. From Alexandria she went to Taranto in Italy, where she was rebuilt in the floating dry dock. HMS *Kimberley* was a destroyer.

12 MAY 1944

Logbook: Hurricane 11A – 8 aircraft of 72 Squadron destroy 9 Me109s over Lake Bracciano!

News reached Rodney that his former 72 Squadron colleagues had been hugely successful in a mission north of Rome. In the official press release at the time:

> Six Spitfire pilots of 72 Squadron shot down 9 Me109s in a four-minute air battle north of Rome. The Spitfires were flying back from an uneventful sweep when they saw 18 Me109s flying north over Lake Bracciano at 1,000 feet. The Spitfires dived on them from 11,000 feet and four minutes later there were nine blazing wrecks in the woods fringing the lake. F/O R.B. Hendry from New Zealand with two aircraft, Sgt J. Bird of Peterborough with two aircraft, Lt P.J. van Schalkwyk of South Africa with two aircraft and Sqn Ldr C.I.R. Arthur the CO, F/Lt B.J. Blackburn and F/Sgt J. Aspinall all with one aircraft each.

A grand total of nine destroyed with no damage to their own aircraft. General Barcus USAF and OAC of the 64th Fighter Wing (72 Squadron was by now attached to the US 64th Fighter Wing) sent his congratulations. 'A splendid show this morning. I am proud of 72 Squadron. Please relay my best wishes.' Rodney's short stay in May culminated in the final entry in his logbook for that month.

24 MAY 1944

Logbook: Spitfire VB. Formation Fly Past Alamein Club on Empire Air Day. 12 Spits escorting 6 Baltimores over Cairo.

28 MAY 1944

ORB: Postings affected during the day involved the departure of F/O C.R.S. McKay for SAAF Base Depot and F/Lt R.D. Scrase for the gunnery school at El Ballah. Pupils of 61 and 62 Courses assembled today in readiness for their training the following day.

MIDDLE EAST CENTRAL GUNNERY SCHOOL, BALLAH, JUNE 1944

Rodney was posted to the Middle East Central Gunnery School at El Ballah and provided instructor duties on No. 24 Pilot Gunnery Instructors Course. The course was an interesting and an educational period with plenty of flying, lectures and training films. Air-to-air gunnery practice was usually done by a pair of planes both carrying cine cameras, which were used instead of guns for obvious reasons. Both pilots would shoot at each other using the cameras, the films of which were analysed later in the station theatre. The courses were designed to teach pilots the finer arts of shooting at enemy planes in flight. By his admission Rodney was his own worst critic; he had felt for some time that his most serious drawback as a fighter pilot was his own perceived inability to hit an enemy aircraft. Instructing on a course for improvement of air gunnery techniques he felt would give him the skills to do the job even better.

> June brought a welcome change – I was posted to the Central Gunnery School at El Ballah. There I was to take the Pilot Gunnery Instructors' Course. Just as my colleagues in Italy were being equipped with the new gyroscopic gun sight that automatically computed the amount of deflection to allow when attacking an enemy plane, I was being trained in the use of the standard drogue!
>
> The one-month course – 29 hours flying time and covering air-to-air firing, air-to-ground firing and brisk evasion in handling overtaking attacks was designed to help me prepare newly graduating pilots for their role on an operational squadron.

At the end of a busy month after he had flown nearly 29 hours instruction he was assessed as 'Above Average' as an instructor in air gunnery and his logbook was signed off by Sqn Ldr Lyne DFC. Rodney returned to Ismailia via Fayid.

> So I returned to No. 71 OTU to take charge of the Air Firing Flight. That was a post I would hold for the next three months. Much of my time would be flying from the backseat of a Harvard. A training pilot occupied the front seat. This was very often a young man from Rhodesia or someone who had earned their wings in one of the FTSs in that country. Others came from South Africa. Our itinerary was a fixed one and I regretted we had so little opportunity to cover operational aspects of their flying training.

71 OTU ISMAILIA JUNE–OCTOBER 1944

30 JUNE 1944

ORB: Recent spate of accidents maintained when Sgt J.T. Lawrence bounced heavily on landing and crashed causing Cat 2 damage to his Hurricane, again the pilot was withdrawn from flying.

P/Os Tilston and J.T. Connolly from the Royal Australian Air Force returned to the unit on completion of their FIS Course at Shallufa. 'Con' had been with Rodney in 72 Squadron in North Africa, right through Sicily and Italy before his operational tour had ended in February and he had been posted to be a test pilot at HQ RAF Middle East before he joined the OTU at Ismailia on similar duties. There was much catching up to do, as there now seemed to be a '72 Squadron reunion going on' with Rodney, Danny Daniels, Barney Barnfather and Con all back together again.

1 JULY 1944

Logbook: Hurricane II air test.

ORB: The month started rather inauspiciously with two flying accidents first day. The first caused Cat B damage to a Spitfire when W/O Greenwood saw black and white smoke escaping from the engine which was also making an unhealthy grating noise so he belly landed near Quantara. The other involved Sgt P.J. Addis a pupil of No. 63 Course when he stalled the engine in his Hurricane and caused Cat A damage. The pupil seemed to be incapable of judging his circuits and landings and was withdrawn from flying.

3 JULY 1944

ORB: Ground looping was the cause of an accident when a Spitfire piloted by Sgt H.A. Firminger, a pupil on No. 62 Course suffered Cat B2 damage. This was the pilot's first solo on type. A Hurricane was also involved in an accident when it suffered Cat A damage when the pilot Sgt C.W. Riley, coming into land, touched down off the runway and damaged the oleo leg. Although he became airborne again he had to belly land because of the damage to the oleo leg.

The low points of life in the desert became the cause of most of their work. Dirt, filth and flies were constant enemies. Wherever there were Arabs or Egyptians around the station, they had the same problem. Their idea of sanitation was rudimentary to say the least, which may have been alright in the middle of the desert, miles from anywhere but in the station, any lapse from the sanitation standards they were used to in the UK produced countless swarms of flies. The other hazard was sandstorms and it could be a clear, fine windy day one minute with a large bank of cloud on the horizon and then the wind would pick up, become gale force and the sand would blow in from everywhere. It even could get to the stage where it was impossible to put your face outside, such was the strength of the wind in combination with the sand.

The high points for Rodney were the rest days and being able to sail with the RAF Sailing Club on the Great Bitter Lake or the evenings at the Greek Club where he could relax and enjoy drinks. It was also apparent to him that the course was noteworthy for being extremely cosmopolitan in nature and he had pupils from Egypt, Rhodesia and a number of South Africans.

> The Suez Canal and its side waters were an excellent place in which to learn how to sail a dinghy. Mark you, there were risks. Young lads – very often the offspring of French families were only too ready to show you they were really the sailing experts – sailing across your bows and giving you something to think about!

6 JULY 1944

Logbook: Harvard II To Aqir and return to base.

ORB: Noteworthy for the number of visitors. Wing Cdr Stan B. Grant of 203 Group collaborated with the Chief Instructor in connection with training matters whilst the visits of Sqn Ldrs Deuchas and Smith of HQME concentrated on the site for the MF–DF station. The WAAF accommodation was the reason for the F/O J.M.E. Adams visit from the Middle East and F/O Moore visited to attend the signals section.

8 JULY 1944

Logbook: Fairchild Argus to Maryut and return to base.

ORB: Still another course passed through our hands and today pupils of No. 61 Course and No. 19 Conversion course successfully completed their training and were now ready to take their places in operational squadrons on the various fronts.

The pilots had radios to keep in touch with the outside world. They were not supposed to have them, but the RAF had people from all walks of life, clerks, shopkeepers, journalists, poachers, burglars and people who could liberate equipment and construct radios, it was inevitable that demand could be met. The end product was a master set in one tent and the speakers were earphones, modified by soldering a pin onto the diaphragm, and sticking a cone on the pin.

They had the World Service from England, and it was always a pleasure to hear the calm, measured tones of Alvar Lidell beamed across all those miles saying 'This is London', and of course popular songs such as 'We'll Meet Again'.

11 JULY 1944

Logbook: Harvard II Sgt Coomber and Sgt Close air-to-air demonstration.

ORB: Inexperience on type was considered the reason for the accident today when Sgt P.S. Mayne a pupil of No. 63 Course swung on landing in a Spitfire causing Cat A damage.

12 JULY 1944

Logbook: Harvard II Sgt Witt, Sgt Ely and Sgt Gill air-to-air demonstration. Bruce Ingalls from No. 72 Squadron killed some days ago strafing.

ORB: The lull in the posting of instructors was interrupted today when F/O P.D. Jones and F/O Fakhry both of the Royal Australian Air Force reported from 203 Group for instructor duties.

16 JULY 1944

ORB: Two flying instructors F/O G. Garnham and F/O D.L.S. Wood both of whom had put in a considerable amount of time on the unit left today for 22 PTC to wait for air passage to HQ Mediterranean Allied Air Force.

17 JULY 1944

Logbook: Harvard II Sgt Proctor, Sgt Hall and Sgt Lewis air-to-ground.

ORB: The station commander and chief instructor had every reason to be happy over the progress of the course, as we had gone through a complete week without an accident.

This amazing state of affairs was short-lived; the inevitable happened and there were two accidents. The first resulted in Cat B2 damage to a Spitfire piloted by Sgt A. Marshall who carried out a forced landing near Fayid. The pilot had just completed an aerobatics exercise when he noticed smoke pouring from the engine, which immediately cut and as he was unable to restart it, he had no alternative other than to carry out a forced landing. The second accident involved a Hurricane piloted by Sgt R.A. Golding who came into land with a certain amount of drift which resulted in the undercarriage to collapse, the damage being assessed as Cat B2.

Two officers F/Lt J.B. Orr and F/Lt J.A. Gray were attached to the engine handling course at Heliopolis.

21 JULY 1944

Logbook: Fairchild Argus Ismailia to Maryut. Barney, Hoot and Bill.

A few days leave, rest and recuperation were in order, happy times sunning and swimming on the Aboukir beach. The station at Aboukir was peaceful, there was a slight hill surrounded by scented herbs and Rodney remembered that when they used to walk in the evening the scent was one that he never forgot.

> One very welcome aspect of our period as an instructor was the weekend breaks. The Spitfires and Hurricanes at Ismailia needed servicing. This was carried out at Aboukir quite near Alexandria. So a welcome break was possible over a number of weekends. We [Barney Barnfather, Hoot Connolly and Bill] spent the weekend in Alexandria. Two days later I had Danny Daniel, until recently our CO of 72 Squadron to show what training we were giving the new boys.

22 JULY 1944

ORB: Another accident, this time to Spitfire that resulted in Cat B2 damage. The pilot Sgt D.S. Armitage RCAF, a pupil of No. 63 Course was carrying out a normal landing until he hit a bad patch on the runway that caused the aircraft to swing and ultimately ground loop.

23 JULY 1944

ORB: The formation of the Air Firing Squadron called for further qualified gunnery instructors and F/Lt W.E. Schrader RNZAF and P/O R.S. Gray RCAF left for this course at RAF Ballah.

24 JULY 1944

Logbook: Spitfire VB Aboukir to Ismailia.

29 JULY 1944

ORB: The unit's 36th fatal accident occurred this morning when Sgt S. Mountzis Royal Hellenic Air Force was killed in a Hurricane aircraft. The pilot was carrying out a pin pointing exercise and was due back at base at 08.15 hours. As he was overdue a search was instituted and the remains of the crashed aircraft and his body were found about 7.5 miles from base. It is

believed that the accident occurred because at the time, there was 10/10 cloud at 2000 feet with its base at 200 feet, and the pilot may have broken cloud cover at high speed and low level and unable to pull out and went straight in. A Court of Enquiry has been convened.

No. 62 Course and No. 20 Conversion Course departed for 7 days leave prior to reporting to their respective personnel transit centres. The record of No. 62 Course during their stay is worthy of a commendation; they were involved in only one accident, one Cat B in a Spitfire. No. 20 Conversion Course maintained the good standard; that also left with a clean record. All the pilots of both courses successfully completed them and no one was withdrawn from training.

31 JULY 1944

Logbook: Harvard II Sgt Petit and Sgt Brigyen air to ground.

ORB: The month ended again on a sad note with another accident, this time involving Sgt Green of No. 63 Course who was piloting a Hurricane. He was proceeding on a cine exercise and as the engine was running a bit rough, switched over to the reserve tank, but forgot to switch over back to the main tank, and when the engine stopped he was under the impression that it had seized. He eventually switched back to the main tank but the engine would not start and he forced landed about 13 miles east of the base near the Palestinian Road, with Cat B damage.

Statistically the month of July showed a high standard of achievement, two OTU courses and two conversion courses successfully completed their training, representing an output of approximately 115 pilots all of whom were ready to take their places on various operational fronts. The general health of the station remained satisfactory in spite of the apparent increase in the malaria mosquito, precautionary measures preventing an epidemic.

2 AUGUST 1944

Logbook: Harvard air-to-air x 4 sgt pilots.

ORB: The month started badly with another accident that caused damage to two aircraft. It appeared that a Havard piloted by F/O T.A. Jowett, Flying Instructor with Sgt T.E. Bladun a pupil of No. 65 Course had touched down and run approx 50 yards along the runway when a Spitfire piloted by Sgt F. Yates a pupil of No. 64 Course collided with it, the wing striking the cockpit cover of the Havard. Damage was assessed as Cat B2 for the Spitfire and the Havard. Sgt Bladun was admitted to hospital suffering from amnesia.

3 AUGUST 1944

Logbook: Harvard air-to-air x 6 sgt pilots.

ORB: The immunity from fatal accidents recently enjoyed by the unit came to an end when Sgt D.S. Shircore, a pupil of No. 64 Course was killed, the units 37th fatal accident. He was flying as No. 2 in a line astern chase and failed to pull out of the dive from 9,000 feet. The aircraft exploded on hitting the ground.

7 AUGUST 1944

Logbook: Spitfire VC air test.

ORB: Another fatal accident when Sgt R.A. Culver a pupil of No. 63 Course, flying a Hurricane, spun in out of clouds causing Cat 2 damage to the aircraft. A court of inquiry was convened to investigate the cause of the accident.

8 AUGUST 1944

ORB: An influx of new personnel to the station, F/Lt N.L. McCulloch, F/O W.F. Raybould and F/O H.S. Smith arrived from 203 Group for instructor duties and F/Lt W.H. Foster from RAF Ballah for engineer duties.

12 AUGUST 1944

Logbook: Harvard II air-to-air x 4 sgt pilots.

ORB: Cat A damage was caused to a Hurricane piloted by Sgt T.C. Austin a pupil of No. 65 Course. The undercarriage collapsed at the end of the runway but as no technical failure could be found, it was presumed that the pilot failed to check with the hand pump.

14 AUGUST 1944

Logbook: Spitfire VC air test.

15 AUGUST 1944

Logbook: Harvard II air-to-air x 2 sgt pilots.

ORB: The discovery of a crashed aircraft confirmed what had been feared for some time from a long overdue Fairchild aircraft that had left Heliopolis carrying Sqn Ldr J.H.P. Gauvain and F/O Terry DFC on board. It crashed 4 miles south of Abu Sueir and both had been killed, but the predatory instincts

of the natives had been satisfied because the bodies had been stripped of all personal effects.

16 AUGUST 1944

ORB: There was a further influx of flying instructors with F/Lt D. Fisher RAAF, F/O J.L. Houle and P/O W. Wheatley both of the RCAF arrived from 203 Group. There was one departure Sqn Ldr S.W. 'Danny' Daniel left for 22 PTC to await air passage for HQ M.A.A.F. The funerals of Sqn Ldr J.H.P. Gauvain and F/O Terry took place today.

Rodney was sad to see his former squadron leader and close friend 'Danny' Daniel leave. Daniel would return to operations later in the year replacing Neville Duke as CO of 145 Squadron. He would finish the war by being awarded the DSO and he remained in the RAF after the war and went onto serve in Korea.

19 AUGUST 1944

ORB: No. 63 Course and No. 22 Conversion Course having completed their training departed on 7 days leave prior to reporting to their various PTCs. Only 3 pupils of No. 63 Course were considered unsuitable and had been withdrawn from training and were posted eventually for re-selection. The OTU course was involved in 12 accidents but the conversion course left with a clean record. With the departure of these course preparations were made to receive No. 66 and No. 23 Course, the pupils of which were assembled today. The termination of the gunnery course also meant that F/Lt W.E. Schrader RNZAF and P/O R.S. Gray RCAF both returned to the unit. Two airwomen were admitted to No. 1 General Hospital yesterday suffering from typhoid fever and a full investigation was at once instigated.

20 AUGUST 1944

ORB: Tour expired personnel of the Royal Canadian Air Force: F/Lt D.B. Rodgers, F/O J.S. Bushe, F/Lt R.L. Hazell, F/O T.B. Percival and F/O F.H. Reid all left for 22 PTC to wait for a sea passage back to the UK and repatriation to Canada.

21 AUGUST 1944

Logbook: Harvard II air-to-air x 6 sgt pilots.

ORB: Two further airwomen were admitted to No. 1 General Hospital reported to be suffering from typhoid and with the cause still unknown, all the usual precautions are being taken.

24 AUGUST 1944

Logbook: Harvard II air-to-air x 2 sgt pilots.

ORB: The elimination of taxiing accidents, which at one time had reached epidemic proportions, reared its head again when Sgt D.J. Cable a pupil of No. 64 Course piloting a Hurricane taxied into a Havard. The latter had been stationary at a marshalling point waiting for permission to take off.

25 AUGUST 1944

Logbook: Havard II air-to-air x 2 sgt pilots.

ORB: F/Lt M.L. Burke RAAF arrived from posting from 203 Group to take up instructor duties.

27 AUGUST 1944

Logbook: Anson Ismailia to Aboukir – round and round went the bloody great shed!

ORB: There was some movement amongst the training wing personnel. F/Lt R.R. Barnfather departed on posting to AHQ Eastern Mediterranean and F/O W.R. Raybould and F/O.H.R. Hall for the engine handling course at Heliopolis. Wing Cdr W.M. Sizer DFC and Bar assumed command of the station during the absence of Gp Capt R.E. Bain on leave.

29 AUGUST 1944

ORB: The termination of the flying instructors course at Shallufa marked the return to the unit of F/O G.P. McCully RCAF. F/O R.A.C. Kendall a pupil pilot of 66 Course was today admitted to No. 1 General Hospital with suspected smallpox. As the officer had only been with the unit for a few days it was felt that the station was not the source of the infection. The usual precautions are being enforced.

30 AUGUST 1944

ORB: Two instructors F/O H.E. Smith and F/Lt D.L.S. Fisher RAAF left to attend the flying instructors course at Shallufa. L.A.C.W. Cooper who had been admitted to No. 1 General Hospital suffering from typhoid died during the night. The ailments of the other airmen suffering have also been diagnosed as typhoid fever, but most are progressing satisfactorily.

Flying during the month of August was probably one of the most successful in the history of the unit. Not only did the unit surpass all previous flying records by amassing the grand total of 5,359 hours of flying time, but accidents in respect of training, which cannot be divorced from results, showed a welcome reduction. Only eight accidents were recorded in the month, which is surprisingly few in the view of the scale of the effort put in.

No. 63 and No. 21 Conversion Course completed their training during the month and approximately 50 trained pilots were turned out. There was a certain amount of wastage, three being withdrawn from training and sickness and other causes necessitated the transfer of other pupils to No. 64 and No. 65 Courses.

ORB: Though the general health of the station is regarded as satisfactory the month was marred by the outbreak of typhoid fever in the WAAF compound that resulted in the removal of five airwomen to hospital, one of which has since died. Elaborate investigations have been carried out to establish the cause and the usual hygienic precautions have been promulgated and are being rigidly enforced to arrest its spread. The segregation of suspected personnel has had a salutary effect and no further cases have been reported.

1 SEPTEMBER 1944

ORB: The month opened very inauspiciously with a mid air collision. Two pupils of 66 Course; Sgt H.P. Rippon and Sgt R. Whittle were practising formation flying when the accident occurred; fortunately it did not prove fatal. Sgt Rippon carried out a forced landing in the desert with resultant Cat B2 damage to the aircraft but Sgt Whittle showed courage and perseverance and was able to land at base in spite of having the trailing edge and aileron of the port wing smashed. His efforts were rewarded with a green endorsement in his logbook.

A few postings were effected during the day; Sqn Ldr J.H. Nicholls arrived to take over the long vacated post of chief flying instructor and F/O R.S. Gray RCAF departed for RAF Station Petah for duty as a pilot gunnery instructor.

2 SEPTEMBER 1944

ORB: The departure of P/O R.L. Abbott MT Officer for No. 10 MT Officers Course at Helwan and the return of P/O N.S. Powell from the pilots gunnery course at Ballah are the only items to report.

3 SEPTEMBER 1944

ORB: The periodic courses at Ballah and Heliopolis claimed the attendance of 3 instructors, P/O P. Wheatley, F/O J.L. Houle and P/O J.R. Andrew all left.

4 SEPTEMBER 1944

ORB: Cat B2 damage to a Harvard aircraft when a pupil of No. 66 Course F/O E.D. Lewis swung on landing. The pilot was not held to blame because on examination it was found that the tail wheel spring had come away thus causing permanent left rudder.

5 SEPTEMBER 1944

ORB: The results of the enquiry into the outbreak of typhoid fever have been consolidated by the SMO. No further cases have been reported though No. 1 General Hospital still houses 5 of our personnel.

6 SEPTEMBER 1944

ORB: Egypt the land of perennial sunshine sometimes belies the title, especially in the early morning! The pupils and instructors found this out to their cost this morning as a thick fog came down at about 7am making it impossible to land on the airfield and the loss of about 100 flying hours. All aircraft landed successfully here or at Fayid with the exception of one, Sgt J.H. Smith who unfortunately got lost and after remaining airborne for two and a half hours, eventually force landed in the Delta. The pilot was unhurt but the aircraft suffered Cat B2 damage.

7 SEPTEMBER 1944

ORB: Today saw the arrival of further flying instructors: P/O D.E. King, P/O R. Pride, P/O R.W. McKernan and W/O A.R. Fulton and W/O T. Hennessy all arrived from No. 203 Group.

8 SEPTEMBER 1944

ORB: The second of our pilots P/O R.H. Hall left for a elementary administration course at Amman.

9 SEPTEMBER 1944

ORB: A Hurricane suffered damage today when the pilot Sgt F.A. Donovan carried out a forced landing 3 miles north east of Abu Sueir. After taking off the pilot felt the engine vibrating violently and saw white smoke from the engine, with the 'post mortem' revealing a glycol leak.

A posting to an operational squadron – any flying instructor's ambition – was the happy news for F/O D. Jackson and F/O T.A. Jowett who were both posted to 94 Squadron via 22 PTC.

64 Course and 22 Conversion Course both completed their training and left on 7 days leave prior to reporting to various transit camps. Their record, viewed statistically was quite satisfactory.

10 SEPTEMBER 1944

ORB: There was considerable movement amongst personnel today. F/O W.M. Eckley left for 22 PTC and F/O L. Houle and F/O W.F. Frost arrived from No. 203 Group for instructor duties.

13 SEPTEMBER 1944

Logbook: Havard II air-to-air x 4 sgt pilots.

ORB: Pupils appear to be getting plenty of experience in forced landings. Sgt R.E. Murphy took off on a reserve tank and forgot to switch to the main tank and in the process earned an endorsement of gross carelessness from the station commander. The Hurricane suffered Cat B2 damage.

15 SEPTEMBER 1944

Logbook: Havard II base to Fayid.

ORB: Another accident this time in a Spitfire resulted in the collapse of the undercarriage, earned another endorsement of gross carelessness from the station commander as the pilot had tried to land in a cross wind with the result that the aircraft swung.

Today being RAF day we took the opportunity of celebrating the glorious 15 September 1940 – The Battle of Britain day. All sections in the station participated in the parade and Wing Commander Sizer DFC took the salute.

20 SEPTEMBER 1944

Logbook: Havard II Fayid to base.

ORB: Finger trouble, an expressive RAF term which characterises many accidents has been frequent of late and has resulted in the commanding officer handing out Red endorsements. Today Sgt F. Moran attempted to land on the wrong runway, realised his mistake and opened up his throttle to go round again. He did so too fast thereby cutting the engine and stalling from 40 feet. Result Cat B2 damage and another endorsement of gross carelessness from the station commander.

The AOC 203 Group, Air Vice Marshall Malcolm Taylor paid a visit to the station.

21–28 SEPTEMBER 1944

ORB: Nothing of interest to report.

29 SEPTEMBER 1944

ORB: Two accidents occurred today. The first Sgt J.H. Park a pupil of 67 Course was doing practice spins when he put his aircraft into a spin from which he could not recover. He made a successful parachute descent and escaped injury but the aircraft crashed and was written off. The second involved Sgt M. Kutas flying a Hurricane, when coming into land, his engine cut and he landed short of the runway causing Cat E1 damage to the aircraft. On inspection it was found the pitch control and propeller were in full coarse pitch.

6 OCTOBER 1944

ORB: Further departures were recorded today. F/O D.N. Hounsfield left for RAF Station Qastina and F/Lt R.D. Scrase Flying Instructor for 21 PTC en route back to the UK.

Logbook: No. 21 PTC Kasfareet 10/10/44–01/11/44.

A short journey from Ismailia took Rodney to No. 21 PTC (Personal Transit Centre), at Kasfareet along the Suez Canal. The camp at RAF Kasfareet was huge, situated close to the Great Bitter Lake and the Sweetwater Canal. The camp was about five miles long by one mile wide and included the main maintenance unit for the whole of the Middle East Air Force, No. 107 Maintenance Unit that salvaged aircraft instruments and serviced and repaired American fighter-bombers from the Tactical Aircraft Group, including Kittyhawks, Warhawks, Mitchells, and P-38s (Lightnings). Squadrons of fighter-bombers from this group bombed German supply lines, first in the Western Desert and later in the Balkans in support of Allied troops during the ill-fated Greek campaign. New aircraft were hastily unpacked from crates, assembled and fitted with British bombsights and oxygen equipment before being dispatched from Kasfareet and Heliopolis. The ground staff on the RAF maintenance flight included instrument makers, flight mechanics, flight riggers, electricians, and armourers, who all battled against the never-ending problem of sand and the shortage of spare parts.

> Whoever gave the canal that name must have had a great sense of humour, because although the Egyptians used to drink it, wash in it and do everything else in it, we were told to report sick for an inoculation against Bilharzia if we were even splashed with it and 10 jabs if you fell in it!

Logbook: DC3 Cairo West, El Adem, Luqa – Malta, Lyneham – Wiltshire 01/11/44 03/11/44.

Many who were posted to RAF El Adem felt that they had done something wrong to be sent there. It was a bleak spot in the Libyan Desert 18 miles due south of the town and harbour of Tobruk, made famous in the Eighth Army Battle against Rommel and his Afrika Korps and was regarded as a Middle East Air Force (MEAF) posting. Fortunately for Rodney his stopover was for re-fuelling only and for the onward journey and his return to Malta.

Logbook: RAF Hospital Wroughton Wiltshire 03/11/44–08/11/44.

> I had got overweight in Egypt and was 15 stone plus and was finding it hard to jump in and out of the back seat of the Harvard so was told to get back to the UK for a medical.
>
> So my 5 months at the OTU had a good ending as I was flown back to Lyneham in Wiltshire. It was immediately adjacent to the RAF Hospital at Wroughton for a full medical. Happily they passed me out as A1 HBH (OK for all operational flying but 'home' based).
>
> My recollections of the brief stay there were as pilots doing our best to meet WAAFs in dressing gowns who were at the end of a long transverse corridor.

Logbook: 14 days leave 09/11/44–23/11/44.

CHAPTER TWELVE

BACK TO ENGLAND, DECEMBER 1944 – NO. 1 SQUADRON

In the last phase of the war between October 1944 and May 1945 the Allied strategic bomber forces played a dominant part in bringing the German economy to the point of collapse. Against ineffectual resistance from the Luftwaffe, they attacked Germany by day and night on an unprecedented scale. The bombing attacks against German rail and water communications were choking German industry to death by the last months of 1944. By September Bomber Command and the USAAF had brought German oil production almost to its knees and aviation and armament fuel was in short supply; production was therefore nowhere near adequate to sustain the German Army and the Luftwaffe.

With the onset of winter weather, precision bombing was impossible and the Germans were able to repair some oil plants and the Allied bomber offensive lost some momentum. During the winter the USAAF 8th Air Force continued to bomb marshalling yards and communications when the weather was too bad for oil targets. The rail and water communication were hit with devastating effect by both the USAAF and RAF Bomber Command but it was not until March 1945 that the effects of bombing communications links became terminal for German industry. In the last 3 months of 1944 the Commander in Chief of Bomber Command waged his last and terrible battle of the war, namely against the industrial heartland of Germany, the Ruhr. Major German cities such as Duisburg, Essen, Cologne Dussledorf, Magdeburg, Leipzig, Dresden, Nuremberg, Munich and Berlin were all hit with devastating effect.

In December Rodney joined No. 1 Squadron at Detling and again flew the Spitfire IX on escort missions and fighter sweeps. The Squadron had seen the new Spitfire XXI at the beginning of the month when the new aircraft had flown in and they were given the chance to have a real look over. On the 18th came the move to Manston with No. 165 Squadron leaving and going to Bentwaters. At Manston they joined No. 91 Squadron and the Wing now consisted of Nos 1, 91, 124 and 504 Squadrons. Each unit provided a section for early morning weather reconnaissance and a readiness section during the hours of daylight.

With No. 1 Squadron was a familiar face for Rodney as F/Sgt Ken 'Red' Weller had also joined the Squadron earlier in the year following his tour with 72 Squadron in North Africa, Sicily and Italy. He had flown with the Squadron since May when the Squadron had been re-equipped with Spitfires to replace the Typhoon fighter-bombers they had been flying. The CO was Sqn Ldr H.P. Lardner-Burke DFC. Lardner-Burke came from South Africa and was known as 'Pat'. In 1941 he had flown off the aircraft carrier *Ark Royal* to Malta where he enjoyed success and earned his Distinguished Flying Cross.

The Germans had begun firing their new V1 rocket bombs that were to terrorise southern England earlier in the year and the Squadron had been involved in dive-bombing the V1 sites. Now the Germans had begun to launch their new 'doodlebugs' which fell indiscriminately all over the South. Preparations had been made to defend against them: RAF fighters would attempt to intercept them over the sea then a bank of anti aircraft guns followed by more fighters and then a string of barrage balloons on the outskirts of London, but all these precautions were of little use. The flying bombs were codenamed 'divers', had speeds of between 320 and 400mph and had a range of up to 250 miles and carried a 2,000lb warhead. They were smaller than a fighter and it generally took a measured piece of flying to get anywhere near them. Red Weller recalled the V1 rocket bombs:

> The closest call I had with one was the day I was vectored towards one in cloud. Control kept saying our two radar plots were together so you must be on top of it. I just said I was in cloud and couldn't see a bloody thing. Suddenly the V1 came whoosh right by me within feet of my Spitfire and immediately disappeared again. Scared me fartless!
>
> We patrolled over the Channel, sometimes as far as the French coast trying to pick them up. They would come over at speed so we were trying to get around 2,000 feet higher than they flew so we could pick up some speed to catch them. Then we got 150 octane fuel which gave us about another 30 mph or so but this made it necessary for our Spits to have an engine change about every 60 hours flying time.

Anti-V1 sorties had continued into August 1944 when the V1 menace began to slacken but the Squadron role was changed from shooting down the doodlebugs to flying escort missions again. The Squadron had also been involved in Operation *Market Garden* where they had been tasked with escorting aircraft carrying airborne troops at low level as well as gliders and glider tugs. As one pilot quipped 'The sky was 10/10ths Allied aircraft'.

Operation *Market Garden* was the codename for the Arnhem and the Rhine road bridges that were the target for airborne troops in an operation, which if successful would have helped shorten the war. Despite heroic attempts by the airborne troops the operation failed and despite poor weather RAF squadrons and crews had ably supported the airborne troops.

The Luftwaffe fighter squadrons were being rapidly decimated by the overwhelming Allied air supremacy and had by now mostly withdrawn into the borders of Germany. Resistance to the bomber onslaught had weakened to a point where Bomber Command felt it prudent to switch its effort from night operations to daylight operations. Many fighter squadrons were allocated for escort duties to the bombers but the biggest issue with the escort required was the limited range of the Spitfire. One solution was to carry jettisonable external long-range tanks under the fuselage. These had capacities of either 45 or 90 gallons of fuel. The 45-gallon tank increased flight time to about 3 hours but the 90-gallon tank reduced the Spitfire's performance to barely an acceptable level. One remedy was to install an internal fuselage tank behind the pilot as the Americans had done with the hugely successful P51 Mustang, but on the Spitfire this upset the aircraft's center of gravity to almost a dangerous level and the idea was scrapped. It had been a similar problem when Spitfires had to operate from Malta when Sicily had been invaded and in turn from Sicily when Italy had been invaded so Rodney was already familiar with the issues of long range flying. The range capability was improved dramatically when the RAF was able to set up airstrips at Maldegem and Ursel in the Ghent area of Belgium following its liberation by the advancing troops. From these two airstrips they were able to cover most of the strategic targets in western Germany that Bomber Command had scheduled for destruction.

The offensive by Bomber Command gave the Spitfire and escort fighters the opportunity, weather permitting, to see at first hand the devastating effect of their efforts on the ground. Efficient as the heavy boys were, they did not at times seem able to fly in neat formations that would have made the task of escort so much easier. Some made half-hearted attempts to close up but most operations saw night tactics adopted for daylight operations and resulted in gigantic streams of heavy bombers stretching for up to 60 miles at a time. This made protecting the vulnerable flanks difficult and often the entire resources of Fighter Command were required to protect the larger raids.

The strength of the operation depended on the priority of the target. Any number of bombers might be required and it was not unusual to see up to 1,000 bombers in the air at any one time with an equal number of fighters providing protection. From the ground, because of the altitude the aircraft were flying, you could see dense contrails that traced a path of the bomber stream. Operations were as frequent as the weather conditions permitted. Isolated long-range targets such as Munich or Berlin were rare so targets tended to be concentrated around the Ruhr and the industrial heartland of Germany. The Ruhr became known as 'Happy Valley' because the flak was so intense. The fighters were not by and large targeted by the flak but clearly the bombers were and it was inspiring to witness the guts and courage of the bomber crews who had to fly straight and level on their bombing runs and provide an easy target for the flak. All too frequently one of the heavies took a direct hit. Sometimes the bomber might erupt in an instantaneous explosion so at least death was quick. More often they took a hit to some vital part of the airframe or engine and the bomber would fall out of formation and begin its slow tortuous spiralling death throes. As it lost height you might be lucky and see one or two parachutes deploy as the crew got out but one can only imagine the sheer terror of those trapped inside a twisting, turning and often burning airframe as it fell to the ground.

With the arrival of winter many airfields became unserviceable and this included the Squadron's former base at Detling and may have prompted the move to Manston. November had also seen the departure of the Wing Cdr Peter Powell who had been replaced by another face familiar to Rodney, his former squadron leader at 72 Squadron, now Wing Cdr Bobby Oxspring DFC and Two Bars. After his tour of operations in North Africa he was getting used to operations in Europe again and apparently on his first show he had led the Squadron over Cologne right through the flak belt!

He had also had a couple of lucky scrapes following his posting to the wing commander role. Just before Rodney joined up with Squadron they had escorted the heavies in an attack on an ammunition dump at Heimbach. On their return they landed at Brussels as they were short of fuel. By the time they set course for Manston it was late afternoon and almost dusk. They crossed out over the North Sea near Ostend but had to switch the navigation lights on to keep the wing in formation. At Manston the final installation of 'Fido' had been completed a couple of days before hand. 'Fido' was a name given to fog dispersal equipment and consisted of a set of trenches that burnt contaminated petrol and provided intense heat down the sides of the runway thereby lifting the fog and providing illumination that was visible at heights of several hundred feet. In the gloom that the pilots now faced, any help at all was appreciated so the 'Fido' was flared up and Manston was able to provide a beacon to the incoming aircraft and they all landed safely.

The next morning all the Spitfires were lined up ready to depart back to Detling when Oxspring took off and his engine cut dead after he had almost gained flying speed. He only just managed to avoid colliding with Pat Lardner-Burke who was formatting on his wing and it was only because Pat hauled back on his stick and quite literally bounced over the top of Oxspring that he was able to avoid a serious accident. His reactions had avoided a messy pile up.

On the ground in Belgium, the Battle of the Bulge otherwise known as the Ardennes Offensive lasted from 16 December 1944 to 28 January 1945. Over one million men fought the battle including some 600,000 Germans, 500,000 Americans and 55,000 British soldiers. This German counter-attack was to be Hitler's 'last stand'.

Believing the Allied lines to be sufficiently weak, Hitler thought he had enough men left to launch a surprise attack on the Western Front through a thinly held line in the Belgian Ardennes forest. He also believed that factors such as bad weather, bad terrain, and the Christmas holiday would help him to catch the Allies by surprise. The Allies dangerously regarded the Ardennes as unsuitable for an attack.

Hitler had planned to re-capture Antwerp. This would cut off a main supply base for the Allied armies on the Western Front. He would then be able to surround Canada's 1st Army, Britain's 2nd Army as well as the US 1st and 9th Armies. This would result in the northern forces of the Allies being surrounded and cut off from their supplies. The southern forces would then be pushed out of Germany. Regardless of vocal concern from his generals, the Nazi leader expected an easy victory.

On the morning of 16 December the German General von Rundstedt attacked with the 5th Panzer and 6th SS Panzer Armies comprising nearly 24 divisions. After a two-hour bombardment the Germans pushed the Allies back. The element of surprise, lack of communication, and the fact that troops were outnumbered, all led to initial German success. However, after two days of fighting the Allied line, despite having a 'bulge', remained intact. Of the three main US divisions, two remained undefeated and the Germans surrounded only the least experienced division of the US VIII Corps.

Much of the battle was affected by the weather. As the fighting carried on, fog over the battlefield meant that the Allies were unable to respond with superior air power. They were then hindered as snow fell on the German lines, hiding enemy positions. The Allies had to wait desperately for the weather to clear before launching air attacks.

18 DECEMBER 1944

Logbook: Tiger Moth – Detling to Manston.

ORB: Manston – At last we were able to get away to Manston. The Squadron took off shortly after lunch arriving at Manston at approx. 15.00 hours. The fellows soon settled in and during the evening joined Sqn Ldr Bond and the pilots of our new wing mates from No. 91 Squadron.

19 DECEMBER 1944

ORB: A wing show was laid on this morning. The role being that of escort to target and withdrawal for 50 Lancasters bombing target south east of Arnhem. Towards midday the weather clamped down however, and the show was at first put back an hour and finally cancelled.

20 DECEMBER 1944

ORB: A preliminary warning of a show was passed through Intelligence early on but the thick fog that prevailed during the morning persisted through the day and in consequence the show was scrubbed.

The first week of fighting had gone so badly for the Allies that Hitler, on 22 December felt confident enough to demand surrender from the besieged Americans at the strategic city of Bastogne. The weather by now had improved and as the skies cleared, the Allies began an air bombardment of enemy tank positions. This allowed the VII Corps to move down and enlarge the US line thus allowing Patton's 3rd Army, on 23 December, to counter-attack against the Germans surrounding Bastogne and push them beyond the town.

23 DECEMBER 1944

ORB: At 13.15 hours the Squadron took off on Ramrod 1414 to act as target and withdrawal cover to a force of Lancasters bombing objectives at Trier.

No Huns were seen and heavy flak came up from the target area. The Squadron returned safely at 15.35 hours.

Bomber Command attempted to attack the Trier railway yards through cloud. The bombing appeared to be accurate and concentrated and Trier suffered, as it was the town's worst raid of the war.

24 DECEMBER 1944

Logbook: 1. Spitfire IX local flying 2. Ramrod 1416 escort 20,000ft. 150 Lancasters and Halifaxes to Dusseldorf.

ORB: This afternoon at 13.25 hours the Squadron escorted 150 heavies bombing Dusseldorf. One aircraft returned early with engine cutting out and the rest of the Squadron landed safely at 15.45 hours. Bombing was difficult to assess owing to ground haze. Weak but accurate flak encountered.

The purpose of the raids was to hinder the movement of supplies by transport aircraft from the Ruhr to the Ardennes battle area. German attacks continued unabated on the ground. On 24 December they launched the first air strike by jet aircraft, and bombed factories making machine parts, then attacked rail yards supplying the Allies. Combined with ground assaults the Allies were at points pushed back almost 60 miles.

25 DECEMBER 1944

Logbook: Rodeo 407. Sweep 17,000ft Aachen and Bonn. Saw 2 Me262s.

ORB: Today, Christmas Day, the Squadron carried out Rodeo 47 sweeping the Aachen–Bonn–Liege area. One aircraft aborted with a jammed hood and two Me262s were seen patrolling over Bonn at 18,000 feet, otherwise the operation was uneventful. Squadron landed safely at 15.30 hours. Unluckily the Bar was closed and there was little food to be had so they had to survive on the odd sausage roll until the evening. Xmas night was fairly quiet although a few of the fellows went out on sorties to local hostelries in the vicinity.

The Me262 was the 'first German jet fighter' and had Hitler not insisted that it be produced as a bomber it could have had a much greater impact on the war. It was the production of the engine that had slowed the numbers being built. It was an incredible technical achievement in itself.

It had first flown on 25 March 1942 and by the time of the fourth prototype's flight in April 1943 the plane had an impressive performance, although the engine needed perfecting. Hitler had demanded that it was to be able to carry bombs and this slowed its development down until 1944 when the first test planes were delivered to German squadrons. Unlike the other early German jet fighters the Me262 handled very well but the short engine life and continued problems with its guns jamming hampered it in combat.

In Belgium, fighting on Christmas Day was intense. By now, with the element of surprise gone, the Germans tried to blast through the Allied lines. However, even with a considerable 'bulge' straining the front the US and British troops refused to allow the Germans any advantage. Instead of a retreat the Germans sent forward more and more artillery to try and expand the 'bulge' as far as possible.

26 DECEMBER 1944

ORB: A show was put on in the morning but after a postponement of an hour it was finally cancelled. In the late afternoon the Squadron were invited to our previous station, Detling, where they spent a most enjoyable evening. A good spread was provided together with plenty of drink. We were very happy at Detling and the station ranks very highly with all Squadron members.

28 DECEMBER 1944

Logbook: Ramrod 1419. Returned with leader.

ORB: After lunch the Squadron took part in Ramrod 1419 sweeping the area covered by Cologne Marshalling Yards in close proximity to Lancasters. The operation went as planned, no Hun aircraft were seen. There was some heavy accurate flak for the bombers from the target area. Our aircraft returned safely at 16.25 hours.

167 Lancasters of No. 3 Group had attacked the marshalling yards at Cologne and Gremberg with accurate bombing. No aircraft were lost.

29 DECEMBER 1944

Logbook: Ramrod 1420. Escort 19,000ft to 200 Halifaxes to Coblenz. W/O Royds PoW.

ORB: This afternoon the Squadron escorted a force of 200 Halifaxes bombing the Marshalling Yards at Coblenz. On the way home Blue 4, W/O D.M. Royds called up when 30-40 miles west of Coblenz saying his engine was cutting. He was flying at 20,000 feet at the time but was last seen at 15,000 feet going down in a steep angle of dive with his engine obviously dead. Blue 3 turned back to search for him but there were no signs and nothing further was heard over the R/T. It is hoped that he was able to bale out successfully, though it is doubtful whether he will make our forward lines and the fear is that he will become a PoW.

W/O D.M. Royds did get down successfully and was later reported to be a guest of the Germans. He would be the Squadron's last casualty in the war. Two separate forces had bombed the railway yards in Coblenz, one of the main centres serving the Ardennes battlefront. No aircraft were lost during either operation. At least part of the bombing of each raid hit the railway areas. The Coblenz-Lützel railway bridge was out of action for the rest of the war and the cranes of the Mosel Harbour were also shut down.

On 29 December the Allies launched a major counter-offensive in the Ardennes. The counter offensive involved the US 3rd Army striking in the north and the US 1st Army in the south. The plan was to meet at the village of Houffalize and trap all the German forces in their way. This was ultimately successful, but the Germans showed exceptional resistance, giving the Americans a tough time.

Hitler hoped to start the New Year by eliminating all Allied air power in the region. The plan, 'The Great Blow' involved sending swarms of German fighter planes over Belgium, Holland, and northern France to bomb Allied airfields. The plan was, in part, a success. Over 200 Allied planes were destroyed, as were many air bases. However, the price paid by the Germans was also high as they lost over 300 planes and about 250 trained pilots that they could not afford to lose at this stage of the war.

As the US 1st and 3rd Armies advanced towards Houffalize the weather again began to deteriorate. This time the Germans suffered worse. In the biting cold men were fighting to escape the elements as well as the enemy and the German fuel shortage meant their advance ground to a halt. The Allied air forces' destruction of Germany's oil resources was chiefly responsible for the breakdown of the offensive and must have hastened the end of the war by several weeks.

30 DECEMBER 1944

Logbook: Attempted return to Manston.

ORB: A show was to have taken place today but bad weather intervened and it was cancelled. Our CO Sqn Ldr Lardner-Burke who had been away the past two days returned with news that he had been promoted to Wing Cdr and as of January 2nd 1945 is due to take over the Coltishall Wing of 4 Squadrons and their Spitfire XVIs whose role will be that of bombing and ground straffing. Whilst we will be very sorry to see him go we heard the good news that F/Lt D.G. Cox DFC & Bar who came to the Squadron several weeks ago is to assume command of the Squadron with our whole-hearted support.

F/Lt David Cox DFC and Bar CdG (French Croix de Guerre) who had arrived as a supernumerary took over and was vastly experienced as a fighter pilot having seen action in the Battle of Britain and the North African campaigns. His third operational tour had been in 1944 in command of 222 Spitfire squadron.

> I was CO of 222 Squadron but had this bloody car crash and then, being only an acting squadron leader I went down to flight lieutenant again. Then I was sent to Group Support Unit testing Spitfires and things, but was posted to No. 1 Squadron because I created about not going back onto operations. TAF didn't like me very much because of my car crash so finally on new year's day Lardner-Burke who had been in 19 Squadron in 1941 when I had still been with them, was posted out. I remember he called into his office and said 'Two things, first you are the new CO and second you will have to write a letter to the parents of a chap we lost the other day.'

It was a very cosmopolitan squadron by now, as they appeared to have every nationality under the sun. The letter that Sqn Ldr Cox would be writing would be to the parents of W/O Royds.

31 DECEMBER 1944

Logbook: Ursel to Manston. Sqn Ldr Lardner-Burke posted as Wing Commander.

ORB: In the afternoon the Squadron took off to act as target and withdrawal cover to Ramrod 1423, a force of Lancasters bombing Volwinkle Marshalling yards near Solinlgen. The bombers were a bit late over target and bombing results could not be observed due to cloud cover. Two of the Squadron, F/Lt Scrase and P/O Hastings, landed at Ursel owing to fuel shortage but the remainder landed safely back at Manston at 15.50 hours. In the evening after several drinks in the bar the Squadron made tracks for the Westgage where a New Year's Eve party was being held with a call into the popular Halmar Castle en route. A highly successful evening and the old year was ushered out in excellent style.

CHAPTER THIRTEEN

THE END IN SIGHT, JANUARY–SEPTEMBER 1945 – NO. 1 SQUADRON, MANSTON

1 JANUARY 1945

ORB: At 08.15 hours this morning the Squadron was briefed for an escort show to Lancasters bombing Ledbergen on the Dortmund-Ems Canal near Munster. Take off was scheduled for 09.20 but at 09.15 the weather closed in and we were unable to take part. The heavies went out, escorted by Mustangs from Andrews Field. The whole Wing stood by for a 'rush job' until 10.30 when 'Ops' instructed us to return to normal state. About mid-day the Squadron was released together with 91 Squadron so a game of football was organized between the 2 squadrons. Owing to leave and sickness however we were unable to turn out a strong side and we were beaten 3-1. During the evening the mess was almost deserted as most pilots adopted an early to bed policy in order to catch up on sleep!

Lancasters and Mosquitos acting as pathfinders for No. 5 Group carried out an accurate attack on a section of the Dortmund-Ems Canal. Half a mile of the canal banks were pitted with bomb craters with some parts breached. The Dortmund-Ems Canal, as its name implied, linked the North Sea port of Emden with the Ruhr but also, through a junction with the Mittelland Canal near Rheine, carried all the inland water-borne traffic between the Ruhr and central and eastern Germany. The traffic amounted to some thirty million tons a year and consisted largely of coal and coke being moved from the Ruhr and raw materials, such as iron ore, being carried to the furnaces and factories. There was one point where the canal was particularly vulnerable to air attack, namely in the neighbourhood of Landbergen, where the canal was carried over the River Glane in an aqueduct. Well aware of the danger, the Germans had constructed a second branch also across the river on an aqueduct; thus, should the first be blocked, there would be an alternative channel. At the same time elaborate camouflaging of the course of the Glane was attempted and safety gates were built on both branches of the canal to prevent long stretches being drained if the embankments were breached.

After the clear weather over the Christmas period which had proved so much to the advantage of the RAF, the Luftwaffe made a decided attempt to neutralise the air effort by an all out attack on Allied airfields in Belgium and Holland. These attacks succeeded in causing considerable losses to the Allies but were in no way comparable to those suffered by the Luftwaffe.

3 JANUARY 1945

ORB: Shortly after first light, 2 sections took off on weather reconnaissance missions over Holland, Belgium and France. All 4 aircraft returned safely after an uneventful trip under heavy cloud conditions. Two V2 contrails were seen in the Hague area. Two Ramrods were laid on today both of which were cancelled due to the bad weather. This afternoon we said goodbye to F/Lt W. Batchelor a most popular member of the Squadron. He joins 229 Squadron at Coltishall as a flight commander.

On the ground General Patton's 1st US Army launched attacks against the Germans in the south who were well organized and dug in. The weather had deteriorated with visibility on the ground reduced to two hundred yards or less and while advances were made, heavy snowfall bought their progress to a halt. Meanwhile in the north General Bernard Montgomery launched his offensive against Houffalize in an attempt to link up with Patton's army in the south.

4 JANUARY 1945

ORB: Ramrod 1425 to Ludwigshaven was put on for a first light take off this morning with the Squadron detailed to land and refuel at Ursel. Had the show taken place it would have constituted our deepest penetration to date, but due to bad weather over the target, it was cancelled.

On the right of the US 1st Army, British troops also attacked the Germans. In the south the 6th Airborne Division had flown in from the UK and secured the area around Bure after fierce fighting.

5 JANUARY 1945

ORB: Yesterday's show with a few minor changes was again laid on this morning and at 10.40 hours the Squadron led by our new CO Sqn Ldr Cox took off for Ursel where they refueled before they set course for Ludwigshaven Marshalling Yards. F/Lt Marshall returned to base with an oxygen leak, F/Lt Still returned with a rudder slightly damaged when taxiing out and F/Lt Stewart and his No. 2 returned as their overhead tanks were cutting. The remainder went to target and patrolled at 20,000 feet. Bombing appeared very good and concentrated with good visibility over the target. Intense heavy flak was put up over Ludwigshaven. On way home all remaining aircraft landed at Ursel owing to fuel shortage and they spent the night there and will return tomorrow.

160 Lancasters of No. 3 Group attacked the railway-yards at Ludwigshaven. Two Lancasters were lost. The Germans continued to press further south in the Ardennes after repeated attacks in the north had failed to provide a breakthrough. Central to

their plans was the capture of Bastogne and its road network. However dogged resistance by the Americans continued to pull German divisions away from the northern sectors until there were no less than 10 German divisions, including 3 crack SS divisions fighting for Bastogne by the 6 January. The German failure to capture Bastogne was the signal that their offensive in the Ardennes should be called off. They had not been able to get to the River Meuse, so vital to their plans and were not likely to in the face of increased Allied reinforcements.

6 JANUARY 1945

ORB: At 14.00 hours all 8 a/c took off from Ursel to return to base. Five of them landed back at base with weather closing in fast. The group captain and F/O Crocker had to put down at Frinton where they spent the night and F/Lt Pederson returned to Ursel.

7 JANUARY 1945

ORB: Two sections carried out 'dogs body' patrols shortly after first light and reported pretty poor weather the other side, also it is expected to close in over base around mid-day. At 10.15 the group captain and his No. 2 landed at base from Frinton and 15 minutes later F/Lt Pederson returned from Ursel. We were not surprised when a release from training came through at 11.00 hours. The Squadron gunnery officer F/O Darry lay on some practice air firing. We are pleased to report that yesterday W/O McKenzie became P/O McKenzie. 'Mac' has been with the Squadron for nearly 12 months having joined the Squadron at Lympne when they were on Typhoons. Besides being a capable and experienced pilot he is a most popular member of 1 Squadron and all concerned welcomed him to the officers mess. At 11.25 hours, Yellow Section, F/Lt Dalley and F/Lt Brown were scrambled to escort a Lockheed aircraft conveying a VIP to Brussels. They rendezvoused over base at 1,500 feet and crossed just west of Ostend. Losing height down to 300 feet below cloud base they reached Brussels safely at 12.30 hours and returned to Manston at 13.15 hours, flying back through a snowstorm and very poor visibility with 10/10 cloud and fog.

The VIP was the British Prime Minister Winston Churchill who together with his Chief of the Imperial General Staff (CIGS) spent two days with Generals Montgomery and Eisenhower who conveyed their thoughts that whilst they felt the Battle on the ground heavy, they were still confident of success.

8 JANUARY 1945

ORB: Today dawned with very poor visibility and a warning of snow so the Squadron was released from training at 11.00 hours.

On the ground and having realised his forces had failed to break the Allied front in the Ardennes Hitler ordered a retreat from the Ardennes on 8 January.

9 JANUARY 1945

ORB: One inch of snow fell during the night and heavy cloud in the morning with a cloud base of 600 feet. preventing operations. The Squadron was given a release and a football match was laid on between 1 and 91 Squadron Wing and 124 and 504 Squadron Wing. Our Wing won well and truly 6-0!

10 JANUARY 1945

ORB: A further heavy snowfall during the night and the weather made it quite unsuitable for flying. Keen snow fights between the pilots and ground crew ensued during the morning. In the evening the whole Squadron moved out to a local hostelry to toast the health of F/Lt Joe Dalley who on the 13th takes the dreaded plunge into marriage. Circumstances permitting as many pilots as can get away will attend the wedding ceremony.

11 JANUARY 1945

ORB: Ramrod 1430, an escort job to Lancasters bombing Krefeld Railway Traffic Centre was laid on for the early afternoon. The Squadron took off as planned but were recalled when just over the Dutch Islands in view of bad weather inland and returned to base with other Spitfire Squadrons also operating on the show. We welcomed back F/Lt Batchelor who landed here from a ground strafing show. 'Batch' is apparently very happy with 229 Squadron at Coltishall and will probably be able to return to them tomorrow, weather permitting.

152 Lancasters of No. 3 Group carried out a raid on the railway yards in the Uerdingen suburb of Krefeld.

12 JANUARY 1945

ORB: Preliminary warning was received during the night of a show for today but high winds approaching gale force with rain and low cloud put paid to all plans.

13 JANUARY 1945

Logbook: Cine gun formation.

ORB: Low cloud and poor visibility prevailed during the morning but a show was laid on for the afternoon with the Squadron acting as target cover to

150 Lancasters. Briefing took place but at lunchtime our part in the show was cancelled.

14 JANUARY 1945

Logbook: Ramrod 1433. Sweep Saarbrucken, Halifaxes bombing. Recalled bad weather.

ORB: An early briefing for Ramrod 1435 took place with the Squadron role that of fighter sweep in conjunction with 100 Halifaxes bombing Saarbrucken. Unfortunately the weather closed in and the Squadron was ordered to return home after being airborne for only 15 minutes.

A combined force of Halifaxes, Lancasters and Mosquitos from Nos 4, 6 and 8 Groups attacked Saarbrucken. One Halifax was shot down in France. The bombing on the railway yards was extremely accurate and effective.

15 JANUARY 1945

Logbook: Ramrod 1434. Escort Langendreen, 200 Lancasters bombing. Recalled bad weather.

ORB: Another escort show was put on this morning. This time the Squadron role was to provide escort to 75 Lancasters bombing marshalling yards at Langendreen.

Nos 6 and 8 Groups attacked the railway yards at Langendreen, a heavily populated district of Bochum in the Ruhr which had one of the largest railway stations in the city. Bomber Command continued to attack German industrial cities, communication centres, and rail marshalling yards to disrupt transport. No fewer than 50,000 tons of bombs were carried to these targets in both day and night raids during the first eight weeks of 1945.

The British bomber force was now at the height of its power and efficiency and, even though January and February brought particularly unfavourable weather, there was a higher average total of sorties for these months than in any previous winter of the war. With ground stations established on the edge of Germany and with the enemy air defence largely impotent, aircraft could now attack distant targets with a certainty of success, so the offensive was carried into industrial Saxony, where towns that had been previously untouched were largely destroyed. These attacks, particularly those directed against marshalling yards and bridges in the Ruhr, increased the confusion wrought throughout Germany by the earlier raids on rail and water transport. With this sharp deterioration in the transport position, the coal situation became so catastrophic that it was impossible to avoid the severe disruption in the whole of the German armaments industry.

16 JANUARY 1945

Logbook: aircraft test.

ORB: Another escort show to Lancasters bombing an oil plant in the Ruhr was laid on this morning but heavy cloud and mist the other side caused its cancellation.

By 16 January, the 1st and 3rd US Armies had joined up at Houffalize and the Allies controlled the original front before the German offensive in the Ardennes. The battle had dire consequences for the Germans; it cost them dear both in terms of men and equipment. Hitler's last-ditch attempt to turn the tide of the war had failed. During the battle the Germans had lost most of their remaining air force and their manpower had been significantly reduced. The Allies remained well equipped with no shortage of soldiers and a superior air force. That said, the German offensive had been mounted with skill and the attempt to drive a wedge between the British and US forces and to strike at the Allied main supply bases of Antwerp, Liege and Brussels had been a bold but desperate attempt to upset Allied progress towards the heart of Germany. They had played for time as they were under pressure on both the Eastern Front from the Russians and the Western Front from the British and US armies.

17 JANUARY 1945

Logbook: Rodeo 409. Fighter sweep Rhine. Return to Ursel.

ORB: The Squadron was briefed for a Rodeo fighter sweep at 15,000 feet. with a landing back at Ursel where they spent the night. The sweep was uneventful.

18 JANUARY 1945

ORB: The airfield strafing show laid on from Ursel was cancelled due to more bad weather that in turn prevented the Squadron from returning to Manston.

19 JANUARY 1945

ORB: Squadron weather-bound at Ursel.

20 JANUARY 1945

Logbook: Ursel to base.

ORB: Ten of the Squadron returned from Ursel this morning looking pretty cold and fed up with several days' growth of beard. F/O Thiele took off, lost his way and had to land back at Ursel. P/O McKenzie's aircraft needed a prop change so he too stayed behind.

21 JANUARY 1945

ORB: A further heavy snowfall during the night so nothing was laid on in view of the bad weather.

Following the failure of the German push in the Ardennes the US armies continued the bitter struggle to push them back from the Siegfried Line defences. Plans were now in hand to clear up the area between the Rhine and the Meuse from Dusseldorf to Nijmegen and establish a bridgehead north of the Ruhr. The operation was called Operation *Veritable* and involved the 9th US Army and the 8th Corps and 12th Corps from the British 2nd Army. In addition the 1st Canadian Army was to attack towards Nijmegen.

22 JANUARY 1945

ORB: Ramrod 1437 escort to 'heavies' bombing Sterkrade oil plant was laid on and then cancelled due to bad weather. Moved to new quarters the other side of the airfield and within close proximity to our wing mates No. 91 Squadron. The quarters are pretty restricted but our position for taking off is much better and our aircraft can stand on excellent hard standings with no fear of bogging down. F/Lt Dalley DMR returned from his honeymoon looking radiant and very happy. F/O Thiele and P/O McKenzie returned this afternoon from Ursel, mighty glad to be back with the Squadron again.

23 JANUARY 1945

ORB: The Squadron provided' dogsbody' sections and pink readiness today. AT 09.00 hours Pink Section was scrambled to investigate shipping in the estuary and the North Sea, all of which proved friendly.

24 JANUARY 1945

ORB: A rise in temperature bought a thaw but considerable mist so all airfields both on this side and over the water was clamped. Shortly after lunch the Squadron was given release and most of the pilots took advantage and visited Ramsgate or Margate.

25 JANUARY 1945

ORB: During the night temperatures dropped considerably and there was 22° of frost in the straits. The snow on the ground has frozen over and the roads are treacherous with ice.

26 JANUARY 1945

ORB: The Squadron provided 'dogs body' sections this morning but the weather was so bad with more snow and low cloud, they were cancelled.

By the 26th the British 12th Corps had completed its task of clearing the Roermond Triangle. It had been a large-scale mopping up operation carried out under extremely difficult circumstances. The Germans again suffered heavy losses and apart from a small bridgehead near Roermond had been pushed back east of the Roer so that the captured area was handed over to the 9th US Army. The weather however remained poor and whilst there was a thaw in temperature, the floods played havoc with communications.

27 JANUARY 1945

ORB: Snow fell during the night and so the Ramrod that was laid on was scrubbed. During the past 16 days only one show has taken place and we are apparently going through one of the worst spells of bad weather with intense cold for many years.

28 JANUARY 1945

ORB: An escort show to heavies bombing Cologne marshalling yards was laid on this morning, take off being schedule for 13.20 hours. The Squadron was briefed and were ready in their cockpits when it was cancelled.

29 JANUARY 1945

ORB: A further escort and Ramrod laid on was cancelled due to bad weather just as the Squadron was to take off again.

30 JANUARY 1945

ORB: A sudden rise in temperature together with heavy rain rapidly disbursed the heavy snow and ice that has been lying about for many days, but poor visibility prevented any flying.

31 JANUARY 1945

ORB: The rise in temperatures was maintained throughout the day, but again nothing was laid on.

FEBRUARY 1945, NO. 1 SQUADRON MANSTON

1 FEBRUARY 1945

Logbook: Ramrod 1448. Flank sweep. 160 Lancasters bombing Munchen Gladbach.

ORB: Shortly after 15.00 hours the squadron took off to act as flank sweep to Lancasters bombing railroad crossing at Munchen Gladbach. This was the first show to take place since the 17th of last month and now that the weather has taken a definite turn for the better perhaps we shall see more activity with less cancellations. The bombers bombed through 10/10th cloud at 4–5,000 feet. so no results were observed. It was a bit tricky landing owing to poor visibility and low cloud. We also today, welcomed a new member to the Squadron P/O Bahadurji who hails from India and was previously with 63 Squadron. His name was more than we could cope with so we nicknamed him 'Barry'!

160 Lancasters of No. 3 Group attacked the general town area of Munchen Gladbach through 8-10/10ths clouds so the results of the raid could not be seen. 1 Lancaster crashed in France.

2 FEBRUARY 1945

ORB: A Rhubarb escort show was laid on today for an early afternoon take off but was cancelled later in the day owing to bad weather. The Squadron did provide a 'dogs body' section to Eindhoven, Rotterdam and Amiens area that proved uneventful.

3 FEBRUARY 1945

Logbook: Rodeo 411. Fighter sweep 13,000ft Rheine airfields. Return to Ursel. Cooks tour of the front line!

ORB: The Squadron with Wing Cdr Oxspring took off at 14.10 hours to carry out a fighter sweep of the Rheine area. One aircraft returned early with a hood jammed but the rest swept the area according to plan but uneventfully. There was a little heavy flak over the front line. The Squadron landed back at Ursel where they spent the night ready for another show the following morning.

4 FEBRUARY 1945

ORB: The show fixed from Ursel did not take place owing to bad weather.

5 FEBRUARY 1945

Logbook: Ursel to Manston.

ORB: The Squadron returned from their abortive stay at Ursel.

6 FEBRUARY 1945

ORB: A weakened Squadron, we could only muster 7 aircraft carried out a sweep in conjunction with Lancasters bombing railway viaduct near Paderborn without incident and then returned to Ursel and then to base.

7 FEBRUARY 1945

Logbook: Ramrod 1454. Withdrawal cover at 24,000ft for 150 Lancasters bombing the oil installations at Wanne Eickel. Cloud cover over target so failed to rendezvous.

ORB: 12 aircraft took off at 14.45 hours to cover Lancasters bombing a fuel oil target in the Ruhr but owing to extremely bad weather, thick layers of cloud, they did not make their rendezvous and returned to base at 16.45 hours.

100 Lancasters of No. 3 Group to attack the oil plant at Wanne-Eickel. Only 75 aircraft were able to bomb in wintry conditions that scattered the force.

By now most of the synthetic oil plants in the Ruhr were no longer operating. Two notable developments marked the opening of the final stage in the campaign against German oil supplies. Firstly, the US 15th Air Force had carried out over a period of ten days the most remarkable series of sustained operations in the whole offensive. In particular, they achieved the immobilisation of the Silesian synthetic plants clinched four weeks later by their capture by the Russian Army and stopped production in the synthetic plant at Brux, which was working up to a substantial output after it had been heavily damaged in 1944. Secondly, RAF Bomber Command continued its successful attacks on the synthetic plants at Politz and Leuna and the oil campaign in particular. Strong forces of Lancasters made further attacks on Leuna and Politz and also bombed the large oil plants at Brux, Wanne-Eickel, and Zeitz. In addition, the Benzol plants at Dortmund, Castrop-Rauxel, Fortsetzunge, and Langendreer were also subjected to heavy raids. By the beginning of February the plant at Wanne Eickel had been reduced to 'a shambles of wrecked buildings, shattered tanks and buckled piping.' It did not resume production again.

Extensive preliminary air operations were undertaken against railways, bridges and ferries serving the battle area that would be the push across the Rhine and the Battle of the Rhineland. During the night of 7 and 8 February Bomber Command delivered heavy raids against Cleve and Goch and on the main communication centres to the Germans rear. Sqn Ldr David Cox recalled:

One of the longest penetrations we did was to Paderborn, well into Germany. Another was to Mannheim, very picturesque with snow on the ground. Of course we had the 90 gallon drop tanks and would refuel at Maldegem in Belgium or Ursel in Holland.

8 FEBRUARY 1945

ORB: Unsuitable flying weather, kept our aircraft on the ground.

A heavy artillery barrage preceded the launch of infantry attacks across the front from the Reichswald Forest and Nijmegen and Cleve and Goch in the north where the 1st Canadian Army attacked, to Geldern in the middle where the 2nd British Army attacked and the south towards Munchen Gladbach and Cologne where the US 1st and 9th Armies attacked. The biggest difficulties on the ground were the extensive minefields and the appalling weather conditions.

9 FEBRUARY 1945

ORB: The Squadron with the usual long range tanks carried out a fighter sweep in the Osmabruck area without incident, no flak, no guns no nothing. They landed at Ursel where they stayed the night.

10 FEBRUARY 1945

ORB: 10 aircraft operating from Ursel took off on a fighter sweep to the Munster – Zuider Zee area. One aircraft returned with engine trouble, the remainder swept through the area as planned. Intense accurate light flak was experienced in the Leiden area. A V2 was seen leaving the ground near The Hague. All aircraft returned to base.

Flooding around the Nijmegen – Kranenburg areas prevented operations on the ground as some of the road network was under at least two feet of water.

11 FEBRUARY 1945

ORB: Two aircraft returned from Ursel.

12–13 FEBRUARY 1945

ORB: Bad weather prevented any flying.

This was the night, despite bad weather at Manston, that the RAF and USAF dropped tons of bombs on Dresden. The name has become synonymous with the brutality of war. The Russian advance towards Berlin had reached within 50 miles of the outskirts of the city and the Allied Chiefs of Staff had discussed the possibility of assisting the Russian advance through further heavy bombing. Dresden was reported to be a vital command centre and the centre of its rail network linking Eastern and Southern Germany with Berlin, Prague and Vienna. A series of heavy attacks by night upon these administrative and control centres was likely to cause considerable delays in the deployment of troops to the front and cause panic and chaos within the Cities selected. Communications came as a secondary target and in this respect Dresden's fate was sealed. Whilst bad weather prevented the US Eighth Air force and the escort to be provided by the Squadrons at Manston from taking off, weather cleared during the night and nearly 800 RAF Bomber Command planes let loose 650,000 incendiaries and 8000lb of high explosives and hundreds of 4,000lb bombs in two waves of attack. They faced very little anti-aircraft fire. The Bombing caused horrific damage and fires everywhere with a concentration in the centre of the city. In the city people huddled in shelters and basements against the onslaught form the skies. Roofs and buildings crumpled under the weight of the bombs and the emergency services were paralysed as roads became blocked and buildings reduced to rubble. Flames leapt from building to building and people were either vaporised or suffered slow suffering deaths as they suffocated in the smoke and scolding air. The flames provided a beacon for the second wave of bombers as smoke also rose to a height of nearly 15,000ft. This time, the bomber crews aimed for the centre of the fires. The flames consumed everything, Roads that were not blocked turned to rivers of tar as this melted and people were sucked into the fires by convection currents. Emergency crews and people trying to escape choked to death in the streets as Dresden collapsed around them. The fires could be seen from 200 miles away. It was not the end of the misery. The two-night time attacks were followed by another attack in daylight by 311 USAF heavy bombers, which reached the smouldering city just before noon. Pilots witnessed fires and reported they were still blazing from the night before. According to reports following the raids, nearly three quarters of the city centre's nine square miles were simply obliterated. Of 220,000 houses nearly 86,000 were either completely destroyed or heavily damaged. Estimates of the number of dead ranged wildly and German propaganda played up the carnage to demonstrate the extent of Allied brutality claiming nearly 400,000 people had died. Post war the estimates of the dead range from 25,000 to 40,000. From a strategic point of view the destruction of Dresden prevented the city from becoming a control centre for German forces on the Eastern Front but the end results remain questionable. The attack did little to weaken German resistance in the East against the Russians who did not capture Dresden until the 8 May. Perhaps the greatest impact of the Dresden raid was on the post war opinion of Bomber Command itself that took the brunt of the blame and the barometer by which its actions became judged.

Post-war it became clear just how vital Manston had been. An emergency landing ground in the Battle of Britain, Manston became the most important forward base for the RAF. Besides the Spitfire Wings based there when large-scale operations began over the continent and its ability to cope with as many as 14 Squadrons taking off and landing in any one day, hundreds of fighters and bombers, damaged or short of fuel after RAF raids into Germany were saved by the huge concrete runway that had been built. Work had begun in June 1943 and the huge runway 3,000 yards long and 250 yards wide had been completed just a few weeks before D Day in 1944 and they coped with thousands of emergency landings of returning Allied aircraft. The 'radio-telephone' conversation was often carried on over 7 different channels and when they were all operating at the same time the tower looked like an American film studio representation of a Wall Street office. The busiest period was the afternoon of 13 January 1945 when between 3 and 4 p.m., 64 Fortresses and 67 P 51 Mustangs were all landed safely. It was also at Manston that FIDO, the device for landing in fog was first installed. It is remembered as a lifesaver by returning aircrew:

> The Manston people below had the FIDO. (Fog Intensive Dispersal Of). Always, everything described in a backwards manner. This was a complete necklace of burning gas around the huge mile square asphalt landing area, burning a beautiful bright light and dispelling the ground fog and rain. I brought our plane in very fast and low over the edge of the field, dumping the throttles in the process. Waited impatiently for the speed to burn off, then down went the under carriage and flap … told George to 'drag his feet at the rear.' We finally touched down … a three pointer! As we taxied in, the nicest snowflakes started drifting down and a land rover arrived to lead us clear of the huge 'parking lot' runway. By the next morning a foot of snow covered the base, and we had a lovely two-day holiday from the war.

14 FEBRUARY 1945

ORB: At 09.30 hours, the Squadron took off on a fighter sweep in the Osmabruck area in conjunction with a Lancasters raid on rail targets. F/Lt Brown in Yellow 1 saw 2 jet aircraft 20 miles south east of Zwolle at 15,000 feet. They approached to within 4 miles of the formation and then dashed away eastwards. V2 contrails were seen in the Hook and Ruhr areas about 100 wagons were sighted in sidings just east of Zwolla and a large number of barges were seen on a canal nearby. Red 2 P/O Weller also saw a large number of covered trucks on the road south east of Zwolla. Squadron landed at Ursel.

15 FEBRUARY 1945

ORB: Squadron weather bound at Ursel.

16 FEBRUARY 1945

ORB: At 15.00 hours the Squadron took off to cover 150 Lancasters bombing targets at Wesel. One aircraft returned early with engine trouble, the remainder covered the bombers as planned. Bombing results excellent. Spasmodic heavy flak from Wesel. All landed back safely at Ursel.

17–18 FEBRUARY 1945

ORB: No flying owing to fog and mist over base and in the Channel.

February brought the most intense period of evacuation of ground troops and wounded from the Continent.

> One day 200 seriously wounded American Infantrymen in 8 C47s were diverted into Manston because of bad weather, which closed down throughout the United Kingdom. The station hospital had only 30 beds available, and there were no British or American hospitals within 70 miles. With an advance radio warning of only 25 minutes, all local ARP ambulance crews and civilian ambulances responded with a fleet of 20 vehicles. These ambulances transported the overflow of 175 patients to the Margate hospital within half an hour of the aircraft landing, despite the driving rain and sleet. Next day the process was reversed and the wounded soldiers were transported back to the C47s that took off, but the weather suddenly closed in again and they returned to Manston where the sequence was repeated. Because of continued bad flying weather they were eventually evacuated to hospitals on trains.

19 FEBRUARY 1945

ORB: An escort show to a Skymaster conveying the Right Hon Winston Churchill back to Northolt from the Continent was laid on today, but at the last moment Group decided to allow a Bentwaters Squadron to do the job. A Ramrod came through in the afternoon target cover to Lancasters bombing the bridge at Wesel but this was also cancelled.

20 FEBRUARY 1945

Logbook: Practice Formation. Visit to Brighton.

ORB: No flying.

21 FEBRUARY 1945

Logbook: 21st Roy Hussey killed.

ORB: A show was laid on this morning but was later cancelled owing to bad weather the other side. Squadron formation flying took place in the afternoon when the G.C. led the Squadron over Brighton. No. 1 being Brighton's own Squadron were soon spotted by the local inhabitants with the result that the local press published photographs the following day of No. 1 in formation flight.

The entry in Rodney's logbook records the death the day before of his good friend Roy Hussey and Rodney felt his tragic death keenly. Roy was completing his second tour of duty flying P 51 Mustangs with No. 19 Squadron who had just moved the week beforehand from Andrews Field in Essex to Peterhead in Scotland. The Squadron had flown to Dallachy a nearby Beaufighter Station for tea and a talk with the guys there. Dallachy and Banff were the homes of what had become known as the Banff strike Wing and the Squadrons there flew operations against German U-Boats and ports in Germany and Scandinavia. The losses incurred by the Strike Wing were heavy. As the Squadron was coming into land Roy's plane stalled off his turn, spun in on the approach and he was killed.

The Official Record Book for No. 19 Squadron records – 'Good weather and in the afternoon as there was no show on it was decided that the Squadron should do some practice flying and then land at Dallachy, the Beaufighter Station for tea and a talk with them. A most unfortunate accident occurred there as the Squadron was coming into land, F/Lt Hussey DFC and DFM, our B Flight Commander, spun in on the approach and was killed. His loss will be very deeply felt on the Squadron.'

F/Lt Roy Jack Hubert Hussey DFC and DFM is buried at Christ Church Churchyard, Coxley in Somerset, the village where his family lived. Rodney still visits Roy's grave to this day.

22 FEBRUARY 1945

ORB: We provided 'dogsbody' section today when 2 aircraft carried out a weather reconnaissance to Amsterdam – Eindhoven area that proved uneventful. In the afternoon the Squadron provided escort to 80 Lancasters bombing Gelsenkirchen power station. Operation went to plan and the bombing appeared well concentrated. Heavy accurate flak directed at leading bombers was encountered over the target and one Lancaster was seen to blow up after being hit. No fighters were seen and the Squadron landed back at Ursel where they spent the night.

US troops attacked across the River Roer after an improvement in weather conditions meant the ground was drying out.

23 FEBRUARY 1945

ORB: Squadron airborne from Ursel to provide escort to 180 Lancasters bombing Gelsenkirchen. Four aircraft returned early, 3 with mechanical problems, one as escort. The remainder rendezvoused with the bombers who were extremely straggled at 18,000 feet and in an attempt to formate better with the bombers climbed to 22,000 feet without reaching cloud top. They finally orbited to the west of the target at Krefeld area. Markers were seen but no bombing was observed. Moderate heavy flak came up from the target bursting in cloud. Squadron returned to Ursel at 16.10 hours where they spent the night.

24 FEBRUARY 1945

ORB: At 15.30 hours 10 of the squadron took off to act as escort to 290 Halifax bombing Kemen near Dortmund. Bombers were late at the rendezvous and at the target. No bombing was seen owing to 10/10th cloud over the target. Intense heavy flak accurate for the front of the bomber stream over the target area and one bomber was hit and seen to break up over the target. One Spitfire landed at Ursel short of fuel. The rest returned to Manston.

US 1st Army assault against Duren, with at least 4 divisions across the River Roer.

25 FEBRUARY 1945

ORB: A fighter sweep in conjunction with a Ramrod to Dortmund was laid on for this afternoon with the Squadron due to sweep the Rheine area. Show cancelled due to poor weather.

26 FEBRUARY 1945

ORB: At 15.00 hours the Squadrons 12 aircraft took off for Waldegen the other 11 Group forward airfield where they will stay the night with a view to operating from there tomorrow.

The bridgehead established by the US was some twenty miles wide and ten miles deep. The towns of Erkenlez and Munchen Gladbach were captured after the US 9th Army had broken through.

27 FEBRUARY 1945

ORB: Today we welcome F/Sgt T. Jeffrey who joins from No. 55 OTU Kirton in Lindsay. At 13.40 hours the Squadron took off from Waldegen to act as escort to 150 Lancasters bombing Gelsenkirchen. One aircraft aborted with engine trouble, the rest rendezvoused and went to target as planned. Bombing was not seen. Two Lancasters were hit by flak and seen to go down. Flak was heavy and accurate for height and direction. Squadron landed at Waldegen at 16.00 hours.

The 'Czech Invasion' took place on 27 February when Wing Cdr Hlado led in Nos 310, 312 and 313 Squadrons which were to operate from Manston as the 'Czech Wing'. They and the Manston Spitfire Wings were soon providing escorts using Maldegem and Ursel on the continent as their forward bases.

28 FEBRUARY 1945

Logbook: Magister 1. Manston to Hawkinge. 2. Hawkinge to Manston.

ORB: Twelve aircraft took off to act as escort to 300 Lancasters bombing Gelsenkirchen. Bombing was unobserved owing to 10/10th cloud at 5,000 feet over the whole area. Fairly intense accurate flak was directed at the bombers from the target area.

MARCH 1945, NO. 1 SQUADRON MANSTON

1 MARCH 1945

ORB: 12 Spitfires took off at 13.00 hours to escort 150 Lancasters bombing Karen near Dortmund. One Spitfire returned early with technical trouble, the remaining rendezvoused as planned at 15,000 feet and escorted bombers to target. Bombing was unobserved due to 10/10th cloud at 7,000 feet over the whole area. Spasmodic but heavy flak experienced over the target area and landed back at base at 16.35 hours. At 17.25 hours they took off again for Northolt where they spent the night in preparation for an escort to a VIP the following morning. That evening the CO led the boys into London on a successful sortie that provided a rare break for all concerned.

Ground Troops reached the River Rhine in two places from Neuss to Nijmegen and were preparing for the crossing. The Germans were faced with being encircled by the US and Canadian Armies and pulled back across the Rhine but huge numbers of prisoners were taken. Conditions on the ground were appalling, with mud and slush everywhere. The heavily wooded areas lacked decent roads and tracks and low-lying areas remained flooded. The crippling losses sustained by the Germans brought the end of the war forward to a matter of weeks. They did not have the manpower to raise new reinforcements and their industry was taking such a pounding from the bombing attacks that it could not have supported fresh divisions. The remaining oil refineries and storage plants together with transportation links were being subjected to increasingly heavy air attacks and were being reduced to a state of chaos.

2 MARCH 1945

Logbook: Spitfire Hawkinge to Manston.

ORB: The escort mission for the VIP turned out to be for the Right Hon Winston Churchill and went without hitch this morning and the Squadron landed back at base at 13.40 hours. There was a fierce cross wind blowing at the time of landing and the CO's aircraft swung slightly and dipped a wing, was caught by the fierce gust of wind and turned over. Sqn Ldr Cox was extricated and luckily only slightly injured, but it was a pretty near thing. He should be ok in a day or so.

Sqn Ldr David Cox was lucky to survive what proved to be a nasty crash. It came at a time when the Squadron was asked to escort a number of VIPs to the Continent including Winston Churchill. It was thought that he had specifically asked for No. 1 Squadron because they had escorted him to France in 1940. David Cox recalls:

> We did a couple of escorts to Winston Churchill but the bloody stupid part about it was that we were ordered to wear our best uniforms which was pretty ridiculous as the PM never saw us but at least it got us a free trip to the West End. The US president had loaned him his Skymaster to fly across and the CO of the escort – me – had to go in and see the captain. The man said to me 'Keep your bloody silly fighters away from my aeroplane.' I replied that he might be better employed as a trolley-bus driver! Anyway, on the escort some P 47s came close and being curious we had to weave our silly bloody fighters around the Skymaster to fend them off.
>
> Concerning the crash, taking off from Ursel I felt we hit material on the runway and managed to damage my tail wheel. When I landed at Northolt I quickly discovered the tail wheel was jammed at 90 degrees and this resulted in a cartwheel in which I lost a wing and smashed up the aircraft quite a bit, becoming trapped in the cockpit. Talk about the longest two minutes of my life. The Squadron sent a two-seat Auster for me as there was a squadron party that evening but Flying Control would not let us take off on a night flight. I wasn't about to miss the party, so off we went. It soon got dark and my Aussie pilot, F/O Harrison, started to get worried. I told him to head south until we picked up the sea. Luckily some Mosquito aircraft were landing at Lympne and the airfield lights were put on, so we landed amongst the Mossies and got to the party. It was only some time later that I discovered that I had been considered for a Court Martial for flying in the dark and against regulations.

3 MARCH 1945

ORB: An early show was laid on with briefing at 07.30 hours but after being put back twice, our role in the Ramrod was cancelled. On Monday the 5th the Squadron will be holding a squadron party at the Westcliff Theatre, Ramsgate. The gathering will comprise Squadron and echelon ground personnel and all told we should muster about 400 including guests.

4 MARCH 1945

ORB: Another early show as escort to Lancasters bombing Wanne-Eichel was put on this morning but the weather changed and the show was cancelled.

5 MARCH 1945

Logbook: Dogsbody 12,000ft to Ostende, Amsterdam, Felixtowe, Manston.

ORB: No operational flying but the Squadron party at the Westcliff Theatre was a thoroughly good show with ground crews enjoying themselves to the utmost, drinking and dancing. Our late CO W/C Burke was there with a small party of other officers including F/Lt Batchelor. The 'show' drew to a close at about 11.30 p.m.

Bomber Command launched nearly 900 bombers in two daylight raids against Cologne. When American troops entered the city a few days later they found it also in ruins.

6 MARCH 1945

ORB: At. 09.35 hours, 2 Spitfires took off from Northolt to escort VIP to Le Bourget. They flew through 8/10th cloud for 85 minutes and escorted VIP to his destination landing back at base at 12.05 hours. No further operational flying.

7 MARCH 1945

ORB: No operational flying.

The US 9th Army secured the Bridge at Remagan, the importance of which was vital in the ensuing operations to cross the Rhine.

8 MARCH 1945

ORB: Today we learned that F/Lt Ian 'Mick' Maskilll our 'A' Flight Commander has been appointed CO of No. 91 Squadron. Mick has been with us for approximately a year and is held in the highest esteem by everyone concerned with the Squadron. He is a fine pilot and a most able leader and leaves us with the best wishes of all concerned. In taking over 91 Squadron we shall still be seeing quite a bit of him as the Squadron are of course, our Wing mates.

9 MARCH 1945

Logbook: Manston to Maldegem.

ORB: At 10.00 hours the Squadron moved to Maldegem where they landed at 11.10 hours. Just over an hour and a half later they took off as escort to 150 Lancasters bombing an embankment of the Dortmund-Ems Canal. The operation went off as planned, the bombers bombed the target through cloud. A fair amount of heavy accurate flak was put up from the target area.

Meanwhile US 3rd Army advanced towards the Rhine at Coblenz and subsequently established a bridgehead south-west of the city across the River Moselle.

10 MARCH 1945

ORB: F/Lt Dalley and F/Lt Harrison took off at 10.10 hours and escorted a VIP to Brussels without event. At very short notice the Squadron was instructed to move to Maldegem to spend the night there in preparation for a show tomorrow.

11 MARCH 1945

Logbook: Ramrod 1490. Target cover at 23,000ft for 1050 Lancasters and Halifaxes bombing Essen. Return to Maldegem.

ORB: At 14.15 hours the Squadron took off from Maldegem to act as escort cover to 1050 Lancasters bombing the Marshalling Yards at Essen. Squadron covered the raid without incident and landed back at Maldegem where they again spent the night.

Bomber Command carried out its largest daylight operation of the war. A daylight raid to bomb Essen would prove to be the last Bomber Command attack on the already heavily-bombed city. Most of the city already lay in ruins. 7,000 people had been killed in air raids and the population of 648,000 had fallen to 310,000 by the end of March. It proved to be the largest number of aircraft ever dispatched to concentrate on one target, and comprised 1079 bombers (750 Lancasters 293 Halifaxes and 36 Mosquitoes). 4,661 tons of bombs were dropped on Oboe-directed sky markers through complete cloud cover. The attacking force was escorted to the target by 18 Mustang squadrons. No. 1 Squadron from Maldegem together with another 6 Spitfire squadrons operating from other continental airfields covered the bombers withdrawal. The attack was very accurate and virtually paralysed Essen until US troops entered the city later in the war.

12 MARCH 1945

Logbook: Ramrod 1492. Target cover 19,000 ft for 1050 Lancasters and Halifaxes bombing Dortmund. Return to Maldegem. Returned with No. 2 with faulty fuel line. Some flak.

ORB: A further show laid on today and at 15.25 hours the Squadron led by Wing Cdr Oxspring took off to escort Lancasters and Halifaxes bombing targets at Dortmund. F/O Still returned to Maldegem with fuel feed trouble that developed over the Ruhr and had to use his hand pump right through the return journey. He made a good landing but was on the point of collapse when getting out of the cockpit. F/Lt Scrase accompanied him back. The remainder escorted the bombers as planned. One heavy went down over the target, as flak was intense, heavy and accurate for the bomber stream. Squadron returned to Maldegem.

Another 1108 Bomber Command aircraft – 748 Lancasters, 292 Halifaxes, 68 Mosquitos attacked Dortmund. This was another new record to a single target, a record that would stand till the end of the war. Another record tonnage of bombs – 4,851 – was dropped through cloud on to the unfortunate city. The bombs fell mainly in the centre and south of the city. This final raid on the city stopped production so effectively that it would have been many months before any substantial recovery could have occurred.

13 MARCH 1945

Logbook: Ramrod 1493. Escort at 18,000ft for 285 Halifaxes and Lancasters bombing Barmen. Return to Manston.

ORB: Ramrod 1493. At 15.00 hours the squadron led by Wing Cdr Oxspring took off from Maldegem to escort in front of 285 Lancasters and Halifaxes bombing target at Barmen. Although markers were seen over the target, the bombing was unobserved owing to cloud cover. There was slight inaccurate flak over the target. When 10–15 miles east-south-east of Brussels, Yellow 1, F/Lt Brown called up saying he could only get 'minus boost' so the Wing Cdr told him to land at Brussels with his No. 2. This he managed to do. The rest of the Squadron landed back at Manston.

Bomber Command sent 354 aircraft – 319 Halifaxes, 24 Lancasters, 20 Mosquitos – of Nos 4, 6 and 8 Groups to Wuppertal and Barmen. The attack took place over a cloud-covered target and the bombs fell slightly east of the area intended, covering the eastern half of the Barmen district and extending into Schwelm.

Bomber Command had dispatched over 2,500 sorties by daylight to Ruhr targets in a 3-day period. Approximately 10,650 tons of bombs had been dropped through cloud with sufficient accuracy to cripple two cities and one town. The bomber losses were only five aircraft, a casualty rate of 0.2 per cent. The results showed the great power wielded by Bomber Command at this stage of the war, its technical efficiency and the weakness of the German defence.

14 MARCH 1945

Logbook: Ramrod 1496. Escort at 21,000 ft for 90 Lancasters to Heinrichshuttel Benzol Plant near Recklingshausen. Given the cloud little to see.

ORB: We provided the 'dogsbody' section this morning to Dutch Islands and both sections carried out their tasks uneventfully. AT 15.15 hours the Squadron left Manston to escort 90 Lancasters bombing targets on the Dortmund-Ems Canal. No bombing observed due to cloud cover. There was intense and accurate flak over the target area. Squadron landed at Maldegem where they spent the night.

15 MARCH 1945

Logbook: Ramrod 1497. Escort at 22,000 ft to 70 Halifaxes bombing benzol plant at Castrop Rauxel. Wonderful bombing.

ORB: Today's show was to Castrop Rauxel Distillery Plant and the Squadron role was to escort 70 Halifaxes bombing the target. Bombing appeared good and black smoke and flames were visible from the Dutch Islands on the way out.

On the ground, the US 3rd Army pushed forward from the bridgehead established at Coblenz and eastwards from Trier while the 7th Army attacked between the Rhine and Saarbrucken.

16 MARCH 1945

ORB: No shows today but two spots of excitement in the form of scrambles, one to escort a 'distressed' Mosquito into base and the other to investigate an 'X' raid which turned out to be a friendly Meteor. Congratulations are in order to F/O Bob Bridgeman on his promotion to F/Lt having been with us nearly a year and following hard on the heels of his fellow Australian and friend F/Lt Pete Crocker.

17 MARCH 1945

ORB: Ramrod 1500 took place this afternoon. All 12 aircraft with the usual 90-gallon tanks took off, 'hopped' over to Maldegem, dined and then hurried off to escort 75 Lancasters bombing Dortmund coking plant. P/O Bahadurji 'Barry' returned early with de-icer trouble otherwise the operation was uneventful. Again no bombing was seen, as there was 10/10th cloud up to 20,000 feet. There were a few bursts of heavy flak from the target area and the Squadron returned to base after a trip lasting all told 3 hours 20 minutes.

18 MARCH 1945

ORB: Today dawned bright and clear with everyone expecting an early show – nothing doing and the Squadron was released for training.

19 MARCH 1945

Logbook: 1. Manston to Ursel. 2. Ramrod 1500. Escort at 21,000ft to 75 Lancasters bombing benzol plant at Recklingshausen.

ORB: Squadron escorted rear of 75 Lancasters bombing benzol plant at Recklinghausen. They landed at Ursel on route. The bombers were 15 minutes late on target but the bombing appeared concentrated and five large

explosions were seen in the target area, intense flak put up which broke up the bomber formation and the Squadron landed back at Ursel where they spent the night.

20 MARCH 1945

Logbook: Ramrod 1506. Escort 20,000ft to 120 Halifaxes bombing railway workshops at Recklinghausen. Return to Manston.

ORB: Squadron took off from Ursel to escort rear of 120 Halifaxes bombing rail workshops at Recklinghausen. 1 Spitfire turned back with technical trouble and the remainder escorted as planned. No bombing observed owing to cloud over the target. There was heavy and intense flak again. The Squadron landed back at Manston.

21 MARCH 1945

Logbook: 1. Manston to Ursel. 2. Ramrod 1507. Escort at 23,000ft for 150 Lancasters bombing marshalling yards and viaduct at Munster. Return to Manston.

ORB: Shortly after first light, the Squadron 'hopped' over to Ursel where they landed at 08.20 hours. At. 12.00 hours they took off to escort 150 Lancasters bombing the Munster area, one Spit returned with mechanical trouble and the bombs were late at the R/V and target. Just before reaching Munster they split up into 3 sections and bombs were seen to go down on the airfield, railway and town. Several large fires were started and one bomber was hit and seen to crash. Flak was heavy and accurate. Squadron landed back at Manston 14.55 hours.

22 MARCH 1945

Logbook: 1. Manston to Ursel. 2. Ramrod 1511. Escort at 10,000ft for 100 Lancasters bombing Bocholt. Return to Manston. 3. Manston to Northolt.

ORB: Another show via Ursel was laid on this morning following closely on the cancellation of 'dogsbody' sections for which the Squadron was providing 4 aircraft. Squadron took off and landed at Ursel from where they were airborne again at 13.15 hours escorting 100 Lancasters to Bocholt. The bombing appeared concentrated and a pall of black smoke covered the target area. Squadron returned to base at 15.35 hours. They were given sufficient time to refuel, eat and change before becoming airborne again for Northolt where they landed a little after 6 p.m. under conditions of much haze and poor visibility. F/O Recile had back luck in landing and ran off the runway. His aircraft is badly damaged but he is ok. The Squadron is staying at Northolt tonight in

preparation for a VIP escort tomorrow. A sortie into London and Sheppards in particular was laid on by the CO.

23 MARCH 1945

Logbook: The Squadron acted as VIP escort to Mr Churchill!

ORB: At 14.40 hours the Squadron took off to escort a Dakota conveying the Right Hon Winston Churchill to Volkel. This is the Prime Minister's second visit to the Continent recently and each time the Squadron has escorted him there. We seem to be singled out for this purpose and regard it as a great honour and credit to the Squadron. The escort was carried out uneventfully and according to plan. The Squadron circled Volkel whilst the Dakota landed safely.

Churchill wanted to be with General Montgomery for the preparations for Operation *Varsity*, the Rhine crossing the following day. He recalls in his memoirs:

> I desired to be with our Army at the crossing and Montgomery made me welcome. Taking only my secretary Jock Colville and 'Tommy' with me, I flew in the afternoon of the 23rd by Dakota from Northolt to the British Headquarters near Venlo. The Commander in Chief conducted me to the caravan in which he lived and moved. I found myself in the comfortable wagon I had used before. We dined at 7 o'clock and an hour later we repaired with strict punctuality to Montgomery's map wagon. Here were displayed all the maps kept from hour to hour by a select group of officers. The whole plan of our deployment and our attack was easily comprehended. We were to force a passage over the Rhine at ten points on a twenty-mile front from Rheinsberg to Rees. All our resources were to be used.

24 MARCH 1945

Logbook: Spitfire 21. Experience on type. Landing of airborne army between Wesel and Rees. The Squadron escorted the tug and glider stream from Brussels to Lille.

ORB: A big day dawned: Operation *Varsity* took place a little after first light and the biggest airborne invasion in history. Over 1,500 Halifaxes, Stirlings and Dakotas with a similar number of Horsa and Hamilcar gliders flew across the Rhine to Wesel. Large forces of glider troops and paratroops were dropped in that area and are successfully mopping up enemy resistance. The Squadron's role was patrolling along the stream en route to its objective. No huns came up. There was a fair amount of flak. All our aircraft returned safely to Ursel and finally Manston. We learnt today that our CO Sqn Ldr Cox DFC and Bar has been offered a Wing Commander Flying Post in the Far East and he has accepted it. Our best wishes from all members of the Squadron go with him over his appointment.

Operation *Varsity* was a joint American–British airborne operation and involved more than 16,000 paratroopers and several thousand aircraft. It was the largest single airborne operation in history. It formed part of Operation *Plunder*,the effort by 21st Army Group under Field Marshal Bernard Montgomery to cross the Rhine and from there enter northern Germany. The operation was meant to help the British 21st Army Group secure a foothold across the Rhine in western Germany by landing two airborne divisions on the eastern bank of the river near the towns of Hamminkeln and Wesel.

The plans called for dropping two airborne divisions by parachute and glider behind German lines near Wesel. Drawn from US XVIII Airborne Corps, they were instructed to capture key territory and to generally disrupt German defence to aid the advance of Allied ground forces.

The British 6th Airborne Division was ordered to capture the towns of Schnappenberg and Hamminkeln, clear part of the Diersfordter Wald (Diersfordt Forest) of German forces, and secure three bridges over the River Issel. The US 17th Airborne Division was to capture the town of Diersfordt and clear the rest of the Diersfordter Wald of any remaining German forces. The two divisions would then hold the territory they had captured until relieved by advancing units of 21st Army Group, and then join in the general advance into northern Germany.

Pilot error caused paratroopers from the 513th Parachute Infantry Regiment, a regiment in the US 17th Airborne Division, to miss their drop zone and land on a British drop zone instead. However, the whole operation was a success, with both divisions capturing Rhine bridges and securing towns that could have been used by Germany to delay the advance of the British ground forces. The two divisions incurred more than 2000 casualties, but captured about 3,000 German soldiers. The operation proved to be the last large-scale Allied airborne operation of the Second World War.

25 MARCH 1945

ORB: Led by Wing Cdr Oxspring, 12 aircraft took off and landed at Ursel to refuel. At 09.25 hours they took off again to act as escort to 150 Halifaxes bombing Munster. They went to target as planned and the bombing appeared concentrated. Two Halifaxes were hit by flak, both were seen to go down in flames, though five chutes were seen to leave the second aircraft. The usual heavy accurate flak was put up, both from the target area and on the way in from the front line. Control called up to say there were bandits in the area. A formation of high flying aircraft were seen at 35,000 feet but could not be identified and went without interfering. The Squadron landed again at 11.50 hours.

US troops completed the clearance of Dinslaken and a heavy counter-attack by the Germans north of Wesel was defeated. Street fighting in Wesel continued.

26 MARCH 1945

ORB: Today dawned with much low cloud and drizzle after heavy rainfall during the night. No operational flying was carried out but the whole Squadron was kept at 30 minutes readiness throughout the day.

US troops advanced nearly 6 miles and captured Bruckhausen and Ringenburg.

27 MARCH 1945

ORB: An escort job to Hamm coking plant was laid on this morning but cancelled ten minutes prior to briefing due to bad weather. There was a chance of the weather clearing later and the show could have been laid on then, but the weather did not improve and the Squadron was released.

US troops reached the Dortmund-Ems Canal.

28 MARCH 1945

Logbook: Spitfire Mark IX cannon and aircraft test.

ORB: More rain with cloud right on the deck and therefore no flying. Land forces in the Rhine area are making splendid progress and we hope their progress will not be hampered or made any harder by our inability to provide air support during the past few days.

29 MARCH 1945

ORB: One section carried out a 'dogsbody' this morning but did not take off until 09.00 hours and covered the areas of Ostend, Amsterdam, and Eindhoven but with nothing to report.

30 MARCH 1945

ORB: A considerable improvement in the weather today but no shows were laid on. It looks as if the marked progress the land forces have made during the past few days have precluded the Squadron from participating in attacks against strategic targets that are now well beyond the range of the aircraft unless we are allowed to use airfields deeper in Belgium and Holland than Ursel and Maldegem for refueling.

31 MARCH 1945

ORB: This morning the heavies went to Hamburg. We were included in the show, our role being that of fighter sweep from Maldegem to Munster and the

Wesel area. This was right on the fighter's endurance and well to the south of the bomber stream. The sweep was uneventful and the Squadron returned to Maldegem after being airborne for nearly 2.5 hours where they refuelled and later returned to Manston.

APRIL 1945, NO. 1 SQUADRON

1 APRIL 1945

ORB: Another non-operational day with the wind reaching gale force. The Squadron was released at midday so the football enthusiasts laid on a match against our Wing mates from 91 Squadron. A hard-fought game resulted in a worthy victory by 3-0.

By now the Allied advance on the ground had been so rapid that the Ruhr had been encircled and the remaining German Army in it was trapped. Following the crossing of the Rhine, Montgomery gave orders that the objective of the army would be the capture of airfields for the continued operations of the RAF and in particular the 2nd Tactical Air Force. It was not possible for the RAF to provide full air support because the advance had been so rapid without the provision of forward airfields until now.

2 APRIL 1945

ORB: No operational flying but the Squadron was kept on 30 minutes readiness. Three new operational pilots arrived this afternoon from No. 154 Squadron flying Mustangs. They are W/O Vickery, W/O Murphy and F/Sgt Snowball. We welcome them all to No. 1 Squadron as they will help swell our depleted ranks.

3 APRIL 1945

Logbook: Dogsbody, Ostend, Schouwen, Rotterdam, Felixtowe, base.

ORB: Our 'dogsbody' section was airborne at 07.15 hours and carried out a weather reconnaissance of the Rotterdam area. Ramrod was 1527 was laid on for this afternoon and at 09.35 hours, 12 aircraft took off for Maldegem from where they operated in the afternoon. Their role was to provide top cover to 250 Lancasters bombing Nordhausen. The Squadron arrived at the rendezvous point slightly ahead of time, orbited but could not find the bombers, so returned along the bomber route and landed back at Maldegem where they spent the night.

4 APRIL 1945

Logbook: Local flying Taylorcraft Auster Manston, Biggin Hill.

ORB: W/O Cameron arrived today to join the Squadron from 57 OTU. At 08.40 hours 12 aircraft took off from Maldegem on Ramrod 1528 to provide top cover on withdrawal for 250 Lancasters attacking Nordhausen for the second time in two days. This time they rendezvoused as planned and provided cover for them as planned and uneventfully. The CO Sqn Ldr Cox leaves us tomorrow for his Far East posting and he was given a good send off after a heavy session in the bar in the evening.

5 APRIL 1945

Logbook: Wing formation.

ORB: No operational flying but the new Squadron personnel carried out some practice flying.

6 APRIL 1945

Logbook: Escort 133 VIP Dakota to Gils Rijen near Tilburg.

ORB: Nothing laid on today. Word has been received that we are on the move again. Coltishall this time and we have to be there by the 8th so everyone is busy packing up. Nothing is known of our role there but it looks like we shall operate under the guidance of our old CO now, Wing Cdr Lardner-Burke. At 15.35 hours a section led by F/Lt Scrase took part in Transport Escort No. 133, escorting a Dakota to Gils Rijen. The operation went as planned and was uneventful under fair weather conditions.

7 APRIL 1945

ORB: No operational flying. A Wing Balbo took place in the afternoon and photographs of the Squadron, which were extremely good, were taken.

8 APRIL 1945

Logbook: Manston to Coltishall.

ORB: Today the Squadron moved to Coltishall. The aircraft took off at 12.00 hours and arrived for lunch. The ground crews and station personnel set course after breakfast and arrived early evening!

Coltishall had originally been planned as a bomber station as early as 1939 but the ferocity of the Battle of Britain in the spring and summer of 1940 had brought about an abrupt change of mind and it was decided to make it a fighter station. Throughout the war its closeness to the sea made it a ready spot for the arrival of damaged aircraft returning from operations when damaged or short of fuel. Its Spitfires had renewed their offensive role in the latter stages of 1944 when they began attacking V2 rocket launcher sites and supported the land forces in Normandy. The Squadron's task was to mount armed reconnaissance by Spitfires around the Hague area, although by the time of No. 1 Squadron's arrival in April 1945, much of the resistance on the ground had ended and there was little threat from any surviving V2 sites.

9 APRIL 1945

Logbook: Sector reconnaissance.

ORB: The morning dawned with considerable sea fog and mist so no operational flying, which gave the Squadron time to unpack and settle in. After lunch the weather cleared and the sun came out. Several pilots went off on sector reconnaissance. A section of 2 aircraft carried out a reconnaissance of the Amsterdam area watching out for road, rail, sea or canal traffic. Nothing of any note was seen other than a few lorries. No flak, weather was perfect with visibility close to 50 miles. At 18.10 hours a section was scrambled to bring in a Spitfire with mechanical trouble but they were recalled shortly after taking off. Two further reconnaissance flights of Amsterdam took place with excellent visibility but again nothing of any note was seen.

11 APRIL 1945

Logbook: Ramrod 1537. Escort cover 19,000ft to 120 Lancasters bombing Nurembourg. Return to Petit Brogel.

ORB: At a little after 08.00 hours 12 aircraft including Wing Cdr Douglas took off and landed at B90 Petit Brogel, a new forward airfield on the Continent. At 13.40 hours they were again airborne to act as escort to 100 Lancasters bombing rail targets around Nurembourg. The bombers were late to R/V but the bombing appeared concentrated. The bombers encountered moderate to heavy flak over the target area.

12 APRIL 1945

Logbook: 1. Spitfire IX Petit Brogel to Coltishall 2. Taylorcraft Auster Coltishall – Hatfield.

ORB: The Squadron returned to Coltishall.

Rodney's last few days with No. 1 Squadron at the beginning of April were spent at Coltishall in Norfolk. On 16 April he moved to the Royal Navy air station at St Merryn in Cornwall on attachment to the School of Naval Air Warfare to join the No. 3 Air Combat Instructors Course.

St Merryn had been opened in 1937 and surveyed by the Admiralty in 1939 and deemed suitable for an airfield that was taken into Royal Navy control as HMS *Vulture*. Whilst the airfield saw operations right throughout the war, by December 1944 the emphasis had changed to training and concentrated on the Pacific Theatre of the war. Students were given the benefit of experience gained by the Fleet Air Arm and the US Navy during the offensive against the Japanese and the school there was renamed the School of Naval Air Warfare. The type of aircraft available to the students was very varied as the school was responsible for strike and torpedo squadron training as well as fighters. These intensive courses were to continue right up to the end of the war in Europe and then with Japan. Rodney joined the No. 3 Air Combat Instructors Course.

He flew the Seafire L3 throughout his time there in April and May and had one flight in a Corsair III JS 619 'P' for 60 minutes for 'familiarisation on type' and was able to fly most days. The Seafire was the naval derivative of the Spitfire and had entered service in June 1942 and first saw action in the Mediterranean the following year. It had become clear that the Seafire was not really strong enough for carrier operations. There were problems with control near the stall and a landing speed higher than was the norm for carrier-based fighters, so the Seafire rapidly gained a reputation as a poor naval fighter. However, improvements were made and the Seafire Mark III showed a great improvement in performance over its earlier Marks with the introduction of the Merlin 55 engine and then the L III variant that Rodney flew for most of his time at St Merryn, which was fitted with a Merlin 55 M engine that had a cropped supercharger impeller for low altitude work and was ideally suited for the Air Combat Instructors Course.

In command of the station at St Merryn and the renamed School of Naval Air Warfare was Lt Cdr R.E. 'Jimmy' Gardner DSC, RNVR. Jimmy had joined the Fleet Air Arm in 1939 and was one of the FAA pilots to be loaned to Fighter Command in the Battle of Britain. There he flew with 242 Squadron under the command of Sqn Ldr Douglas Bader. After a brief sojourn flying Beaufighters with Coastal Command, Gardner joined No. 807 Squadron on HMS *Ark Royal* in the Mediterranean and later No. 889 Squadron flying Hurricanes from land bases in North Africa.

Rodney flew most days and typical entries in his logbook were as follows:

1 MAY 1945

Logbook: Seafire L3. 1. Tracking 250 yards 2. Tracking 400 yards.

2 MAY 1945

Logbook: Seafire L3. Tracking and ranging 200–800 yards – German forces in Italy surrender and ceased hostilities.

Locally there was a range at Treligga known officially as HMS *Vulture 11* which was a satellite of HMS *Vulture* at St Merryn. In all some 240 acres of coastland between Tregardock and Backways Cove were requisitioned by the Admiralty and laid out as an air-to-ground and an air-to-sea firing range.

Because of the difficulty in carrying out an emergency landing in the area – there were no large fields or runways – some 'wheels up' landing strips were constructed on the range. This involved a lot of earth moving and heavy machinery was brought in to complete the work. To the north of Treligga village three grass landing strips were laid out. Each of these strips were over 650 metres and marked out for possible landings by aircraft suffering engine failure or ricochet while firing on the range. This arrangement led people to think that *Vulture 11* was a relief landing ground for St Merryn but this was not possible because the ground was quite rough and intended for belly landings. Later the surface was improved and some traffic did use the landing strips.

Several buildings were constructed, the most obvious being a control/observation tower about 10 metres high in the middle of the area. Towards Backways Cove and nearer the sea there was a heavily reinforced observation hut. This housed quadrant equipment to record the angle of dives and the accuracy of attacks made by aircraft.

Off the site there were other associated buildings; at Treligga Downs near the Poldark Inn a building was used for counting holes in drogue targets. These were dropped on the old Trelliga Downs by towing aircraft, retrieved and laid out on long tables where the holes were counted. A reward of 5 shillings was offered to any member of the public who found one. There was a further dive angle hut at Trebarwith village and targets were positioned in Port Isaac Bay for air-to-sea attacks. Near the cliff at Dannon Chapel was an observation tower that was used to gather hit information on the floating targets. Accommodation for the Wrens was built on the Delabole side of Port Gaverne and early in its life HMS *Vulture 11* was unique in being run entirely by the WRNS.

Later action moved to the Japanese war in the Pacific and as a result the Treligga range was made to represent a typical area of Japanese-held territory and was modelled on the island of Tarawa. Real and dummy tanks, a bridge and a road convoy were located near an airstrip and a small railway was constructed to provide moving targets.

6 MAY 1945

Logbook: Seafire L3. Attacks from opposite course – German forces opposing 21st Army surrender.

8 MAY 1945

Logbook: Seafire L3. Downward roll attacks –VE Day.

ORB: A blank day from the point of view of flying but in every other way a great day. VE Day, the occasion for which we have all worked and waited for, for over 5 years. Surprisingly enough the evening was spent quietly in the Mess and although a good quantity of beer was consumed, no organised celebration was laid on.

> VE Day did not come as a surprise. Earlier in the month news had come that the German forces in Italy had surrendered unconditionally. Two days later this was followed by the announcement that German forces opposing the 21st Army Group had surrendered to Field Marshal Montgomery. So our little drive down to the South Cornish coast was a very impromptu affair. Two WRNS and a FAA pilot made up the contingent in my Austin car. It was stop and go at one off licence or another and the odd grocers. The great thing was it was a lovely day and the swimming was wonderful and the beach was virtually empty.

26 MAY 1945

Logbook: Corsair III. Familiarisation on type.

The Corsair was a US Navy fighter built by Chance Vought and universally acknowledged as the most outstanding carrier-based fighter of the Second World War. The first Corsair had been supplied to the US Navy at the end of 1942 and they were in action from the following February. With a maximum speed in excess of 440mph and strongly armed with six 0.5inch machine guns, it carried two 1,000-pound bombs or eight 5-inch rockets. It proved a most formidable fighter. The first Corsairs entered service with the Fleet Air Arm in June 1943 under the Lend–Lease agreement. In action and at full power, the aircraft gave off a distinctive whistling noise caused by the aircraft's air intake and it became known as 'The Whistling Death'.

The School of Naval Air Warfare was now mainly engaged training pilots and crews for the Japanese war in the Far East and the Pacific and each squadron now comprised three flights: Ground Attack, Air Combat and Photo Reconnaissance.

Rodney finished the No. 3 Fighter Combat Course under the School of Naval Air Warfare having completed a total of 78 hours flying and was assessed as 'Average' as a pilot, 'Above Average' as a marksman and 'Above Average' as a ground instructor.

> I did enjoy my time with the Fleet Air Arm. My posting on the course was to bring some of our operational skill to the chaps in the FAA. They did bring me skills too. We were able to use combat film to give evidence of our operational skill. My fixed and gyro gun sight results were all assessed as Above Average. If nothing else it was something to which I could turn. And in my last few months with the RAF I could say, 'Thank you for what you have taught me.'

In June he returned to 1 Squadron who by now were at Ludham in Norfolk flying the Spitfire Mark IX and Mark XXI with the sorties now containing much dive-bombing practice and air-to-air firing around Coltishall and Watnall.

At the end of July the Squadron moved to East Yorkshire and Hutton Cranswick near Driffield in the East Riding where they continued to fly the Spitfire XXI. He recorded his 1,000th flying hour on 10 August in Spitfire 21 LA202 'Y', but the Squadron did not have a good month with two mid-air collisions recorded, one of which proved fatal.

3 AUGUST 1945

Logbook: F/Sgt Jeffery killed after collision with W/O Scall.

Nine Spitfire Mark IXs were bounced by two of the Mark 21s. The IXs broke to port and 30 seconds later F/Sgt Jeffery's aircraft collided with that of W/O Scall. Thomas Jefffery's machine broke up and spun in, but Henry Scall managed to parachute down with only minor injuries.

13 AUGUST 1945

Logbook: Another mid air collision. F/Lt Adams cut off most of F/Lt Bradshaw's tail. Both force land OK.

> A second mid air collision of the month occurred. F/L Bradshaw and F/L Jimmy Adams were involved. Brad flew home with about half his elevators and rudder chewed away, but by keeping the stick well forward he managed to land safely. Adams, with all five blades damaged also managed to get down.

With VJ Day and the coming of total peace, flypasts were organised over various towns and cities and on 28 August, No. 1 Squadron flew over Newcastle upon Tyne in celebration.

15 SEPTEMBER 1945

Logbook: Church Fenton for Battle of Britain Day.

There was a temporary detachment to Bentwaters in mid September in order to take part in the first Battle of Britain flypast. This was a much publicised and photographed occasion and was led by Gp Capt Douglas Bader DSO, DFC who had recently returned from a PoW camp in Germany. 15 of the Squadron's Spitfires took off at 12.00 hours (including three spares) and flew over London and St Paul's Cathedral. It was said that on that day five years previously the Battle of Britain had turned in Britain's favour.

17 SEPTEMBER 1945

Logbook: Class B release through!

F/Lt Scrase 123465 was released from the RAF on 29 September 1945 with a record of 4 destroyed, 3 damaged and a DFC to his credit. After such an eventful war Rodney resumed his civilian life. By his own admission he found the transition difficult.

> The Class B Release was granted to those who had been in full time university education before their war-time service. In my case it meant a return to the London School of Economics to complete my B Com studies. I did find that life as a student four or five years older than my fellow undergraduates was very difficult, especially as many of my ex-service colleagues did not benefit from this arrangement until the following academic year.

CHAPTER FOURTEEN

1946 AND ONWARDS

After he resumed his studies at the London School of Economics Rodney was also able to resume his rowing. He again rowed at No. 6 in the 1946 Head of the River race. This is an annual race over a 4.5 mile course from Mortlake to Putney and is traditionally held a week before the annual Oxford Cambridge boat race and is held on the boat race course. It is a processional race of over 400 boats, the race being based on time to do the course. It is not generally known that there were two Heads of the River races that were not rowed over the full course. In 1932 building work on both Chiswick and Putney bridges had shortened the course to 3.5 miles and in 1946, when consideration had to be given to the under-nourishment of the participants, the course started at Barnes Bridge. Unfortunately for Rodney, his 1946 LSE crew did not perform to their potential and their rivals Trinity College won the race. He married Jean in 1947 and they had two children, Elaine who was born in 1948 and John born in 1949 but the marriage later ended in divorce.

After he finished his studies he joined the company where his father was a sales director, and he and Jean lived in Derbyshire near Bakewell close for work and for the Peak District where they could walk. Within a few years he was able to get a sales management role with the Nestlé Company. Later he became Assistant Manager Marketing for them, heading a sales team of 30 people in the Midlands and Yorkshire. He then went to Nestlé HQ in Switzerland and a had one-year release from work to take his MBA at IMEDE – the International Business School in nearby Lausanne, a city in Romandy, the French-speaking part of Switzerland, situated on the shores of Lake Geneva.

Rodney quickly became dissatisfied so he used his language skills in French and Italian and joined the Rank Organisation as a general manager, who, at the time were building a chain of hotels in Europe. This in turn led to the world of tourism and he became Head of Tourism in Gibraltar and later Chief Executive Officer with the London Tourist Board where he spent the last 15 years of his working life. His service in tourism gave him an interest in London and he felt it only right to see the operation from the ground up and worked to qualify for the 'Blue Badge' as worn by officially qualified London tour guides. He continues as a Blue Badge Guide, and has been made a Freeman of the City of London and of the Company of Watermen and Lighter Men of the River Thames.

Rodney married again, this time to Sue who he met while working in Gibraltar and they have been together nearly 40 years. They have two children, Diran born in

1971 and Christopher born in 1973. Christopher is married to Caroline and they have a young daughter Millie who keeps Rodney and Sue on their toes. Diran lives in a specially adapted home that caters for people with learning difficulties in Wells in Somerset and is run by the Orchard Vale Trust, while Christopher works for the Higher Education Funding Council for England –HEFCE.

Rodney and Sue have lived for most of their married life at Bishops Avenue in Bromley. After retirement Rodney became involved in Environment Bromley (EnBro) that had been established in 1980 with some financial support from the London Borough of Bromley to recruit volunteers to maintain footpaths in the area and a role that involved walking as well.

The combination of his love of rowing and walking led Rodney to organise the Head Day walk. The first was organised in 1999. It started at Putney with the route taking the walkers along the Surrey bank to Barnes Bridge, across the river and then back to Fulham, a walk of some 9 miles in all. The attraction is that after the walk, the walkers can then watch the Head of the River Race. Happily his present state of health until earlier this year meant Rodney could take a full part in walking with the Ramblers, and involved attendance of meetings of the Bromley Probus Club and with the Chartered Institute of Marketing and other professional bodies.

That apart, his RAF activities such as the preservation of Bentley Priory and the Biggin Hill Battle of Britain Supporters Club under the banner of 'The Bump' continue to occupy his free time. Housed at Biggin Hill in a recently refurbished RAF T2 Hangar is a Mark IX Spitfire TA805 named 'The Spirit of Kent' owned by Mike Simpson and Peter Monk and which first flew again back in 2005. The sound of the Merlin engine reverberating around the airfield brought back many memories for Rodney. He also remains an active member of No. 72 Squadron Association as their President and he took a party of veterans to Italy in September 2004 funded by the New Opportunities Fund under the name of 'Heroes Return'. The programme drawn up by Rodney included visits to Salerno, Anzio, Nettuno with the addition of Naples and the present-day Capodichino airfield and lastly, Monte Cassino.

Tracking the locations of their temporary airfields was not easy. The PSP (Pressed Steel Planking) akin to giant meccano pieces that had been laid out to give 100 yard-long strips perhaps 30 yards wide had long since disappeared. Their location at Salerno was near Tusciano and their base at Lago on a beach site by the Volturno river, some 35 miles north of Naples. Both these sites had been returned to agriculture or built over with holiday homes but on the strip close to Nettuno, the Italian military now has a range so entry was forbidden. They did stop where they could, look and remember what had happened in those months from September 1943 to June 1944 and remember their friends who had not been so fortunate and were now buried in military cemeteries.

Of the seven pilots who made the return trip, four had baled out or crash-landed behind enemy lines, two, Tom Hughes and Lawrie Frampton, had also become prisoners of war while another had been plucked from the sea. Two of the seven, Rodney Scrase and Dicky Bird, were awarded the DFC.

It was a time of reflection. Their return to Monte Cassino was especially poignant as their arrival there was timed for the end of the day and their first point of call was to the Commonwealth War Graves Cemetery. With the graves of over 4,000 servicemen it is the largest war graves cemetery in Italy and although there are no graves of 72 squadron personnel there, there are those of 35 RAF personnel. Finally their trip included a visit to the rebuilt abbey of Monte Cassino and again it was time for reflection remembering the many servicemen who fought and died in the five battles for the town and abbey before the Gustav line was breached in 1944.

Another trip is planned for a veterans return in 2010, again with Rodney at the helm and as organiser, this time to take them back to Malta and Sicily. It will be a time of reflection and a time to remember those that were not so fortunate, those that gave their lives, so that today, we might live in freedom.

I don't think anyone realises what those men went through, the friends they lost and the sacrifices they made. It has been my privilege and a pleasure to meet Rodney and his wife Sue, to become friends and see what a gentleman he is. A quietly spoken, truly gentle person, he is very unassuming and always willing to give his time. He should be very proud of what he has achieved.

I hope he feels I have done his story justice.

ACKNOWLEDGEMENTS

My second book has taken two years of research and I am indebted to a great many people in helping me. In addition to RAF and Squadron Records, Rodney Scrase has allowed me time to ask him what must have seemed endless questions and access to his logbook, memoirs and photographs. It has been both a privilege and a pleasure to write his story and I hope he feels I have done a decent job.

I have been able to use the memoirs of other pilots and ground crew still very active with the 72 Squadron Association and who were good enough to record their recollections through the 72 Squadron historian Erik Mannings. The memoirs included in this book with their permission are those of Tom Hughes, Jack Lancaster, Jimmy Corbin and Laurie Frampton. To all of you, thank you.

I would also like to thank Robbie Robertson's grandson for permission to use extracts from his grandfather's diary that were posted on the website www. Pprune.co.uk and to Roy Hussey's nephew Edward Lambah-Stoate in Bath who was willing to share information about his uncle and who is also in the throes of writing a book that will include Roy Hussey's story, a good friend of Rodney and of my grandfather Barney Barnfather.

The National Archive at Kew and the Imperial War Museum in Lambeth deserve a mention as they willingly help anyone trying to do research even if they don't have all the answers, and this book would not have been possible without the help of everyone at The History Press but in particular Shaun Barrington and Miranda Jewess.

Finally, a word of thanks to my wife Sue, who has had to put up with my absences whilst I was researching and writing this book; I could not do without her support and love.

EPILOGUE, BY ANGUS MANSFIELD

I first met Rodney 13 years ago in 2005 when I was doing the research for the book about my grandfather, Barney Barnfather, *Life on a Spitfire Squadron*. My grandfather and Rodney had flown together on the same 72 Squadron for about 18 months during the war. I remember being quite nervous about meeting him for the first time but I need not have worried: 'Young man, how nice to meet you, now please, please do sit down and we can talk, I would love to be able to help you!' And that was Rodney, always made time for you and always willing to help. He was good enough to write a foreword for my grandfather's book; indeed he thought it special I had asked him. It was a privilege to have met him, to become good friends, and for him, then, to ask me to write his story.

One of my favourite photographs of the two of them together on 72 Squadron was taken in North Africa. Barney, my grandfather, is far left; Rodney is in the middle; and an unknown Australian pilot (maybe Keith Clarkson) is far right. One of the main

Barney Barnfather and Rodney Scrase with an unknown Australian Pilot. (Courtesy of Angus Mansfield)

things I remember him telling me in the time I spent with him and got to know him was the camaraderie on the Squadron and the cosmopolitan nature of the pilots and ground crew drawn from all over the Commonwealth – I remember he dedicated his book to the ground crews: 'This book is dedicated to the Ground Crews who so effectively provided the back up to their pilots, these chaps on the Squadron for years gave the Squadron its teeth. Not glamour but at all times complete support.'

One of the best and most endearing features of Rodney's character traits was how he always thought the best of everyone. Chris Scrase, his son, recalled the same in a moving tribute at his funeral:

> Dad was loving, kind, charming, a gentleman – generous of spirit and with his time, he always thought the best of everyone. He formed and actively maintained lifelong friendships from all parts of his life, sending little notes and newspaper clippings to us all regularly.
>
> Dad also cherished friendships with people he met at No. 5 BFTS, the British Flying Training School in Florida, where he learnt how to fly a Spitfire in 1941, aged 21. As with everything, he dedicated himself to the onerous war-time tasks required of him and was a focused and single-minded pilot who was decorated for his bravery.
>
> Despite the context, Dad developed a love of flying – a love that would continue throughout his life. As would his connections to the RAF, in particular, No 72 Squadron, of which Dad was honoured to be President.

Through the No. 72 Squadron Association and his presidency, Rodney was able to keep him in touch with some of his former pilots and good friends. Sadly Rodney was one of the last surviving Spitfire pilots from the squadron but Tom Hughes, Laurie Frampton, and Jack Lancaster were all at one time active members of the association and sadly are also no longer with us.

Tom Hughes in particular formed a long-lasting friendship with Rodney, and it was Tom that Rodney asked to write a foreword to his book. Sadly, it was received too late for the publication date of the original hardback published in 2010 but it has now been included in this version.

> We met at the Operational Training Unit at Grangemouth and Balado Bridge where we both flew the Spitfire. Rodney had been trained in America and I had been a flying instructor at RAF College Cranwell before I managed to wrangle out of Training Command by way of a Night Fighter Training unit. It was easy to pick out the pilots who could fly a steady formation and Rodney was one of the best.
>
> I returned to university in 1945 from my prisoner of war camp in Germany and as I walked down King's Parade I wondered at old friends who had survived. I went one day to try the lunch in the Air Squadron Mess. There, in the visitors' book, was a name I dearly wanted to find. Rodney had written in very small print, his decoration. He certainly deserved it and we have remained friends to this day.
>
> F/Lt Tom Hughes DFC– August 2010

Laurie Frampton, Jack Lancaster, Rodney Scrase and Tom Hughes. (Courtesy of Angus Mansfield)

Sadly, Tom Hughes passed away on the last day of December 2010 but Rodney attended the funeral and memorial service for his good friend in Pontelland where Tom had lived in later life. Rodney later recalled in the 72 Squadron newsletter, 'The life of Tom Hughes was recalled with great admiration and affection at a memorial service held at St Mary's Church in Ponteland. The church was packed with many people standing at the back. They had come from far and wide to say farewell to a well-loved man of diverse talents.'

The Reverend Peter Barham took the service and nephew Peter Jackson in his tribute recalled the conjuring tricks performed by his uncle when he was a teenager. Another nephew read a poem by Kahil Gibran and Rodney paid tribute to Tom's flying ability, portraying a man of integrity but who was not afraid to have a tilt at authority when called for.

> Tom was a Spitfire pilot engaged in the build up to the invasion of Sicily and then in the battle for Monte Cassino where he was shot down, badly burned and lucky to survive. The Germans transferred him to a military hospital where he was held as a POW for more than a year before coming home in early 1945 as part of a prisoner exchange.

72 Squadron based at Linton-on-Ouse in Lincolnshire, mounted a colour party with Flight Lieutenant Chris McCann carrying the colours into the church and a fly-past

with two twin-seat prop trainers, Tucanos, which flew east to west over Coates Green after everyone left the church. A fine tribute to a true gentleman!

After the war Tom took up electronic design and engineering and worked for AEI and Ronson. He died after a short illness on 31 December at the Royal Victoria Infirmary, Newcastle, and was survived by his widow Joan, whom he married in 1949. Squadron Leader (retired) Eric Mannings Squadron historian for No. 72 Squadron, said:

> Tom was a true gentleman of the old school and very modest about his flying career. When asked once what he rated as his greatest achievement, he replied: 'I married Joan and designed Prince Philip's electric razor' – no mention of his combat flying, injuries or imprisonment and experimentation. He will be greatly missed.

The Scrase family had moved to Bromley in Kent when Rodney became Chief Executive of the London Tourist Board. He qualified for the 'Blue Badge' worn by qualified London guides and would occasionally 'drop in' on their tours to keep them on their toes. He travelled the world promoting tourism in the British capital and was later made a Freeman of the City of London.

Mike Bugsgang, marketing manager, recalled with fondness their time together at the London Tourist Board during the 1980s:

> During my tenure as marketing manager of the London Tourist Board in the eighties, I have many fond memories of working with my then boss, Rodney, who was the director of the company at the time.Stories from this period at the tourist board abound but I have selected two that Rodney frequently reminded me of during our conversations over subsequent years.
>
> The first relates to the summer that London was so crowded with visitors that most of its hotels were overbooked and some groups were being transferred to accommodation as far away as Birmingham! Ever resourceful, Rodney arranged for us to meet with the people running Tent City, which as the name suggests, was a canvas accommodation facility located on the football pitches outside Wormwood Scrubs Prison. We agreed that in the absence of available hotel beds, LTB's Tourist Information Centres at points of entry to the country and around the capital would book tourists, mostly students and youth travellers, into Tent City.
>
> After finalising the details, Rodney and I, suited and booted in our business attire, were invited to join the operators of Tent City and some of the residents, in their shorts and T-shirts, under canvas, for the dish of the day – Spaghetti Bolognese. Well, this meal must have been 90 per cent garlic because for days afterwards, Rodney and I were breathing fire on our colleagues back at the office.
>
> My second tale highlights one of Rodney's traits at work which was to cut things very fine for meetings. It was a Saturday morning and we were at the office at Grosvenor Gardens in Victoria. I kept popping in to Rodney's office that was

Tom Hughes. (Courtesy of Angus Mansfield)

adjacent to mine to remind him that we were scheduled to meet a group of American travel agents at Westminster Pier to host them on a riverboat trip.

Well, at the very last minute, we dashed down to Rodney's Triumph Stag parked outside the office and flew down Victoria Street to Westminster Pier. Having parked the car on the Embankment, miraculously directly opposite the Pier, we sprinted down the gangway to see the boat disappearing with the travel agents waving sarcastically at us in fits of laughter. Not to be beaten, we rushed back to the car for another hair-raising drive down to the Tower of London to greet the group as they disembarked at Tower Pier.

Looking back, I think my time at the London Tourist Board was probably the happiest period in my career and that was mainly attributed to Rodney. I will miss the chats we used to have about our days promoting the greatest city in the world, but I will continue to hold the memories dear forever.

Chris Scrase continues:

But even after Dad retired from the London Tourist Board in 1981, nearly 37 years ago, he stayed active, never gave up his interests, and was forever busy. At first he focused on setting up his own tourism consultancy, working with the likes of Westminster Abbey, and with boating companies on the Thames.

> But he also got to spend more time at home, developing new strong friendships with members of the church at St Marks in Bromley, reigniting his links with 72 Squadron and joining the local business and walking groups Probus and Enbro. Walking had always been a passion for Dad – usually from the front, with me, Diran and Mum trailing behind. On the occasions when as a teenager I sped off in front, he would quickly catch up, with his long stride, telling me to walk faster and 'step it out'. Similarly, when he led walks with Enbro, several walkers confided in Mum that they were delighted when she came too, so that she could tell him to stop for regular breaks. Later on in life, he even adopted a similar approach to his mobility scooter, invariably turning up the speed on the scooter so that he sped off in front with the rest of us trotting on behind, but he was also delighted to give rides to his grandchildren Millie and William when their young legs got too tired!

The mobility scooter had a story in its own right but it is also a measure of the esteem with which Rodney was held and the friendships that Rodney was able to build – after his original scooter was stolen from outside his house the local community twice rallied round to help him. When Geoff Nutkins, Curator of the Local Shoreham Aircraft Museum, heard about the original scooter being stolen, he contacted all the museum volunteers who agreed to club together and buy him a new one. Rodney was a regular at the museum and signing events and was astonished at their generosity. He was presented with the new scooter and David Jones from the museum commented, 'he was last seen negotiating Shoreham High Street at speed!'

When the new scooter then broke down almost a year later the Biggin Hill community came together this time. Ady Shaw, from the Group 'Spitfire Britain's National Treasure' and a good friend of Rodney and Sue after meeting him at an event some years beforehand, had planned to raise the funds for a second scooter by auctioning a signed Battle of Britain Canvas. However, when he contacted the owners of the Spitfire Café in Biggin Hill, Sally and Barry O'Connor, they put Ady in touch with Julia Stevenson from Ride of Respect, a group of bikers who holds events throughout the year to help ex-serviceman, and the group generously handed over the funds to enable a second new scooter to be purchased. This was handed over to Rodney at the aptly named Spitfire Café in Biggin Hill.

I remember I 'borrowed' Rodney for the day to go to the RAF Museum in Hendon back in 2012 as I never had the chance to go there with my grandfather. Sue Scrase had kindly agreed I could 'borrow' Rodney for as long as I wanted to and by then Rodney had asked me to write his story and had arranged to sign a few of his books – it was great to be able to spend the day with him, made all the more memorable because he met a Cub Scout Group on the tube train, who then recognised him at the museum and were all in awe of a real live Spitfire pilot. He made time for each and every one of the boys, who all wanted their photo with him or wanted something signed by him. Very humbling and the mark of a true gentleman and a gentle person.

Rodney and his scooter. (Courtesy of Shoreham Aircraft Museum)

Rodney with replacement scooter at the Spitfire Café Biggin Hill. (Courtesy of Ady Shaw)

Rodney signing books at RAF Museum, Hendon. (Courtesy of Angus Mansfield)

Photographer Ady Shaw first met Rodney in 2013 while visiting the Biggin Hill Heritage Hangar to sit in a Spitfire.

He recalled:

> There I met a gentleman who would change my life forever. Sitting at a table I nervously approached Rodney, who looked up at me and said 'Hello young man, how lovely to meet you.'
>
> From there we engaged in a conversation that left me spellbound. Later joined by several others, we sat cross-legged on the hangar floor while Rodney regaled us with his exploits for over an hour. Grown men were hanging on every word.

Ady added:

> Then I was amazed to have the honour to escort Rodney out on to the apron to photograph him with a Hurricane. From there, Rodney took a shine to a picture I asked him to sign for me and a few days later I was in Rodney's front room meeting the lovely Sue and enjoying tea and biscuits. Having converted my garage into a Spitfire study, I asked Rodney to come along to cut the ribbon – once we managed to tear him away from the ladies.

Ady Shaw and Rodney Scrase in front of a Hurricane. (Courtesy of Ady Shaw)

> Everyone loved Rodney and Sue. Rodney's passing has left a big hole in countless lives.

One of Rodney's greatest ambitions was to get back into the seat of a Spitfire and fly in it. Sadly it was not possible to achieve this, even though there are a number of two-seater variants still flying in the UK, due to Rodney's mobility. However, he did manage the next best thing and with the help of Aero Legends Ltd, Virgin Experience Days and F/Lt Anthony Parkinson MBE, Rodney was able to fly in a de Havilland Dove alongside a Spitfire flown by Parkinson from Headcorn Airfield in Kent in November 2016. Rodney remembered the day with fondness: 'The Spitfire had a silky smooth engine, it was absolutely wonderful. It had a lasting memory on me and you don't lose the sense or the feeling. It was most graceful and you are at one with the machine.'

Chris Scrase continues:

> Another fond memory was to do with Dad's love of a gin and tonic, or more specifically, a gin and martini, in the evening. When he was in hospital last year, having, by then, been diagnosed with dementia, the nurses reported he often asked them hopefully for a gin and tonic or a glass of beer, to go with his dinner. The first time Caroline came to Bromley, as a 19 year old with a year's experience of working in a pub whilst studying at Exeter University, she offered to make him a gin and tonic – only to have it, politely, sent back because it 'had no gin in it'. Needless to say, it did have a serving of gin, but Dad wasn't necessarily used to pub measures, and Caroline quickly learnt to pour a bit more in future.

Rodney and Sue Scrase with Sue in the cockpit of the Spitfire. (Courtesy of Rodney Scrase)

> Similarly, when Dad came out of hospital last year, he was under strict instructions to drink more water so that he stayed hydrated. So early one evening I decided to give him a glass of water in order to carry out the doctor's orders and thought no more of it. A couple of minutes later – 'Sue,' he called out, weakly. 'This ... is ... water.' The glass was removed, then brought back – gin, martini, ice, slice of orange. 'Much better!' He remained consistent, even throughout his illness.

In her own words, Charlotte Moore also recalls:

> My Grandpapa, my Grandpa in London, my POGR (Poor Old Grandpa the Rod) died yesterday evening 25/02/18 with those he loved closest around him.
>
> It was so hard to be in Dubai, so many miles away. Like everyone in the family, it was a time to grieve, be still and reflect. My tears flowed from loving a man so much yet loving him with deeper tenderness in his later years as he became the epitome of the two values I hold so dear: gratitude & positivity.
>
> I raised a glass to him and all he was and I was thinking of his life, his achievements and the hearts he had touched and the hearts he had broken. His legacy professionally and personally – imprinted and living on in us all.

And in her own special tribute to her grandfather, Charlotte also read this poem at the private family ceremony before his funeral – I will leave the last words as hers in loving memory of her 'Granpapa' – it's a poem called *Remember Me* by David Harkins:

> You can shed tears that he is gone or you can smile because he has lived
> You can close your eyes and pray that he will come back or you can open your eyes and see all that he has left
> Your heart can be empty because you can't see him or you can be full of the love that you shared
> You can turn your back on tomorrow and live yesterday or you can be happy for tomorrow because of yesterday
> You can remember him and only that he is gone or you can cherish his memory and let it live on
> You can cry and close your mind, be empty and turn your back or you can do what he would want: smile, open your eyes, love and go on.

Rodney Scrase, DFC, fighter pilot and tourism chief, sadly passed away from the effects of Alzheimer's disease on 25 February 2018, aged 96.

Dear Grandpa – Rodney with his granddaughter, Charlotte Moore. (Courtesy of Charlotte Moore)

ACKNOWLEDGEMENTS TO THE PAPERBACK EDITION

This final chapter and epilogue would not have been possible without the help and/or blessing of the following for which my sincere and heartfelt thanks: Sue Scrase, Christopher Scrase, Charlotte Moore, Ady Shaw, Mike Bugsgang, Simon Pearson – *The Times*, Tom Docherty, Tom Hughes, Erik Mannings, Amy Rigg and Alex Waite at The History Press and David Harkins, author of the Poem *He is Gone*, who gave permission for it to be quoted in the epilogue.

INDEX

The History Press
The destination for history
www.thehistorypress.co.uk

9 780 7524 5580 8

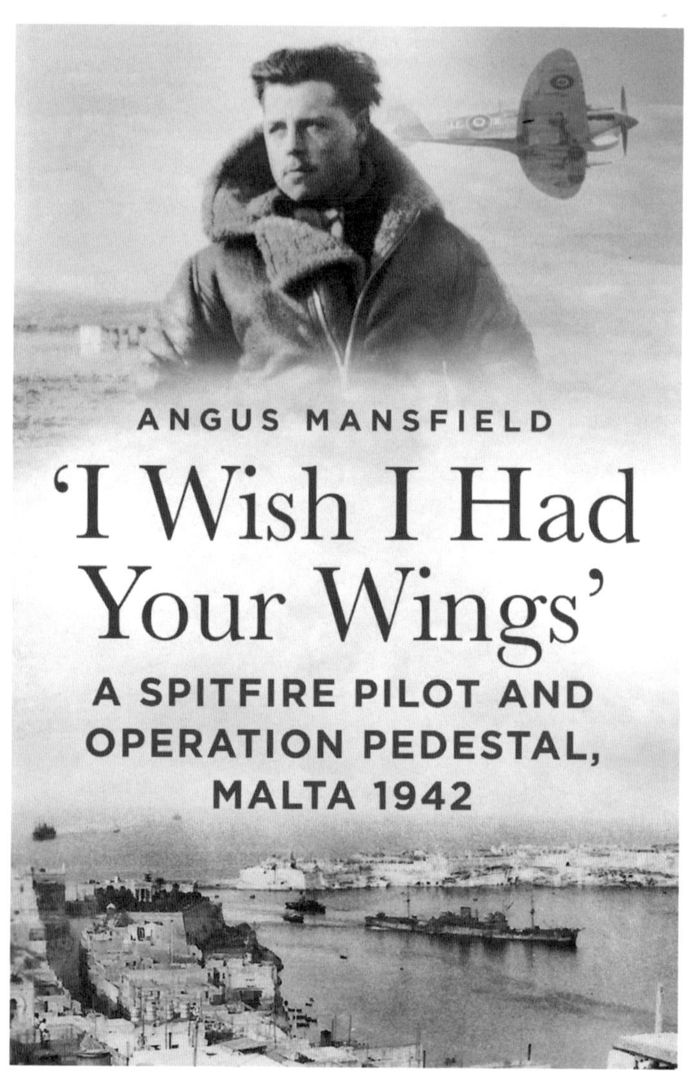

9 780 7524 9782 2